Let Not the Waves of the Sea

Let Not the Waves of the Sea

SIMON STEPHENSON

JOHN MURRAY

First published in Great Britain in 2011 by John Murray (Publishers)
An Hachette UK Company

1

© Simon Stephenson 2011

A CIP catalogue record for this title is available from the British Library

Hardback ISBN 978-1-84854-558-8
Trade paperback ISBN 978-1-84854-559-5
Ebook ISBN 978-1-84854-560-1

Typeset in 12.5/15 Monotype Bembo by Servis Filmsetting Ltd, Stockport, Cheshire

Printed and bound by Clays Ltd, St Ives plc

John Murray policy is to use papers that are natural, renewable and recyclable products and
made from wood grown in sustainable forests. The logging and manufacturing processes are
expected to conform to the environmental regulations of the country of origin.

John Murray (Publishers)
338 Euston Road
London NW1 3BH

www.johnmurray.co.uk

To begin to comprehend what happened that day on Ko Phi Phi, you first need to understand the island's geography. You best achieve this by climbing to a rocky outcrop atop a hill on the island's eastern side, a spot known locally as 'Viewpoint'.

Be warned, though, that the journey to the top is an exhausting one. Steps have been cut into the hillside, but their gradient remains steep and treacherous enough to take your breath by exertion or fear. You climb to Viewpoint early in the morning before the day is warm, or at sunset when it has again started to cool. You do not go if you are pregnant, prone to breathlessness, or suffer from any kind of heart condition. Most importantly, you do not undertake the trip if you are feeling anything other than emotionally robust.

If you wake young and healthy and in good spirits, you follow the road that leads east from town, past Tara Inn and the Rimkao Store. You take care to ignore the first rustic signpost that claims to lead you to Viewpoint – it will do so, but by a torturously circuitous route – and instead continue on, past what was once the town's reservoir but now, planted over with reeds and rushes, is the water treatment plant, and then take the road that forks to the right.

This narrow street is cobbled, and rises steeply as it passes Mr Bau's Garden Home Restaurant on one side and the high, stilted bungalows of Pichamon Resort on the other. Walk for another few hundred yards, around a corner and down a gentle slope, and abruptly you will find yourself in a strange, close part of town; the buildings here two and sometimes three storeys high, they lean forward as if to shade the people on the street, and in their cool dark much of the day's business is indeed accomplished. It is here, a little way beyond the beach towels that billow like prayer flags from the balconies of the US Guesthouse, that the stairway appears and your journey to Viewpoint truly begins.

Here at their foot the steps are set close and you climb them as you climb a mountain: trudging upwards you can see only all the distance still to travel, but glancing back during a pause for breath, you find a patchwork quilt of corrugated iron rooftops has spread itself beneath you and a thin fringe of sea is already visible at its edge. Such early and tangible progress quickly reinvigorates you, and you clamber on.

Upwards, ever upwards, but for their own part the steps grow ever deeper, and soon you must stop once again. From here you can see down into the valley where Mr Bau has his restaurant, and beyond it to the dusty road from which you were careful to take only the second turning.

You push on. One foot after the other, and repeat. Sometimes a hand must be planted on a thigh to gain further leverage, sometimes a curse must be uttered. The thought that this is impossible toil creeps back insidiously, but some families make their home here on the hill, and now one of their number hurries past you, an elderly lady carrying bags of rice over each shoulder as if they were no more than foam guesthouse pillows. Chastened, you vow to carry on.

One foot after the other, and repeat. Overhead a jungle canopy quietly weaves itself together, and when next you turn to check on your progress its knitted branches and leaves are all that you can see. It is cooler here in this shade but, robbed of the visible reassurance that your efforts are not in vain, the going becomes exponentially harder. After a dozen more steps you begin to believe that you really can go no further, that you must turn back to the consolation of Mr Bau's banana pancakes. But right when you are on the very cusp of doing so, when you have reconciled yourself to your excuses and made a silent vow that you will tell nobody that you attempted this ascent today, the steps smooth themselves into a path.

The people that have warned you about the climb to Viewpoint have spoken only of the steps, the endless cursed steps, so when halfway up the hillside the land suddenly plateaus, you initially assume it to be a mirage. Yet it is no illusion: here the path truly is a ribbon of poured concrete that winds past ramshackle homesteads and through jasmine groves; here you find yourself strolling through glades of butterflies that flutter on the breeze like the confetti of a stranger's wedding you stumble across in the city.

The path soon steepens, turns to steps once again, but such things are now irrelevant. If ten minutes ago you could not have walked another yard, now you could continue all day. You climb without fear and fifteen minutes later the canopy above you abruptly disappears. Ahead of you, a hand-painted sign announces that you have reached your destination, its triumphant fresh white letters on faded driftwood proclaiming this place to be PHI PHI VIEWPOINT. Behind this sign is a lean-to shop selling juice and water, and beyond that is an immaculate rose garden where a black and white cat sprawls in the warming sun. You barely notice any of this, for you are transfixed by the view beneath you.

You are stood on solid rocks and these fall away to bushes, which in turn give way to the tops of tall trees. Beyond these, the island sits like an architect's scale model: two miniature mountains joined in the middle by a slender strip of a sandbar that is concaved on each side by the symmetrical emerald bays it divides, Tonsai and Loh Dahlum.

3

Travellers who make it to Viewpoint write in their journals that Phi Phi is another butterfly, its twin bays the perfect wings of a Tropical Greenstreak, its sandbar the fragile creature's torso. Geographers reason that Phi Phi is technically an archipelago, the sandbar an isthmus. Friend Ben says that his island home is an alien, and if you turn a north-orientated map through a hundred clockwise degrees, the outline does indeed begin to look like the elongated head and underdeveloped body of a Roswell figure.

What Phi Phi most closely resembles, though, is this: a lush cartoon apple gnawed almost to the core by some hungry Tom or Jerry in a long-ago Saturday morning cartoon. The yellow sands that line the bays mark the boundaries to which the apple has been eaten, the two verdant mountains its untouched top and bottom. The fragile core that remains – the sandbar, the isthmus, the elongated alien's neck – is barely half a mile across. Its highest point sits no more than a dozen feet above sea level, and yet thereon perches the entire town.

Standing on the rocks at Viewpoint, you can pick out its landmarks like a deity playing a celestial game of I-spy. Something beginning with 'P': pier; something beginning with 'S': school; something beginning with 'H': hotel. There is Mr Bau's Restaurant, and there is the Rimkao Store. There are the resorts and the guesthouses, the Cabana Hotel's glistening blue pool, the covered stalls of the Thai market. There is the Front Street with its dive shops, its souvenir stands, its hundred–baht massage parlours. There is the water treatment plant and there is the power station, the post office and the ice factory.

It takes your breath, but not by its beauty. To look out on this view early in the day is to understand a terrible truth: that if some evil genius ever wished to construct a place utterly defenceless against a tsunami, any blueprint they came up

4

with would likely look a lot like the little island of Ko Phi Phi in the Andaman Sea.

Now, as it was that day, it is coming on for ten thirty on a cloudless morning in the busy season. In Tonsai, the dive boats are idling and the longtails have already begun their ceaseless buzz back and forth to Ko Phi Phi Leh; at the pier the Phuket ferry sounds its horn impatiently but then waits, as it always does, for the last late risers to hurry through the town. Across the sandbar in Loh Dahlum, kayaks and deck-chairs are being arranged in neat rows in preparation for the busy day ahead; from this height, the matchstick people moving amongst them are the only ones that you can properly pick out, but you know that there are five thousand more down there. Five thousand more: doing laundry, sleeping in, making coffee; watching over children, sweeping up in restaurants, writing postcards in which every sixth word is 'paradise'. Five thousand human beings, and not a single one of them stood more than a dozen feet above sea level.

A framed photograph hanging from a nearby tree now catches your eye and you walk over to look at it. The man who tends the rose garden has daubed the words AFTER TSUNAMI PHI PHI in dripping red paint on the ramshackle frame. He did not need to do this, for it is self-evidently a scene from the recent apocalypse.

The view is immediately recognisable as the same one you have just been looking out on – there are the twinned bays, there is the sandbar – and yet everything else about the picture is wrong. On all of Tonsai Bay there sits not a single boat. The emerald waters are now yellowed as old bruises, the fine sandy beaches all but devoured by their swelling. The isthmus is littered with debris. The town itself appears to have been razed.

From a pyre near the middle of the island, a dark column

of smoke creeps into the sky. An identifiable focal point, it draws your eye further into the picture and you now see that across the ravaged land half a dozen similar fires are burning. Soon you pick out a yellow mechanised digger, a line of white-shrouded bodies laid out on the pier, and six men spread across the narrow remnant of Loh Dahlum beach, walking it like investigators after there has been a murder.

You stare at this picture for a long time and, when the moment comes, you walk back down the hill from Viewpoint in silence. You put one foot after another, all the way down, but this day is broken before it has even begun.

Three evenings a week on Phi Phi, a tall Thai man with a pair of boxing gloves draped around his neck commences a slow promenade around town. As he goes, he rings a hand-bell and passes out flyers to the tourists: *Tonight at Reggae Bar, Thai Boxing.* He makes no verbal pitch whatsoever, but this man, whose name is Mr John, is a difficult person to resist: fifty years old yet buzz-cut and trim, his military bearing and silence combine to inform you that he is not the sort of person to waste his time or yours.

But if Mr John wins your trust at first sight – and you accept one of his flyers and later find yourself following the hand-drawn map on the back – his place of employment does exactly the opposite. Painted in a migrainous shade of fire-engine red, Reggae Bar is the dirty beating heart at the centre of Phi Phi's famously hedonistic nightlife, an inter-minably pulsating mass of muscle and sweat that pumps out plastic bucketfuls of Thai whisky and cola until the small hours of the morning seven nights a week. It is too noisy, the drinks are overpriced and even by Thailand's forgiving stand-ards the toilets are a public health hazard. If it were in your town, Reggae Bar would be the dive that you love to hate but somehow find yourself in at the end of every big night out.

And yet beneath everything, in a place the drunken tour-ists and even the closing-time broken glass can never penetrate, lurks the knowledge that Reggae Bar does have a soul, and a great big one at that: when the water came, these garish walls stood strong. The only solid structure in a part of town dominated by shanty bars and kitchen restaurants, Reggae Bar was one of few places on the island capable of providing refuge to those in mortal need of it. On a busy night when the music is blaring, the huge television screens are showing an English premiership football match and the pool balls are clicking and spinning into the corner pockets, this can seem like a faraway notion, but once you know the place's history, you never entirely forget it.

By the time he was finishing primary school, my brother Dominic had already worked his way through several martial arts: judo, ju–jitsu, tae kwon do, and even an unnamed discipline of his own creation that primarily seemed to involve chasing me around the garden with a set of nunchucks he had bought by mail order. For many years afterwards, Mum carried in her purse a photograph that seemed to capture Dominic in his element at nine or ten years old: karate-kicking his way over a bonfire in our back garden, his leading leg projects horizontal to his waist and his face is a picture of preternatural concentration.

This photograph, however, told only half of the story of Dominic's love for the martial arts. The business with the nunchucks excepted, he had always been as drawn to the mythologies and traditions of the disciplines he studied as to the actual combat. If this distinction was mostly wasted on the unlicensed instructors that sublet the gymnasiums of our youth, it at least meant that Dominic knew the martial art for him when he and his friend Graham stumbled upon it at twenty years old.

The national sport of Thailand, Muay Thai places great emphasis on honour and tradition, and requires its students to learn as many ritual dances as combat moves. This is not to imply that it does not get violent: towards the end of their inaugural lesson, Graham accidentally fractured one of Dominic's ribs. Neither of them was put off, and as the cracked bone fused itself solid over the next weeks and months, so did their shared dedication to the sport.

The ring at Reggae Bar is endearingly ramshackle, open on three sides to the street and above to the night sky; if a fighter is made to see stars here, he literally does so. Occasionally the combatants have been brought over on the ferries from Phuket or Krabi, but usually they are local: teenage boys and young men you might have played football with on the beach or glimpsed through half-closed doors, toiling in the hot backrooms of restaurants. Mr John acts as Master of Ceremonies and referee both, and his decisions and time-keeping are invariably scrupulously fair.

The show begins sometime before midnight. Bob Marley is abruptly and unceremoniously silenced, the scratch-pop-hiss of ancient vinyl fills the bar, and then the music starts.

Music is the correct word for it, but only just. Produced by the *pi chawa*, a Siamese snake charmer's flute of a clarinet, it is a weirdly intoxicating sound: atonal yet melodic, it is spiked with a rhythmic repetition unfathomable in quavers or semi-quavers but instantly captivating. The first time you hear a pi chawa you start to ask what it is; before you have even got the words out, the sound has you in its grasp.

And now the fighters process out towards the ring. One is wearing red trunks, the other blue, and a matching braided headpiece tapers backwards from each determined forehead. Each combatant is sleekly bare-chested and sports a length of red thread tied around his upper arm.

The two trainers bear down on the top rope to allow their young charges to enter the ring; once inside, each moves to his own corner and there begins his ritual dance. This is an intimate and holy thing, and to look on it can sometimes feel a little improper, like spying on a monk as he goes about his prayers. Every fighter has his own unique interpretation of the act of communion, but the most popular movements acknowledge the four corners of the ring and pay tribute to the rising sun; one cinematic variant requires the fighter to physically enact the digging of his opponent's grave.

And all around, always, there is the sound of the pi chawa. The volume never changes – the stereo at Reggae Bar is anyway permanently set to eleven – but as the phrases build and repeat, build and repeat, the music becomes more persuasive, as if it were a narcotic that has now built to toxicity in the tissues; by the time Mr John rings the bell, audience and fighters alike are both utterly entranced.

Perhaps this is just as well, for human beings burdened by the everyday could never appreciate movements made with such grace and freedom, much less perform them. The fighters jab and swipe, duck and soar, testing each other's range and sometimes erupting in a mass of angular limbs to please whatever crowd there is with a flying elbow or a forward sweep.

Mr John keeps a watchful eye on proceedings, but rarely has cause to intervene. Occasionally somebody is knocked down, but never out: this is not the televised Saturday night fights that come live from Bangkok's Lumpini Stadium and Chai shows on his snow-storming television at the Rock Backpackers, nor, truth be told, is it even a proper neighbourhood bout. Any single one of the kicks would be enough to send a lesser mortal into neighbouring Trang Province, but here each solid connection is acknowledged with a smile or a bash of the gloves that betrays the fact this is just play, an exhibition match, a semi-choreographed show to ensure that the tourists get their fifty baht's worth.

After five rounds the spent fighters take their bow, Mr John raises the winner's arm and Bob Marley picks up where last he left off. The ring is now thrown open to the floor and any travellers wishing to spar with their friends are invited to pull on the gloves. Mercifully, Mr John continues to serve as referee here and ensures that things never get too far out of hand.

Two months after the tsunami, Graham had found a kind of solace deep in the disciplines and rituals of Thai boxing and had started to keep time at inter-club fights. One weekend a bout is held on the west coast of Scotland in order to raise money for tsunami relief in Thailand, and I travel through with a group of Dominic's friends.

The ring has been erected in a gymnasium much like the ones where Dominic passed so many of his evenings and weekends when we were young: the smell of chlorine drifting up from the basement pool, an empty vending machine, a sign insisting that only indoor shoes be worn here. The assembled company is almost entirely male and many of them are obviously connected with the fighting in some way; even among those who are not, the dress code remains shaven head, sportswear and abundant tattoos. If it sounds at all intimidating, it is precisely the opposite: they are a friendly, smiling bunch, and it is immediately obvious why Dominic – who had shaved his head since his early teens, frequently tormented Mum with his plans for various tattoos and possessed his own thousand-watt smile – would have felt at home amongst them.

We buy cans of lager from a makeshift bar, take our seats

and attempt to make small talk. I am surrounded by some of Dominic's oldest friends, but it is still difficult to be here today. It is the first time since Boxing Day that I have left Edinburgh, and every time I think of how the money raised from this event is to be sent to help communities affected by the tsunami, I have to bite my cheeks to stop myself from crying. I have decided that the solution is not to think of this any more when the day's Master of Ceremonies stands up to introduce the first fight.

This Master of Ceremonies is a striking-looking man: six foot three, yet so fighter lean he must be a flyweight, he too sports the closely shaven head but is dressed in a full kilt and fly plaid. When he speaks, he does so in a strong Glaswegian accent and with a naturally loud voice that is potentiated by a superfluous public address system which sends it booming around the gymnasium.

'Now, as everybody in this room today knows,' I hear this stranger to me say, 'we lost one of our boys over there.'

We lost one of our boys over there. He has flying-round-house kicked me in the gut. He has winded me. I am struggling to breathe.

We lost one of our boys over there. It makes Dominic sound like a fallen soldier in the war films we used to watch together when we were young. All men yearn for fraternity, and if you die far away and later somebody stands up and tells a gymnasium full of your peers that they have lost one of their boys, well, whatever else happened in your life, how-ever abruptly or sadly it ended, you certainly found a place in this world.

He was our boy, of course – his parents' boy, his grand-parents' boy, Edinburgh's boy – but, hearing this west coast stranger say it, I know it to be unquestionably true that he was their boy as well. An entire part of his life that I knew so little about and yet he was their boy too, and they share in our loss.

We lost one of our boys over there. I am still thinking about this when the music starts and I hear the pi chawa for the first time in my life.

On the 26th of December 2004, Dominic and his girlfriend Eileen were staying in a beachfront bungalow at a place called Charlie's Resort on Ko Phi Phi. Four days into their fortnight's holiday in Thailand, they had arrived on the island on Christmas Eve and planned to remain there for a few more days before leaving to explore the north of the country.

Phi Phi is the glittering jewel in the emerald and gold crown that is the coastal south of Thailand, and Dominic and Eileen's trip there was intended as a half chance well taken. At the end of a long and apparently fruitless autumn of Edinburgh house-hunting, Eileen already had plans to travel east to visit her grandmother in Hong Kong and Dominic had some annual leave to use up before the new year. A restorative winter break seemed a good idea, and Thailand the perfect place to rendezvous.

A few weeks after they had booked their flights, they found that they'd had a speculative offer accepted on a flat in Edinburgh. The place was more or less derelict – and hence a dream of a first home for my architect brother and his creative girlfriend – but the deposit alone would consume their savings, and they quickly found that their plane tickets were non-refundable. They had happily concluded that there was nothing to do but go to Thailand, enjoy themselves, and live on bread and water once they returned home.

At lunchtime on Christmas Day, Dominic had phoned Mum's house in Edinburgh from one of the telephone and internet shops that crowd Phi Phi's narrow streets. It was already evening in Thailand, and he and Eileen were on their way out for dinner. When my turn to talk to him came, we wished each other a happy Christmas and he told me that I would need to get out to Thailand soon myself. Phi Phi, he said, was an island paradise and I would surely love it there.

We ate our own dinner, set our pudding on fire, pulled our crackers and read aloud the jokes inside them. Afterwards we sat in the living room, that year half-filled by an enormous Scots Pine a friend of Mum's with a Christmas tree business had gifted us. A week previously, Dominic and Mum had dressed it together and as evening segued into night we complimented their handiwork and worked our way through the leftover spirits that annually emerge from the back of the cupboard.

Early the next morning, I was woken by the telephone ringing. Somehow I had the idea that it must be Dominic, and I hurried downstairs to answer it.

But it was not Dominic, it was his friend Caroline, and she wanted to know if we had heard from him. Still sleepy and only mildly puzzled, I told her that he had phoned yesterday and reassured her that they were having a good time. Caroline hesitated and then said, no, what she was asking me was if we had heard anything from him yet *today*?

I put down the phone and switched on the television. Already, every channel was showing home-video footage of an earthquake in Indonesia and the tsunami that had ensued around the Indian Ocean. Indonesia and Sri Lanka appeared to be the hardest hit countries, but the news ticker at the bottom of the screen said that Thailand had also been affected.

Neither Dominic's nor Eileen's mobile would ring when I called them, but I was not unduly worried: on the television they had said that all communications in the region were down and, anyway, the flooding portrayed in these early pictures seemed relatively innocuous, the kind of thing that a fit young couple like Dominic and Eileen would have little difficulty navigating if it ever really came to it. I sent them each a text message asking them to get in touch when they could and then went through to tell Mum before she heard the news on her radio.

Still sleeping, she stirred when I entered her room. I sat down on the edge of her bed and told her what I thought I knew so far: that there had been an earthquake in Indonesia and some subsequent flooding in Thailand, that the phones were out so we had not yet heard from Dominic and Eileen, that we would do soon.

Mum, however, only stared at me. When I reassured her that it would be all right, that there was really nothing to worry about, she could still only stare at me. Months later she would tell me that as soon as she woke she had felt an overwhelming emptiness in the world, and when she had heard me say the words 'earthquake' and 'Thailand' she had understood what it meant.

We gathered in the living room to watch the television news and await their phone call, but the news was on an unchanging loop and the phone steadfastly refused to ring.

At noon I thought to check my email and felt my pulse quicken as I saw that I had a new message from Dominic. Scanning through it, I found no mention of any earthquake or flood and with dismay realised that it had been sent yesterday, shortly after he and I had spoken on the phone. For everything else this message would later come to mean to me, for now it only did not tell me that they were safe.

Each piece of news that trickled out of Asia over the

course of that first day was incrementally worse: the earthquake that had triggered the tsunami was stronger than initially thought; around the Indian Ocean over a thousand people were feared to have been killed; Phi Phi had certainly been affected, possibly severely so.

By the middle of the afternoon, when the skies blacken in the depths of a Scottish winter, it was already midnight in Thailand. Midnight and we still had not heard from our two missing travellers. Mum was quietly inconsolable, but the rest of us told each other that Dominic and Eileen must simply be stuck somewhere without access to a telephone, that we would surely hear from them before we ourselves went to bed. There was still nothing to worry about, for if nothing else we all knew that Dominic was a good swimmer. When somebody recalled that Eileen had only recently started to take swimming lessons, we reassured ourselves that Dominic would certainly have been able to get them both out of any trouble they might have found themselves in.

Dinner time came and went but nobody could eat. At nine o'clock the television began to give out a telephone number for a casualty bureau that the British government had set up. It took two hours of trying and when we eventually got through they had no information to offer us and instead only wanted to glean ominous details about Dominic and Eileen: their dates of birth, their heights and shoe sizes, their passport numbers and whether they had any birthmarks or other distinguishing features; when I protested, the harried policewoman on the other end asked me what I had been expecting from her.

At midnight we went to bed only to lie awake in our separate rooms. As I fell asleep in the small hours I told myself that there would be good news in the morning. Dominic and Eileen were twenty-seven and twenty-four years old, they

17

had just bought their first home together and it was Christmas time; it was unthinkable that there would not be good news in the morning.

But the morning brought no good news, and the bad news had grown still worse. The time difference meant it was already early afternoon in Thailand; by now, Phi Phi had been evacuated for the best part of a day. The local hospitals had posted casualty lists on their websites and Dominic and Eileen's names did not feature on them. Experts on television were now openly talking of the Indian Ocean tsunami as a disaster on an unprecedented scale.

On the lunchtime news a correspondent walked along Phi Phi's devastated Loh Dahlum beach and delivered a piece to camera. As he spoke, he smashed a balled fist into his flattened palm and said this was how the water hit this island, like this. Mum and her husband Rob, who had together visited Phi Phi the preceding summer, recognised the background for what it was: the empty place where Charlie's Resort had once stood.

We turned off the television, agreeing that we would not watch the news any more, and then snuck off hourly to do so alone. On the internet, Mum found an interview with the owner of Charlie's Resort; he was quoted as saying that he feared many of his guests had been swept out to sea and would never be recovered.

But it remained unthinkable. Quietly, frantically, I searched for a reason that they could not be dead, and eventually settled upon a detail with which to reassure myself. The television, the newspapers, even the hysterical internet had been repeating that there were only nine British casualties and then that there were only eleven, that now there were only twelve. With such a small handful of Britons lost, had

Dominic and Eileen actually been among their number we surely would have had some definitive news from Thailand by now. No news, I decided, must be good news.

For all that, the tasks with which I distracted myself might have told me another story. I obtained Dominic and Eileen's passport numbers. I posted their pictures in newsgroups about Thailand and when those drew no helpful response, searched through online catalogues until I found images of the bags they had carried with them, of the exact model of Dominic's digital camera and a wristwatch that matched the one Dad had given him on his twenty-first birthday. These I forwarded to the survivors who had already started to write internet postings about their experiences, as if the only reason we had not yet heard from Dominic and Eileen was that somebody did not know what their bags looked like, or which model of wristwatch he wore.

By late afternoon the pictures on television had evolved from collapsing buildings and onrushing floodwaters to temple mortuaries shrouded in dry ice and tearful airport reunions. Again, I reminded myself that there were now only fifteen confirmed British casualties, that if anything had happened to Dominic and Eileen we surely would have heard.

At some point that evening, Mum got up and walked over to the Christmas tree that had stood so awkwardly whilst the television spilled its foreign tragedy into our lives. Slowly, methodically, she began to strip off its baubles, its tinsel, its sparkling lametta. Nine days and a lifetime ago, Dominic had helped her decorate it and now none of us could look at it. Later that night, my Uncle Bob stood up and announced his intention to travel to Thailand the next day; for all the reassurance I was still taking from the casualty numbers, I made no attempt to stop him.

I went to bed but again could not sleep. Lying awake at

19

four in the morning, turning it all over in my head for the millionth time, searching for the elusive fact that would provide the indubitable proof that they were still alive, I came across its polar opposite: of the fifteen officially declared British casualties, not a single one of them had been from Scotland. Scots account for around ten percent of the United Kingdom's population, and the implication was clear: the figures to which I had been clinging like a life raft were wrong. There were more British casualties than were being reported, and we had not heard from Dominic and Eileen because they were indeed amongst them.

I put on my dressing gown and went downstairs. Mum was sitting up on the couch, staring into the cold blue flames of the gas fire. Looking up at me, she did her best to muster a smile. Of all the awful things that were currently happening, this was one of the worst, and I can write that because I know Dominic would have agreed with me. Mothers love their sons in ways unfathomable even to those same sons and for two days now my every second thought had been about Mum. With Dominic gone it seemed to fall to me to somehow try to shield her from the worst of this, but I had no earthly idea of how to even begin. I sat down beside her and we cried together.

On the twenty-eighth of December we woke to find that the hospitals had ceased updating their casualty lists. If the notion remained unspoken, we had come to understand that we now had to somehow focus our efforts on the search for Dominic and Eileen's bodies: the only thing worse than for them to be found would be for them never to be found at all.

Nor was the risk solely that the water had taken them. Uncle Bob was already on his first plane to London, but it would be another twenty-four hours before he reached the temples at Krabi and Phuket. Meantime, the internet had been set alight with rumours of bodies being falsely claimed by desperate families. What if even their remains were lost to us in such a way? How, Mum asked quietly, would we ever be able to say goodbye?

The identification websites that began to appear late that afternoon seemed to provide a solution: if I could only here locate them, I would be able to guide Uncle Bob to the correct temple, to the correct bodies. It might be the smallest of mercies for Mum, but it would be a mercy all the same.

But I could not look at the first round of pictures. I waited as half a screen of images of what I took to be tsunami debris loaded then, realising what I was actually staring at, turned the computer off. Battered in the chaos, bloated by the water then scorched black by the sun, the corpses I had glimpsed were barely recognisable as having once been human, let alone the people we loved.

By the next morning, the authorities had learned the technique of blotting out the swollen limbs and the gorged faces. If the change made the images themselves less confronting, the experience remained crucifying. All that you could do was to wish and not wish for some sight of a T-shirt you remembered, a piece of jewellery you had once remarked upon, a wristwatch inscribed with your brother's initials. In these moments I oscillated between loathing myself for praying for the glimpse of a relic that would put an end to our hopeless waiting, and constructing absurd fantasies in which Dominic and Eileen's continued absence from the ranks of these identifiable dead could only be proof that they were still alive somewhere.

This latter made even less sense than my earlier belief in the fifteen British casualties had, because really the only way you could have successfully identified your loved one from these pictures would be if they'd had a tattoo. For all his musings, Dominic had never got round to getting his, nobody recalled Eileen having one and, anyway, I had never seen tattoos like the ones on the screen in front of me. To begin with I could not even comprehend them, could not understand how so many bodies could have been decorated with so much ink.

Coiled cobras and fire-breathing dragons, orchids and galleons, leaping tigers, junk ships, butterflies and unknowable words calligraphed in curlicuing scripts. These were the tattoos of the dead, and as my heart broke apart they were more beautiful than anything I had ever seen. Calming to the point of transfixion, I could not stop myself from staring at them, and when I stepped away from the computer found their forms intruding into my thoughts and haunting my sleepless dreams. In those days of desperate search, these tattoos were like a tantalisingly visible DNA, the scales of dragons and the petals of flowers the whorls and loops of a fingerprint legible to the naked eye. Had Dominic and Eileen only been similarly marked, we would have been able to fetch them home immediately.

The nearest thing Dominic had to a tattoo was a scar from the abdominal surgery he had undergone when he was twenty-two, but even by the fifth day this stigmata was yet to have helped us. Uncle Bob had barely rested since arriving in Thailand, and for our own impotent part we had kept ceaseless watch on the identification sites, but together we had made scant progress. The bodies were simply too battered and too many for those charged with cataloguing the dead to attempt to document each scar, and in the pictures we viewed on the computer such details were obscured unless they happened to abut a tattoo.

By the time Uncle Bob found his way to a guesthouse bed that evening, he had spent two full days scanning the albums displayed outside the temples, hoping and yet not hoping to find a picture of a body that he recognised. These photographs remained uncensored but Bob bore his task with typical avuncular fortitude, signing off from his every telephone call back to me with an instruction to 'Keep on trucking, brother'. Even knowing only as much as the news programmes had been willing to show of the disaster zone that Bob had landed in, to keep on trucking seemed to be the very least that I could do.

On New Year's Eve, something about one of the pictures caught Bob's attention and, as he had done on three prior occasions, he asked to be shown the body that it represented. Once more he donned the protective overalls and once more he pulled on the mask; inside the temple, he again smelled the formaldehyde and steeled himself to view a corpse that shared his nephew's height and shoe size. Once more, he hoped and did not hope that this would be the body he was searching for; unlike on each previous occasion when they took him into the refrigeration unit, this time Bob saw that the abdomen of the body bore a neat surgical scar.

How could it ever come down to this, that the question of whether or not this might be Dominic's body came down to the presence of a simple scar? Surely Bob ought to have known the young man who had inherited his love of reggae music and even his old stereo to play it on, the kindred spirit who had sought him out at every family gathering to listen to his traveller's tales? And yet, the truth is that he could not have. For this is what the water and the things it carried with it did to the people we loved: it took their lives from them, and once that was done it went about rendering them unrecognisable.

When he was nineteen, Dominic was diagnosed with Crohn's disease, an inflammation of the gastrointestinal tract. Later, in his final year of university, the illness flared to such an extent that all his doctors could do for him was to cut out the affected segment of bowel. When Bob telephoned me that evening, then, what he really needed me to tell him was where exactly Dominic's abdominal scar had been.

I did not know, and I hated the fact that I did not know. In France the previous summer we had swum together daily and, though I could picture Dominic standing on the edge of the pool claiming that the scar had been sustained in a knife fight on the mean streets of Glasgow, I could not visualise its location. More correctly: I could visualise it, but having thought about it too much in the past days and nights, I could now picture it centrally, peripherally, vertically, horizontally, even diagonally. I no longer knew where my brother's scar was. I told Bob this, and he told me to keep on trucking, that we would find some other way to tell if this was the body for which we were searching.

Should auld acquaintance be forgot,
And never brought to mind?
Should auld acquaintance be forgot,
And days o' Auld Lang Syne?

Scottish people like to claim that the night when one year passes into the next is a bigger occasion to us than even Christmas itself. Known as Hogmanay, it is an evening saturated in whisky and customs both: the sharing of a forty-percent proof cake known as 'black bun', the communal midnight singing of 'Auld Lang Syne', the calling in on your neighbours clutching a symbolic piece of coal. As we entered

2005, we did none of those things, and instead simply each lifted a glass to a toast that said all that it seemed there was to say.

'To Dominic and Eileen, wherever they are.'

Before I went to bed I returned to the computer and went through the identification sites once again, half hoping I would find the scarred body that Bob had been looking at that afternoon, still half hoping even now to happen across an entirely different kind of miracle: a delayed email that told me of a change of plan, a newly updated hospital casualty list with their amnesiac names on it. I found neither and before I knew it was again lost in pages of tattoos, my stormy sea becalmed once more by their quiet and final beauty.

On New Year's Day I woke to a message from Uncle Bob asking me to call him when I could. Over the course of his own insomniac night he had begun to doubt that the body with the scar was Dominic's. Having been told that a military helicopter had recently flown in what was thought likely to be a final batch of bodies from Phi Phi, he had approached a soldier and told him that he was looking for the body of his nephew, Dominic.

'Dominic!' the soldier had replied, 'Yes, yes, Dominic!'

The soldier had led him to an English-speaking colleague, who in turn had told Bob that one of the bodies recovered from Phi Phi that morning had been found with a wallet containing bank cards in Dominic's name. The bodies were still being processed, and Bob had so far seen neither wallet nor body, but anticipated being shown both in the next few hours.

In Edinburgh, we drove out to my aunt's house on the nearby coast. It was a bitterly cold day, a winter sun set low in a chill white sky and a freezing wind blowing in from the

North Sea. As we walked across the hard wet sand, outwardly indistinguishable from every other family out for their bracing New Year's Day walk, I felt my phone begin to vibrate in my pocket. I knew that it was Uncle Bob, and I knew what he was calling to tell me, but I did not answer it, and instead let my brother's death knell ring out in my pocket.

Somehow I imagined this was an act of kindness, that if I could stop Mum knowing the truth for another half an hour, that if I could give her even twenty more minutes of walking along a beach in a world where she might still have two living sons, that is what I must do. I realise now, of course, that I was protecting her from nothing. At the medical school I attended we were taught how to break bad news and that the bereaved have inalienable rights: the right to hear it at their own pace in a gently lit room, the right to have a friend present, even the right not to initially believe this news if they so choose. If you are a mother who has lost a son, however, you are granted no such privileges, for the first time you wake you feel an overwhelming emptiness, and from that moment on you know exactly what has happened.

And so we walked on, battered by the north wind, each of us wrapped up in memories of Dominic, in thoughts of the impossible grief we had so quickly come to know. As we approached the house, my Aunt Catriona came out towards us.

'Oh Mary,' she said, 'Oh Simon.'

A few weeks after Dominic and Eileen had been searching the city for the fixer-upper flat that would be their first home, we drove around Edinburgh seeking out a place to bury him.

If this was the grimmest of tasks, the day matched perfectly: the sky dark, the wind coming from every direction, the rain sharply freezing. On such an afternoon in early January, even Edinburgh looks awful, her castle gothically foreboding, her cobblestones slicked to a treacherous black, her citizens bowed and weary. The cemeteries we visited that morning were studies in municipal disinterest and private heartbreak: swirling in windblown litter, their grass long since turned to mud and half their headstones knocked down by vandals, their sole pilgrims were the dog walkers for whom the park was too far in such weather. Though we told each other that in summer these places would be different, and knew that in reality the stones had been prostrated not by vandals but by safety-conscious council workmen, there was still no way that we could bury him here.

When Mum suggested that we drive out to the old churchyard at Colinton, I attempted to talk her out of it. Colinton, the sleepy suburb where we had lived until we were thirteen and fourteen, had been everybody's first thought, but the undertaker had been swift to warn us that no new graves had been permitted in the churchyard in years. It seemed that to visit the place would only be to torture ourselves, but Mum was not to be dissuaded.

27

As soon as we exit the car, the rest of us understand why Mum has insisted we come here, for this is the place where Dominic must be buried. Even on a day bleak as this one, the churchyard is starkly handsome, but more than that it instantly feels right, or at least as close to right as anything can be when we are all still waiting for the alarm clock to wake us from this nightmare, for the apologetic telephone call explaining that it has all been a terrible misunderstanding. We will await these things for ever, but later that day Rob calls the council and they tell him that the recent relocation of a path in the churchyard has created some new burial plots.

And then we enter limbo. We go to bed believing that Dominic's body will be arriving in Edinburgh the next day, but what we receive in the morning is a phone call from the Foreign Office informing us that the situation has changed: all the tsunami victims in Thailand must now be identified through an internationally agreed protocol called Disaster Victim Identification.

It is the right thing and we know that it is. Identification has so far proceeded on an ad hoc basis, and stories of erroneously repatriated bodies have already started to appear in the press. Under this new system, all bodies released must now have been formally matched by dental records, DNA, or fingerprint comparison; a single day earlier and Dominic's body would have been returned to us without question, but as a telltale scar and bank cards in a pocket do not feature on this official list, there is now a problem.

Dominic's dental records, faxed from our childhood surgery in Colinton village, have already been effectively matched but a small discrepancy in the nomenclature means that the DVI committee cannot accept them as confirmation of his identity. We now require one of either a DNA or a fingerprint match; very quickly, we discover that these things do not work in the way they do on television.

Take DNA identification. We initially assume that it is a binary science, a matter of scanning something into a computer and waiting a few minutes until the machine beeps with a result. What it turns out to be is a technique, an art, a skill subject to human vagaries and the chance whims of nature.

For Dominic's DNA to be analysed, samples must first be aspirated from the marrow of his hip bone or the pulp of his wisdom tooth, immediately refrigerated and flown to a laboratory in China. There they are irradiated under ultraviolet light, soaked in distilled water, bathed in alcohol and boiled in alkaline solution. The tentative fragments of his DNA this process may release must then be separated by centrifugation, isolated from one another by the cautious addition of priming chemicals, and placed with an alchemic polymerase in a machine capable of rapid heating and cooling. At low temperatures the polymerase will bind to and create a mirror image of Dominic's DNA; at high temperatures these two strands will unwind themselves so that the process may begin again. The heating and cooling is performed thirty times in the hope of obtaining sufficient quantities of a usable sample, and such is the fragile and long-distance prayer of DNA identification.

Fingerprints are no more straightforward, circles and whorls that have been soaked in salt water and scorched under tropical sun having already proven far beyond the reach of any conventional forensic examination. To garner readable prints from the tsunami dead, investigators must first develop and benchmark novel techniques of tissue rehydration. This too takes time.

But even once the precious DNA has been obtained or the elusive print procured, the question inevitably arises of what they might actually usefully be compared with. If a crime were being investigated they could be analysed against the samples of a known suspect or those on a national database, but how can they be used to prove these are the remains of somebody whose only encounters with the law involved being the victim of serial bicycle theft?

It can be done, it turns out, by having two police officers visit the small rented flat Dominic and Eileen shared and examining their home as if it were indeed the scene of a crime. These investigators do not wear the plastic overshoes or the white space suits, but this is otherwise the part that occurs in the way it does on television. For there the two officers will move around Dominic and Eileen's rooms, quietly ignoring the notes on the mirror which say 'Tidy up tonight, please' and 'No, thanks!' whilst patiently gathering up whatever evidence they can find: the forsaken toothbrushes, the discarded razor blades, the glasses on the sideboard that still patiently wait to be lifted up and replaced in the cupboard.

We are equally helpless in our own waiting. Sometimes we manage to be patient, and sometimes we do not. Mum, particularly, wants her lost boy's body home now; when she asks why this simple clemency cannot be granted, it is a question for which none of us can provide an answer. Instead, we make phone calls and write letters – to politicians, cabinet members, even the Prime Minister – but the truth is that we might as well be calling numbers picked at random from the Yellow Pages or writing to Father Christmas care of the North Pole, for our elected representatives are as powerless as we are. The science takes as long as it takes.

We do not know it yet, but for months we will exist in this vacuum, our days empty and endless, our nights still but sleepless. Psychologists say that grieving only starts after a funeral has taken place, and in this they might be right; without Dominic's body, without even the sight of the coffin that contains his body, we begin to feel like lost travellers ourselves. Just as Dominic's body waits in a funeral home in a foreign city, so we wait in a strange land too, walking around the silent rooms of our house, picking things up only to put them back down again.

Alone at night, I drive Dominic's old car out on the city bypass, crank up the stereo playing the last tape he had been listening to and put my foot to the floor. In the daytime I hike in the Pentland foothills and sit by the frozen reservoirs we once knew so well but now seem like places from another continent. Sometimes I cry, but mostly I find myself waiting for the sky to crack open.

It seems impossible that my brother could have left in such a way, even more so that he might have done so without telling me, that I will never now exchange another word with the only soul that was built from the exact same pieces as mine. It seems impossible, and so at a certain point I once again simply stop believing that he is dead. In this new world of chaos it seems no more implausible than any other explanation, and each day that passes without a call to say his body has satisfied the identification requirements only reinforces this. Stories are how I have been earning my living lately and it seems clear to me that fate is playing this one with a twist: the dental records did not match not because of any problem with the nomenclature, but because they were being compared to somebody else's teeth; the body lying in the funeral home in Thailand is not Dominic's, but that of a thief who stole his wallet shortly before the water arrived. Dominic is safely marooned on an island or lying in a hospital somewhere with his transient but utterly fixable amnesia. Soon a passing ship will spot his signal fire. Soon he will come to and recall everything with a start. Soon his name will light up on my phone and I will answer it to hear a voice that asks, 'Alright, Si?'

But the phone call that arrives in the middle of March is not this one that I have again started to expect. A fingerprint on a glass the police officers took from the kitchen of their flat has proven a match and the criteria have been satisfied. Dominic really is dead, and his body is to be flown home overnight.

On what should be Dominic's twenty-eighth birthday, I am sitting in a small room near the centre of Edinburgh, my head rested upon his coffin.

A week ago now, we drove out to the airport and waited at an appointed back entrance. A freezing wind was blowing in from the Firth of Forth as overhead the Airbuses and Boeings roared in and out. We stood together in silence, wishing we were aboard one of them, travelling away to London, to Paris, to New York; wishing that what had happened had not, wishing that what was about to happen would not. After ten minutes the black car appeared, inching its way between the static aeroplanes at a mournful pace. It was a scene from a state funeral or the homecoming of a fallen soldier, a scene none of us ever imagined we would have any part to play in. Behind, on the runway proper, the planes continued to take off and land, but now did so soundlessly.

The hearse drew level with us and stopped. With a slow, martial dignity the driver got out and opened the back door of his vehicle. Each of us took a turn to walk up and place our hands on the coffin, uttering our secret small prayers as we made our communion with the cold wood. This done, the driver quietly closed the door again and we set off for the funeral parlour.

Corstorphine, Haymarket, the Grassmarket, the Cowgate: the familiar streets fell away interminably as we kept our measured pace with the hearse. Impatient following cars – unaware of the black one ahead of us – sounded their horns, but were as silent to us as the landing planes had been. Edinburgh is the smallest of cities, and every street corner we passed brought some memory of Dominic rushing back: here the zoo with its penguin parade when we were young, there the shop where I bought him a beer-making kit for a distant teenage birthday, in that tenement the flat of a girl we knew who gave the best parties. Even the funeral parlour on St Mary's Street in the city's old town was three doors down from the restaurant we had eaten in on the very last night I had seen Dominic.

And Saint Mary: apostle of the sea, patron saint against flooding and of mariners, watermen, yachtsmen and sailors, of travellers, of builders, of motherhood, of childbirth, of the whole human race. The one our own mother was named for. It ought to have made it easier to leave him there, but it didn't.

We watched the funeral parlour gates close behind the hearse and discovered that we did not know what to do with ourselves. To simply return home – to warm rooms, to the food that friends were even now still leaving on our doorstep – seemed somehow disrespectful. Somebody mentioned the nearby cathedral and, non-believers all, we crept inside and each lit two candles. One was for Dominic, now lying a few hundred yards from the altar where we were standing, and one was for Eileen, about whom there had been no news for the past three months.

When we were young, I looked forward to Dominic's birth-day more even than I did my own. Mine brought presents, but Dominic's signified that we were growing up, and fast: at eight years old I overnight knew somebody big enough to merit double figures; at eleven I woke to find a teenager now slept in the next room. Moreover, Dominic's birthday meant that we had made it through winter: through the freezing mornings where even bowls of irradiated sweet porridge offered little incentive to leave our cosy beds, through the endless street-lit afternoons, through the frosted Saturday practices where the impact of a firmly struck rubber football on a cold thigh was universally acknowledged to be immediately fatal.

Yet as much as it was about what we were leaving, it was also about what we were now rushing headlong towards. In Edinburgh, spring arrives dramatically, the city's northerly latitude rendering it not so much a season as a sudden stand-off between the battling gods of winter and summer. One evening you draw the curtains tight against a night as wild as any you have known, and the next morning you open them to find azure skies that stretch all the way to heaven. Stepping outside, you taste the change on the air but though the wakening white sun shines as hard as it can, the north wind remains resolute in its refusal to warm by even a single degree, as if to do so would be an act of treachery against the winter that has allowed it such free rein. It is a day both freezing and glorious, a day to blow the dust from the deepest recesses of hibernating young minds; in childhood memory, it is a day that never once failed to fall on the nineteenth of March. We woke up on Dominic's birthday, pulled the curtains aside, and knew that we were now on the back straight: ahead of us lay the Easter fortnight off school, the short summer term with its camps and sports days and, finally, the promised land of the long holidays themselves.

Joni Mitchell has a lyric that runs 'Come on light the candle in this poor heart of mine' and each time I hear it I find myself flinching with recognition, for she has described exactly how the physical act can feel: as if the candle is being

35

lit not in an empty church or draughty cathedral, but in the hollow chambers of an actual human heart. You touch your dry wick to a flame that burns with somebody else's loss, you watch their fire catch your own troubles and you feel your burden soften as surely as the wax beneath starts to melt and drip to the flagstone floor. It is the simplest of rituals but sometimes the sense of calm it gives you is strong enough to last a whole day, and sometimes even longer.

The day that Dominic's body arrived back was a hard one and the candles I had left burning in the cathedral near St Mary's Street proved no more than a temporary salve, their effects on me sustaining no longer than the wicks themselves would have remained aflame. Their heat and light may have carried me through the late afternoon and early part of the evening, but at seven o'clock the enormity of the things we had seen and done that day abruptly enveloped me: in a rush, I could now hear the deafening roar of the inbound planes, the angry honking of the impatient car horns; suddenly I could understand what a thing a coffin was.

Until I saw it, the whole thing could still have been make-believe, and in a way it was. Up to that moment, my information had come almost entirely from phone calls, from faxes and emails, and therefore was nothing more than simple binary ones and zeroes. In fact, it was even less than that, because the most important information – the call from Dominic and Eileen that never came through – was merely a lack of these ones and zeroes. Whilst I might have gone through the motions of behaving as if he were dead, of sending emails and making phone calls of my own, of arranging other zeroes and ones to carry the details of birthmarks and scars down optical fibre cables, I had still never entirely believed it. And now that I finally had to believe – because I had seen this wooden box that my brother lay inside, because

36

I had touched it with my own hand – the feeling was like nothing I had ever known.

It was a desolation, an emptiness, a sense that a freezing winter wind had snuffed out every burning candle in every church and temple on earth. It was the sudden realisation that several months ago some twisted surgeon had put me to sleep, removed my heart, and sewn me back up without ever admitting what it was that he had done to me. It made a terrible and inevitable kind of sense and came with the certain knowledge that there was nothing I could do about any of it: there was no fire left, anywhere in the world, to even think about relighting any candle with, and anyway no heart in which to do so. Worse, if the removal of my heart was going to kill me, it would surely have done so months ago. I had seen his coffin, had touched it with my hand, and now I realised that I was for ever consigned to wander, alone and without a heart, in a dark and freezing world.

Fashioned from a rich foreign rosewood, Dominic's coffin is absurdly large: too wide to reach my arms around in a bear hug, long enough that when I first saw it at the airport a week ago, I wondered if they had sent us the right body. Since then, we have been informed that the coffin is necessarily this size in order to accommodate the steel casket in which Dominic's body had been sealed before leaving Thailand, a steel casket we have been strictly instructed not to open.

At my medical school I learned too that bereaved families should be gently encouraged to view the bodies of their departed loved ones, that this might help them attain a thing called closure, but the water has rendered that impossible for us. I will not get to see him, to touch his body, to look on his face one last time, to simply see that his eyes have remained closed on the journey home. None of us will. Dominic has a head injury and it took three days for his body to be recovered from the tropical island where he fell; somewhere inside these Russian doll layers of wood, metal and muslin is my brother's broken body, but it has been decreed too damaged, too dangerous for us to see. I want to tell whoever might listen that I do not care, that this is my brother, no matter what has befallen him, no matter what has been done to him, but I do not.

In part, I do not because I am simply afraid, because our police liaison officer firmly warned me against even looking at photographs of him. I have certified my houseman's share of deaths, have placed my stethoscope atop still hearts, shone bright lights into unreacting pupils and touched wisps of cotton wool against unflinching corneas, but I am afraid to look now at the body of my own brother, afraid to see the damage that has been wrought on him.

I am afraid, but more than anything I believe that he should not be disturbed. Three months have passed since Dominic left this world, and to look on him now – to splinter the wood, to grind through the metal and shake his sleeping bones awake – seems an act of unspeakable desecration. Three months ago in the temple at Krabi, Uncle Bob laid a hand on his head; through that touch, I try to tell myself now, flowed the love of all of us; with that touch I must believe that we all said our physical goodbyes.

On his birthday, then, I only lay my head on the alien wood and whisper some of the things I wish I had told him in the restaurant three doors down the street whilst I still had the chance.

I am barely murmuring, but my voice comes reflecting back off the polished wood. I keep talking back at it, telling his rosewood coffin the same urgent things over and over again. They are simple sentiments, easily expressed in the

38

most basic of language, and take mere seconds to say; here, in this sparse room, it is impossible for me to fathom why I never said them to him before.

It is equally too late to be bringing birthday offerings, but that did not stop me buying what may or may not have been flowers. Nowadays I can pick a bouquet of lilies at a hundred paces, but in those first months I hadn't much experience and that morning I had been mis-sold a strange-looking bunch of purple stems that the florist had claimed were all the fashion. I write 'mis-sold' but, really, I had only myself to blame. I had entered the shop hesitatingly and, glimpsing my indecision, she had asked me what the occasion was. Not wishing to have to tell her our whole sad tale, I had said simply that it was a birthday.

Only when I was back out in the car, purple stems on the passenger seat beside me, did I realise that I ought to have asked her for tulips, after the Sylvia Plath poem which takes them as its title. Its opening line had been stuck in my head since first thing that morning when I had looked out of the bathroom window to see a cold grey sky: 'The tulips are too excitable, it is winter here.'

Dominic had studied the poem in his fifth-year English class and had enjoyed introducing me to it.

'Si, you know how much you like all that depressing Nirvana stuff?' he had said. 'Well, you're going to absolutely love this.'

I had not thought of the poem or the conversation in years, but it was a perfect fit. Today was Dominic's birthday, but you could not have looked out on such a sky and claimed this nineteenth of March was anything but winter.

A lucky bag of birthday memories.

Dominic is six today, and our Uncle John has included a

consolation present for me in the parcel that he has posted up to Edinburgh. My gift is a foot-high silver robot that shoots tomahawk missiles out of his chrome-plated forehead. By contrast, the birthday boy's present – a yo-yo that lights up – seems surprisingly meagre.

It takes perhaps an hour for the parental administrative error to be rectified, by which time my relationship with the robot has progressed beyond simple infatuation to purest first love. Divining my distress, Dominic reassures me that if I will only grant him reciprocal rights on the light-up yo-yo, I will be free to play with his silver robot any time that I want.

I am now six years old but Dominic, as of this morning, is eight. It is the first day of spring, and we are driving to town with Dad. The sun is shining, the radio is playing, and we have the windows of our ancient red Escort wound all the way down so that we can feel the fresh, freezing air against our skin. On a long straight, Dad demonstrates the holy paternal art of steering with his knees, and Dominic and I both agree that it is the greatest piece of driving we have ever seen. Later, we will eat hamburger meals at Wimpy with his friends then feed the leftovers to the squirrels in Princes Street Gardens. When night comes we will fall asleep to memories and dreams of a day good as any either of us has ever known.

Dominic is nine years old and I am now eight. En route back from a camping holiday in France, my family are staying with my grandparents. By nine thirty in the morning, the only person yet to give me a present is Dominic; I am looking around for him when I hear the front door open and footsteps running upstairs. A moment later, I hear him shout down for me to come up and receive my birthday present.

I hurry upstairs. Entering the back bedroom, I am puzzled because I can see no present.

'Where is it?' I ask him.

With a theatrical flourish, Dominic produces the bag he has been hiding behind his back. Holding it aloft, he proudly scatters a smorgasbord of corner-shop confectionery on my bed.

'What's that?' I ask.

'It's your birthday present,' he says. 'Happy birthday.'

It would have cost him a fortune in our pocket money currency and I should have been grateful, but instead somehow took it upon myself to be nonplussed; a proper birthday present was a 'Choose Your Own Adventure' book, a cassette tape, an annual. We had arrived back from holiday after dark the night before but he should, I was certain, have had the foresight to buy me something before we left home.

Of course, I think of that birthday now, and the only remotely nonplussing part is my ingratitude. I picture him as a little boy, getting up early after a long journey, walking by himself down to the shops on a summer morning, and spending every last penny he had on chocolate for me. It might well be the very best birthday present I will ever receive.

I am fifteen and Dominic, as of this morning, is seventeen. Mum presents him with a birthday card whose envelope bulges curiously in the middle. I warn him that it is merely a badge that says 'I am 17', but as he opens it something entirely different falls out: an ignition key to Mum's car. It might well have been the very best birthday present he ever received.

I am seventeen and Dominic, as of tomorrow, will be nineteen. I am in my last year of high school, and he is now studying architecture at university in Glasgow. He will be coming home tomorrow evening, but I want something to reach him in the morning at the halls of residence where he has been living this year. Parked beside the post box where

Edinburgh's latest collection is made, I am frantically scribbling a card to accompany the CD I am sending him. When he appears, the postman is kindly and assures me that he will see to it that they get to Glasgow in time, that my brother will wake up to a birthday present.

I am nineteen and Dominic, as of today, is twenty-one. By now I have followed him to Glasgow, and we live two streets away from one another. He would never admit it, but this has been a difficult year for him, mysterious stomach pains that the doctors do not yet know the cause of having wreaked havoc with his social and academic lives both. He needs a break from everything and his friends give him one by hiring a limousine for the evening. They drive around the city streets, drinking champagne and waving at strangers; when they stop at a nightclub, they are ushered to the front of the queue.

A couple of hours after my candle goes out, my oldest friend Barney phones me. I have not yet learned the words, the metaphors, to communicate the emptiness I feel inside, and so I simply describe to him the things I have seen today: a hearse moving through parked aeroplanes, a man in a black suit standing with his hands behind his back, candles burning in a deserted cathedral. It takes a long time for me to recount this; several times, I have to stop talking because I am crying, and there are moments when I suspect that Barney might be too. Only when I have described the whole long day does he finally speak.

'I love you, mate,' he says.

Barney and I have been friends for more than half of our lives, but these are words that neither of us has ever said aloud to each other. They have always been in the background, implied and understood, but we were boys and now we are men, and somewhere along the way we came to understand that we were not supposed to say such things to one another.

And yet here is the thing. Despite all the odds that were against him, despite the coffin that I had seen and touched for the first time, despite the fact that I had not had language to even describe what I was feeling, these words of Barney's lit a candle, and it felt like the first one to flicker in my broken world. By its tentative light, I could glimpse that something did in fact remain of my heart. For tonight, that was everything I needed to know.

I love you.

Three words, and each of them a single syllable long. Written down, they do not seem like they should be a particularly difficult thing to say. Why, then, can I not clearly remember saying them to Dominic, even at least once? Why, for that matter, did I not shout them to him at the end of every single phone call we ever shared?

Perhaps this makes me sound like a character in a television soap opera. 'I never told them I loved them and now they are dead and I won't ever get the chance' – such a sentiment is the way a hackneyed screenwriter might ice genuine tragedy with melodrama in an attempt to wring a few more tears from the sensitive souls in the audience. And yet there is still a truth to it: if in the first year there was one thought guaranteed to move me to tears – and I do mean guaranteed, wherever I was, whatever I was doing – it was the notion that I had never properly told Dominic that I loved him. No matter how much people attempted to reassure me that this was perfectly normal – that men were indeed not supposed to tell each other such things, that anyway Dominic knew I loved him – it still hurt almost as much as anything.

On his birthday, I say it once more for good measure, set

the purple stems where my head has rested for most of the afternoon, and exit the room.

That night, Dominic's friends invite us out to mark his birthday with them. The venue is a bar where Eileen worked when the two of them first met and got to know one another, Dominic ostensibly calling in to see a school friend who worked in the kitchen, but really there to flirt with a sparky student who moonlit there as a waitress.

Tucked inside a tenement building, the bar is run on a Mexican theme, with a décor intended to give it the feel of an adobe hacienda. It does not entirely work – the cracks on the walls have been painted on a little too painstakingly, the overhead lights are kept a little too bright – but it is near the railway station and does a good line in salsa and tequila, so it is always lively.

Yet it is strange to be here at all, let alone to be here in this company and on this night. This is where Dominic and Eileen would have come for his birthday, and the people surrounding us are the ones who would have been there to celebrate it with them. The only people missing tonight are the guests of honour themselves.

But if it is a bittersweet time, it is also a good time. We have long since learned that we always feel particularly close to Dominic and Eileen amongst their friends, hearing new stories and uncensored versions of the old ones.

Approaching midnight, when our thoughts are starting to turn to home and all the trouble the next days are to bring, the music abruptly stops and, a moment later, the lights go out. Assuming we are about to be evicted, we start to gather up our coats and bags, but then notice a waitress moving around the room, lighting candles. It is a big establishment and hence slow work, but corner by corner, alcove by alcove, pockets of it are illuminated; at a certain point, when a quorum of candles are lit, their glows abruptly coalesce and when that happens the place turns magical. In the warm yellow light, and with the black shadows flickering across them, even the painted-on cracks are perfect. The bar now looks like a real hacienda.

We lay our coats back down and pick up our drinks and conversations where we left them off. We assume it will be only a temporary reprieve, but the bar remains open. Unable to operate the till without electricity, the waitress at first asks for exact change but after half an hour, when the beer starts to warm, begins to simply give it away. And in the glow of the hacienda candlelight, we sit there like *vaqueros*, telling the stories and drinking the drinks that will get us through the hard riding days ahead.

What is a candle? It is a light against the dark, but it is something more than that too. It is a tale, a promise, a never-forgotten birthday, a hope that is spread from one soul to another. If you felt inclined, you could put this book down and go out and light a candle; you could do it in a church or a temple, or you could do it simply by telling somebody that you love them.

Tsunami science was not on the syllabus at the school Dominic and I went to, but guidance exists on the internet for any teacher wishing to build a simulator for classroom usage. The suggested design requires only a water-filled basin with a folded picnic plate at one end and a small toy house atop a fixed incline at the other, yet provides an essentially accurate model of a tsunami in action: earthquake, waves, destruction.

In real life it begins not with a picnic plate but with the India and Burma tectonic plates, two massive pieces of the earth's crust that have been grinding against each other for millennia. Shortly before eight o'clock in the morning on the 26th of December 2004, something gives and the India Plate slips beneath the Burma Plate. This movement begins a hundred miles off the northern coast of Indonesia, but the tremors are felt as far away as the American Midwest; above ground alone, the earthquake unleashes energy equivalent to the simultaneous detonation of fifteen hundred Hiroshima-sized atomic bombs.

Still, who alive today can conceive of the effect of even a single nuclear bomb, let alone one and a half thousand of them? Perhaps the event's scale might be better conveyed by writing that this earthquake knocks our planet from its usual axis by an entire degree, but more likely the awesome power involved simply exceeds the boundaries of human imagin-ation. Even Richter scale seismometers – the very tools created by the brain of man to measure such things – are unable to quantify earthquakes of such fearsome size. In earthquakes such as this one, seismologists instead now empirically calculate something called the moment, a number obtained by multiplying the length of the slip on the geographical fault by the surface area that moved. This figure is then presented – in a format reassuringly similar to and more or less comparable with the Richter scale – as a value known as the moment magnitude.

The event that will come to be known as the Great Sumatran-Andaman Earthquake has a moment magnitude of 9.3, making it the second most powerful earthquake ever recorded. Early news bulletins on the twenty-sixth of December report this figure as being 8.0, a far greater inaccuracy than when they proceed to claim this as a reading from the Richter scale. As with its forebear, moment magnitude values rise not linearly but logarithmically; an earthquake measuring 9.0 is not a tenth more powerful than an earthquake measuring 8.0, it is ten times more powerful.

Yet not only has the second strongest earthquake ever recorded just occurred, it has occurred deep below the Indian Ocean. For over a thousand miles, the India Plate has moved beneath the Burma Plate, elevating the seabed above by as much as twenty feet; in turn, this has upwardly displaced cubic miles of water. As the fault line runs in a north–south direction, so the waves thus created will naturally travel to the west and to the east: to Sri Lanka and India, to Indonesia and Thailand.

Dominic and I shared a high school physics teacher in successive years, a man who would make a performance of screwing your homework into a ball and throwing it at you whenever your answers displeased him. Entertaining as this was to a room full of fourteen-year-olds, as a teaching method it was singularly ineffective. In case you had a physics teacher like ours, then, a brief reminder about waves.

In measuring waves, there are three important numbers: amplitude, wavelength and volume. Amplitude is the height of a wave, wavelength the distance between one crest and the next; multiplied together, these numbers give volume. For any particular wave, volume is a constant: if the amplitude increases, the wavelength proportionally decreases, and vice versa.

Tsunami waves are huge in volume but race across the ocean imperceptible as the three-quarters submerged dorsal fin of a great white shark. In deep water they have amplitudes as shallow as a foot and wavelengths perhaps two hundred miles long; sitting on a boat at sea, the sensation would be as if you had bobbed on to the wake of a speedboat that had passed in the far distance.

In truth, if you had been sailboating to the east of the fault line that morning and had been paying particularly close attention, you might actually have first noticed a slight dipping. When the India Plate slid underneath the leading edge of the Burma Plate it pulled down a more landward part of it, drawing with it a body of water.

As positive energy travels through the ocean as crests, so negative energy is conducted as troughs, and it is this trough that first reaches the Thai coastline, seemingly sucking the water out of Loh Dahlum Bay as it arrives. Sometimes people talk of this withdrawing as a warning from nature, and praise the primitive Nicobarese tribes who retreated to high ground at its sight. Such conversation always makes me uncomfortable, for it sounds suspiciously like our dead are being scolded for forgetting some imagined mystical old ways. This was the first major tsunami in the area in generations, and the emptying of the bay was not a warning. A warning is a siren sounding and somebody in a uniform telling you that danger is imminent, that if you value your life you will make for the high ground immediately; the sea slipping away to reveal a beach full of stranded technicolour fish is no more than a particularly cruel trick.

As an ocean wave approaches land, its amplitude increases in proportion to both its own speed and the decreasing depth of the water it now finds itself moving through. Tsunami waves cross the ocean fast as jetliners and Loh Dahlum Bay is shallow indeed; by the time the first tsunami wave reaches the beach, it has grown from one to twenty feet tall.

The submerged shark, then, has risen up to reveal its sharp rows of pointed teeth, but now comes the moment where physics plays a trick that classroom simulators, logarithmic scales and even sardonic teachers can never hope to convey. Because contrary to everything that we have all been taught, a tsunami is not a wave.

At least, it is not a wave in the way that you or I might think of one, for a wave is supposed to have an end. Whilst the wave's amplitude increases twentyfold as it crosses the bay, the corresponding decrease in wavelength means only that instead of a wave that is two hundred miles long, the people perched on the isthmus are confronted with one that is ten miles long. And a body of water that keeps coming for ten miles is not a wave. It is a river.

River. That is the word that the people who were there that day still use, and that is what they all will tell you: that it was not a wave that came and washed over their island, but a river. A Chao Phraya at the Wat Arun, a raging Thames at the Pool of London, a Forth beneath the bridges in whose shadow Dominic and I grew up. A deep and seemingly end-less river boiling with bricks and metal, with glass and timber.

At Loh Dahlum the water roared in twenty feet tall and

kept coming for thirty minutes. In deeper Tonsai, where the bay is more sheltered, the water arrived as a rapidly rising flood tide. Some people ran from one side of the island to the other, but in each place they found only more water.

When after half an hour the trough following the first wave finally arrived, people thought that the danger had passed. Some of them climbed down from their places of safety, to tend the wounded, search out the missing, to weep over the dead. As they were doing this, the second wave arrived; this one was bigger than the first, and the third wave that followed would be bigger still.

I wake early and watch as the creeping dawn slowly lights the room. My pressed suit hangs over the door, downstairs the orders of service sit stacked in boxes, and at precisely twenty-five minutes past ten a black car will turn into our street. There is no job left for me to do but find a way through this day itself. I shower, polish my shoes and check in the mirror that my tie sits straight. And then I tell myself that if only I can break this day down into a succession of such small tasks, I might even make it to evening.

Perhaps the only thing you can say for having to wait three months to hold a funeral is that it at least gives you time to think about how it should be. If these services were the last thing we would be able to do for Dominic, we had all been determined that we would get it right.

The problem was that nobody had been able to tell us what getting it right entailed, nor even if such a thing might be possible. How do you bury somebody who died in a calamity at the age of twenty-seven and get that right? What can possibly ever be right about it?

And still the thing came with other, more practical problems. We had organised the plot at Colinton but Dominic was a member of no recognisable church. On any given day his spiritual ideology might be two parts Rastafarian to one part Buddhist to an eighth part unconfirmed Catholic, this last an essentially nostalgic nod to our maternal forebears. True, he had recently asked Grandma if she could lend him a Bible, but this was just curiosity; if he had thought Grandma likely to have one, he would have asked her for a copy of the Qur'an too.

Who, then, could we approach to conduct the funeral service? The obvious idea seemed to be to ask the resident minister at Colinton, but we had never met him, and naturally worried about just how irreligious we could reasonably ask him to be. I was steeling myself to make this awkward call, my key phrases written on a piece of paper in front of me like a nervous teenager phoning to suggest a hopelessly optimistic date, when Uncle John arrived with a better idea.

There was a man that one of his colleagues knew, an ordained minister who sometimes spoke on the radio to an audience as sceptical and disparate as the one that we ourselves would constitute. I dialled his number, found no need for my carefully crafted sentences, and a day later he was sitting in our living room, explaining to us how he would approach such a difficult task.

He told us that he would naturally wear the robes and collar of his office, but at the beginning of the service he would declare that, whilst he would be using the words of prayer and the vocabulary of his religion, he would not expect everybody present to subscribe to these. Rather, he would say simply that he hoped that people might use them as a means of thinking about their own way of remembering Dominic; when we heard him say this, we started to think that it might be possible to somehow get this right after all.

At Colinton many people are gathered outside the church but the only ones I see are Samantha and Laurie, the older of Dad's children from his second marriage. Eleven and thirteen years old, they live in France and we are today seeing each other for the first time since a week we spent with Dominic the preceding August. For many nights now I have wondered how I might console them at this moment, but have consistently come up with nothing. Instead, we hug each other, and hold the embraces for a long time; they have lost their brother too, and are already old enough to know just what a thing that is.

Inside the church, the other pews have already been filled as we walk to our empty one at the front. I do not look at the surroundings, do not need to: this is the church of our youth, the one I still picture first when I hear the word. Here we gave tuneless thanks for Easter, here we were solemnly invested as Cub Scouts, and here I spent an entire Harvest service wrestling a classmate beneath a pew whilst our mortified parents stared on impotently from the gallery. After so many childhood hours I know every inch of this space, from the eagle atop the lectern to the inscription that runs around its pulpit: 'Wherever two or three are gathered in my name, I am there amongst them.'

At six years old, this had been an impenetrable riddle to me. A name was a word to be spoken aloud or sewn into your school jumper to distinguish it from the thirty identical ones that belonged to your classmates. How could anybody possibly gather in it? When Mum explained that the words were a reference to a time after Jesus died, and that to gather in somebody's name simply meant to think of them together, as the disciples had thought of their departed prophet, this served only to confuse the issue further: if Jesus had died, how could he possibly be there amongst them? Died meant dead like our put-to-sleep cats or Darth Vader at the end of *Return of the Jedi*; at six I thought I already knew that there could be no coming back from dead, whether your friends gathered in your name or not.

I do not see the coffin until I have sat down. If I am already intimately familiar with it, I am struck now by how ordinary it suddenly looks, perched there in the chancel with its out-size spray of lilies robbing it of scale. Outside this church, policemen have been stationed to keep away the photographers, but after all the exceptional circumstances that have brought us to this point, it is strange and somehow relieving to suddenly be at what might now pass for an ordinary funeral. For today, the focus will be on Dominic and not the way in which he left this world.

But there is another unanticipated emotion too: fear. Fear of a simple and a selfish sort: what if I cannot manage to give the reading that I am supposed to? Amidst all the organisation, I had not thought to worry about this, but sitting there on the hard wooden pew, I am confronted by the enormity of the task facing me.

The passage is a short one – a few sparse paragraphs from Khalil Gibran's book *The Prophet* – but surrounding me are Dominic's family and his closest friends, and in that box lies his body. The only saving grace is that I am not to be the first to speak, that daunting task having fallen to Dominic's friend Caroline.

I make a silent pact with myself that if Caroline manages to give her reading then I must also give mine, but do so in the certain belief that she will be unable to complete hers. The minister has a copy of all the lessons and yesterday made a point of reassuring us that he will be on hand to step in at any time; with such an enticing safety net, it will surely be an easy thing for Caroline to allow herself to fall into its embrace.

But when the moment comes she stands up and walks down the aisle, her footsteps echoing around the silent church. She steps up to the lectern, unfolds her piece of paper and reads the poem Mum chose for her. It fits perfectly, the note it ends on redemptive enough that the minister will later compare it to Paul's letter to the Romans in which he declares that neither death nor life nor angels nor principalities can separate the true believer from that which he holds dear. The real lesson, however, lies in Caroline herself, for she has delivered the verse faultlessly: straight of back, dry of eye, and talking to the spot at the very back of the room of which head teacher Mum earlier reminded us all. Later, Caroline will tell me that she drew fortitude from Dominic's memory. This will make sense to me, for when I am called up to speak I will quietly ask him for exactly the same thing.

The Prophet is a strange book, a mystic's fable written with the poetic concision of the King James Bible. The overarching story concerns the voyage of a traveller preparing to depart a city that loves him, but the short section I am to read aloud says everything I wish to say this morning, and does so in language more eloquent than I could have ever hoped to find.

> Let not the waves of the sea separate us now, and the years you
>   have spent in our midst become a memory.
> You have walked among us a spirit, and your shadow has been
>   a light upon our faces.
> Much have we loved you. But speechless was our love, and
>   with veils has it been veiled.
> Yet now it cries aloud unto you, and would stand revealed
>   before you.
> And ever has it been that love knows not its own depth until
>   the hour of separation.

My mouth is dry and the tears close, but I fix on the back of the room as I saw Caroline do, and the thing passes quickly. Only the last line properly catches in my throat.

The minister utters a prayer, and then the undertaker's men approach, shoulder the coffin and carry it towards the door. Out in the churchyard, a lone piper begins to play.

All morning the rain has been falling, and the grass that was still verdant in January has begun to give way to brown battlefield mud. The hole in the ground that was dug yesterday gapes unanswerable, and slowly we gather ourselves around it. When the pipes cease the last notes echo and then the dell quiets, the only sound the rushing of the swollen river nearby.

Taking from his pocket the card I wrote out late last night, the undertaker calls forth the cord-bearers and instructs us that when the time comes we are to simply let the velvet ropes run through our hands, to make no attempt to hold on. Everybody is openly weeping as the minister recites his final blessing and we pick up dank handfuls of the dark Scottish earth to throw into the grave.

And after the earth, the flowers, the red and yellow roses. Mum throws the first in, and I the second. Mine lands atop hers, their two thorny stems forming a cross atop the coffin, a kiss in a long-ago birthday card.

In the afternoon following the burial, there is a celebration of Dominic's life.

A nearby university has provided the venue, a silver space-ship of a lecture theatre on a hilltop overlooking the city. Dominic would have liked its modern design, and an older part of this same building was once the convent primary that Mum attended as a pinafore-wearing schoolgirl. That is the city that Edinburgh is: large enough to be possessed of such institutions, small enough that within them you find such reverberations. Small enough even that Eileen studied at this same university and later today a receptionist will take me aside to tell me that of the thousands of students who annually pass through she yet remembers Eileen for the daily beam of sunshine she was.

By the appointed four o'clock start time people are lining the aisles and a nervous janitor has started to mumble about fire regulations. Here are men and women, children and even occasional babies; here are friends, neighbours, col-leagues, relatives and teachers. At four o'clock on a weekday afternoon in March they have all come to join us, some of them travelling great distances to do so; even in themselves they are a humbling sight, and then the ceremony itself begins.

Since Uncle John first suggested this separate event, we have spoken of this part of the day almost entirely in the abstract. It is as if to dwell on it would have been to acknow-ledge the impossibility of what we would like to happen here this afternoon: our unutterable hope has been that if we only ask people to join us in talking about Dominic, if we only show photographs of him down through the ages, if we only play the songs that he loved; that if we only do these things, that if we two or three only gather in his name, he will somehow be here amongst us.

The lights are dimmed, the blinds closed and a photograph of Dominic appears on the screen at the back of the stage. Mum's husband Rob takes the podium to speak.

Except he is not going to speak. Rob's father was a regimental pipe-major and he in turn expresses himself best through music, pitch and melody coming to him down through his bloodlines. In front of these five hundred friends and strangers, Rob is going to sing, and he is going to do so unaccompanied.

Rob has been a permanent and precious fixture in our lives since we were newly minted teenagers. If I don't use a word like 'stepdad' in this book it is simply because he has always been something far better; that word implies a disciplinary role and Rob has forever been the diametric and glorious opposite of that. Growing up, he was a crucial strategic ally, a powerful advocate for the ways of boys and the fact that they might occasionally need to cause a little mischief. More recently, he has been the one who did the most to welcome Eileen to our family, and had been closely advising the pair of them on the purchase of their flat in Edinburgh.

Taking an old steel harmonica from his pocket, Rob blows a solitary note to find his pitch then opens his mouth wide to sing the Robert Burns' song 'Is There For Honest Poverty'. It is a song of equality and fraternity, a song of Scotland, a song of Dominic. Even in the hubbub of a living room hootenanny Rob is a special singer, but in this silent auditorium his baritone voice quivers with all the loss and love of the memory of a boy he first met by chance on a morning in autumn twenty years ago when the little girl who lived next door brought her shy friend with her to watch him at his woodwork.

Others now take turns to speak. Everybody has something illuminating to say: an unknown fact that sketches out a surprising part of Dominic's life, a memory that colours it in. Mum talks of how Dominic was born on Mother's Day and paints a picture of him toddling through the back garden carrying a Tupperware box of rescued ducklings. She says that she had always thought of those days as the happiest of her life but since the tsunami she has realised that the days we had all been living more recently – days of first proper jobs and first proper girlfriends – were blessed ones too.

Dad is next to speak, and it is a difficult thing for him to do. He and Dominic were always unspokenly close and though in the past few months he has suffered as profoundly as anyone, he has done so almost entirely silently. This is an afternoon for sharing, however, and he does Dominic proud, beginning by recalling the maternity ward in 1977 and finishing by telling us about some adventures he and Dominic enjoyed on a trip to Prague last year; I was invited on that trip too, but somehow let myself think that my new career in television screenwriting needed me more urgently that weekend.

Friends speak and cousins speak. Dominic's tutor from university tells us how Dominic was not only a standout student but a fellow aficionado of reggae music and a judicious end-of-the-day rum and Coke. A classmate recalls a shared project. The director of the Edinburgh architectural firm where Dominic worked reveals how they would confidently send him out alone to meet their most valued clients.

It is a side of Dominic's life that I had known little about. On some level the people you were children with always remain as children to you, and it is hard to imagine this person you think of as your fellow eleven-year-old charming a planning officer or taking charge on a construction site. These, though, are the things Dominic spent his workdays doing, and a glimpse of his talent is visible in the running-order booklets Graham has created. The back page features two examples of Dominic's work: a design for a canalside development in Edinburgh, and a sketch for a private house in the Scottish Borders. The canalside development is a study in modern urban living – all glass balconies and sustainable timber walls – but it is the private house that really intrigues: its central feature is an A-frame, an echo of the modernist churches our maternal grandfather spent his working life designing. At his funeral six years before, Dominic and I had been placed in charge of the offertory; at the back of the church we had anxiously debated as to when we were supposed to carry it up to the priest until Uncle John had turned round and motioned at us to get on with it.

In the auditorium the speakers pause and a slideshow plays, photographs set to an old Bob Marley song, 'Three Little Birds'.

That reggae music, forever coming out of Dominic's room. He had always adored it, and I could never stand it. We used to exasperate each other in equal measure, my inability to appreciate the genre as unfathomable to him as his apparent belief he might change my mind by incessantly playing it was to me. As a teenager, his invariable first act on waking would be to turn his music up loud; I would suffer it for as long as I could, then go through to beg him to turn it down.

And he would not be there. He would already be downstairs, cheerfully eating his breakfast whilst even more reggae music now blared from the stereo on the kitchen sideboard. I used to tell him that the reason he had not apparently noticed that he was now listening to a different song on a different stereo was that every song sounded the same. He would only ever laugh and turn the music up even louder, the better to increase my chances of appreciating it.

Predictably, I love it these days. More than that, I think I have even begun to understand it, and comprehend now that the fact the songs sound similar signifies not any failure of imagination but rather respect for an essential convention of the genre. Dominic used to tell me that the reggae beat was the human heartbeat, but I had always assumed he was being gnomic. It took his own heart stopping for me to come to understand that he was being quite literal.

When doctors place their stethoscopes beside a patient's sternum, we are listening for the heart sounds learned phonetically as *lubb-DUPP*. 'Lubb' is made by the valves of the atria closing, 'DUPP' by those of the ventricles. The two sounds occur in rapid succession, but ventricular valves are under higher pressure than their atrial predecessors, and thus in health 'DUPP' is louder than '*lubb*'. The dictionary on my computer defines the hallmark of reggae music as a 'strongly accented subsidiary beat', but the truth is that if you listen to either music for long enough, the *lubb-DUPP* of a human heartbeat quickly becomes indistinguishable from the muted down–up strum of the rhythm guitar that lies at the heart of every reggae song.

'Three Little Birds', a song with a central mantra that reminds us that 'every little thing gonna be all right', was always one of Dominic's favourites. The photographs projected on the screen, technicolour in a darkened room, are a collage of what in hindsight were indeed all perfect days: Dominic in his high chair, reaching out to feed Mum some of his own lunch; Dominic beating a toy drum on his third birthday; Dominic and I in our uniforms on my first day of school, he helpfully pointing my face towards the camera.

The slideshow holds on this last image and this means it is now my turn to speak. There are ten times as many people here as were at the church this morning but I now feel no nerves, for underneath my shirt I have pulled on an old T-shirt of Dominic's. Unwashed three months on, it still smells of him and bears a picture of Bob Marley, over which is written a phrase that has lately come to be another kind of scripture to me: music goes on for ever.

My eulogy for Dominic is an inventory of cherished secrets. I talk about a spare mattress he used to keep under his bed for when I was too scared to sleep alone. I talk about the nights we used to stay out playing frisbee on the Meadows long after it was dark and each throw and catch had become an act of fraternal faith. I talk about his ability to make friends and illustrate this with a story about an evening when I visited him in the hospital where he was supposed to be on a strict protein-shake diet and found him eating a fish supper that one of the nurses had smuggled in for him. Finally, I talk about how proud of him I am, and of how much I love him, as if telling this auditorium these things might go some way to atone for all the things I never told Dominic in life, as if he might be near enough today to overhear them.

Exhausted, I sit back in my chair. Mum now steps up once again, this time to talk about Eileen. If this has been a difficult day for us, it has been a near impossible one for Eileen's family. Three months after the tsunami, Eileen's body has not yet been found, and with each week that passes it looks increasingly unlikely that it ever will be. Even as we are thankful that Dominic has finally been brought home, so a huge part of the collective heart of this packed auditorium remains lost in Thailand. Five months from now, a phone call will bring us the news that Eileen has at last been identified and is to be brought home, but for today all we know is that she is missing.

Mum uses the words that anybody who met Eileen would recognise – sparkling, confident, beautiful – and adds some lovingly recalled details of her own. That Eileen possessed more clothes than anyone we had ever known and never went anywhere looking less than stunning. That a fortnight into her relationship with Dominic she appeared on the doorstep with a suitcase. That she spoke languages and was learning to play the Spanish guitar. That when we buried our family cat in the garden, she solemnly announced that it was the first funeral she had ever been to.

The afternoon's last song arrives accompanied by more photographs. These pictures are more recent, the blurred sepia and rounded corners of the early 1980s now replaced by crisper modern prints: Dominic and his school friends on their first trip to Amsterdam, looking like an early nineties boy band; Dominic at Christmas with his university flat-mates; Dominic in his graduation robes; Dominic and I sharing a joke at a café in France; Dominic and Eileen looking like a young couple with the world at their feet in the picture that all the newspapers printed.

At the end of these photographs, Mum and Uncle John spring a coup de théâtre I had not known was coming. As tissues are dabbed at eyes, the steel auditorium blinds abruptly flutter open and the room is flooded with light. Suddenly revealed beneath us is Dominic's city in all its glory and tragedy: there is Edinburgh, her castle, her streets paved with memory and love. And somehow, at this moment, in here amongst us two or three or five hundred who have gathered in his name, is my brother.

Wander down through Phi Phi town late in the evening and somewhere amongst the strip-lit beer and cigarette shops, the street-front hotplates and the stalls that sell immaculately polished shells and poorly pirated DVDs, your attention will inevitably come to rest on the tattoo parlours.

The hand-painted signs are deliberately garish, but their dubious enticements – NEW NEEDLE EACH TIME, GUARANTEED NO BLEEDING – are not what catch your eye. For through an open door a customer is visible, prostrated on his belly on an examination couch liberated from some long-ago clinic. Crouched over his quiet patient, backlit by the narrow glare of his bright surgeon's spotlight and wielding his splinter of bamboo delicately as any scalpel, is the tattooist. He is at least thirty years old – it takes a decade to serve an apprenticeship worthy of the name – and, wearing only tight blue jeans, his decorated torso is his own greatest advertisement.

From out on the street you can see that the tattooist is entranced by his work, that he is oblivious to the music playing, to the low chatter of voices emanating from his room's dark recesses, to the bustle passing behind you. It looks a private scene, and yet you find yourself taking a tentative step forward; sensing no disapproval, you take another and then another, over the threshold and into the shop.

You hold your breath and wait for somebody to ask you to leave, but nobody does. From this new vantage, you can see into the darkened corners of the cramped little parlour: the sheets of sample designs that paper the bamboo walls, the sink where the Indian ink is mixed, its chipped white porcelain stained blue over the years. On a bench at the back of the room perch the apprentices, young men jealously watching for the chance to cut a new sliver of bamboo, or dab away a stray drop of blood. Now the boldest amongst them catches your eye and motions towards the couch in a gesture of 'You next?'; when you shake your head at him you do so just a little too quickly, a little too emphatically. It sets them all giggling until a reprimanding glance from their master silences them.

But now he turns his attention back to his operating field and so do you, catching for the first time the silver glint of the tiny metal needle attached to the bottom of the piece of bamboo. The outlined image the tattooist is colouring is of a flower, an eagle, a heart, and you watch rapt as the needle gently moves in and out of the skin, tenting a layer of dermis up with it each time only to drop it once more. It is a minuscule, painstaking procedure, and yet it is utterly mesmerising. There is nowhere else you need to be this evening, and you watch for hours.

A month after Dominic's funeral, the time comes to return to London. If for the last four months we have lived like lost travellers, the world has continued to spin on its new axis and I need to find my place in it once again. Mum, who herself is soon to start back at the Edinburgh primary school where she is head teacher, agrees to come with me for the first weekend. In the days before the trip we spend hours together fabricating complex plans of what we will do in the city. Mum tells me that she suspects I am trying to distract her, but my plan is actually a little bolder than that.

In December, I had left the capital feeling like Dick Whittington at the end of *Puss in Boots*. At medical school I had spent my free time entering every short story and screen-play competition I could find; in my final year of university I had started to occasionally place in some of them, but the transition to working doctor had left no time for such pur-suits. At the end of my houseman year I had taken some time off medicine to write, but this had not begun well: perhaps rightly, the wider world had been little interested in my fledgling short stories and it had quickly started to seem like it would be easier to break into the Bank of England than the screenwriting business. After a year of trying, I had found myself reduced to working at my old teenage desk in Mum's house in Edinburgh, quietly suffocating under a wastepaper mountain of rejected scripts but somehow still too proud to admit defeat.

I ought to have returned to medicine with my tail between

my legs – I had always loved the job, just not its demands for unfailing monogamy – but had instead made the move south in a final roll of the dice. The gamble had paid off almost immediately: a few screenwriting commissions abruptly came my way and six months into my time in London if nobody had quite yet made me Lord Mayor, it had felt as if it could only be a matter of time.

I was living with a friend from Edinburgh, Paul, in a flat in Ladbroke Grove, a neighbourhood that even allowing for the recent upswing in my fortunes was still far too affluent for us. We shared a tiny attic with a platoon of mice and our shower offered only a dribble of hot water between seven and a quarter past, but it was my first London home and I loved it. We subsisted entirely on pizza and beer and at night watched old movies beamed on to the living room wall from a projector liberated from Paul's workplace. When we grew bored of watching old movies we took a bus down to Shepherd's Bush to watch newer movies, and some nights we wandered up to the Portobello Road to drink beer and look up at the Trellick Tower. I had a pretty girlfriend and at twenty-five years old I felt as if I already had the world entirely figured out. If anybody had told me that I would not have been able to return to that halcyon existence, I would have refused to board the plane north for the holidays.

If ever you have taken a train into Paddington Station, you will have seen the Trellick Tower off to the left-hand side: an up-ended rectangle of a housing block seemingly staked to the ground by a much thinner rectangle that supplies its lifts and staircases. It is an odd, Lego-like structure, but seen from the window of the train in from the airport, and subsequently discovered to be within walking distance of our flat in Ladbroke Grove, it became an easy symbol of the city and all the promises it had so quickly seemed to make me. In the long, empty nights of waiting in Edinburgh, I had occasionally thought of the Trellick Tower and all the other things that I had lost along with it: a career, a city, a girlfriend. At a certain point I had surrendered every one of them to the chaos, as if the water having taken the most precious things had to be given everything else I cared about too.

You miss lost cities a little in the way that you miss lost loved ones. You grieve for them too, carry them with you and sometimes picture the people you should have together seen that day, the restaurant you ought to have eaten in, the rooms you should have retired to. Thinking of such things as you lie awake in your exile, you begin to experience a yearning so physical that you can only conclude that what you are feeling is the distant gravitational pull of the city itself; somehow, your metropolis misses you in the same way that you miss it. In your mind it stands now waiting to clutch you back to its warm heart, its empty railway platforms and gaping runways its outstretched arms. You decide that those melodramatic French had it right all along with their inverted verb for 'to miss': *Londres me manque*, London misses me.

But when you do finally manage to return, you disembark from the plane and not one of the cab drivers' whiteboard signs bears your name. Passing through town, you see that the restaurant you mentally dined in every night has become a kitchen showroom, and when you eventually arrive back at your own front door, your key no longer fits the lock. And yet this very thing that is so terrible about a city like London – that enormous, brash confidence that allows it to deny all knowledge of your existence the very instant you leave – is also what makes it so irresistible.

Visiting the city as children, Dominic and I had been puzzled to discover that Uncle John – who had already lived there for a decade – kept an *A–Z* in his rusted white Mini. Returning home late one night, we had been speeding along the North Circular when John had asked his girlfriend Kate which exit we should take; as if it were the most natural thing in the world, she had opened the glove compartment and taken out the little white book with the red and blue letters on the cover.

Coming from Edinburgh, where we could have found our way home from anywhere by the time we were ten and eleven, the presence of this book in John's car baffled us. Was our wise uncle who had gone to a famous university not as wise as we had always been led to believe? Had he really even gone to any university? Or could it actually be possible that a city might be sprawling and intricate enough that a man as educated as our uncle claimed to be could have lived there for a decade and still not yet know his own way home? This last was a thought that shook our world to its core, the red 'A' and blue 'Z' burning themselves into memory like a fiery brand.

I had recalled it the summer I had moved into the attic in Ladbroke Grove and taken possession of my own *A–Z*, a small inheritance from James, the room's previous occupant. James had come to London to study for a Masters degree in design, and the *A–Z* was marked with the annotations, the circles and asterisks, of his own first years in the city: the museums he visited for inspiration, the cheap neighbourhoods where his classmates kept their studios, the warehouses where they threw their parties. I used this *A–Z* of James's almost every day, carried it with me in my bag everywhere I went, added my hieroglyphics to his and eventually came to understand the truth that had eluded us that night all those years before: yes, a city genuinely could be that big; it had to be, if only to house all the dreams us young immigrants brought with us.

Since Mum and I began talking of our trip to London I had been planning to show her the Trellick Tower, the symbol of the life I was determined to regain. Never mind merely distracting her, I intended to use it to convince her to join me in my belief that if we only assumed it would, if we only behaved as if it had no choice in the matter, the good life would somehow resume for us both. Unfortunately, on the train in from the airport I had become so caught up in expounding this theory that I had completely missed the tower as we passed it.

After breakfast on our first morning, we set out to look for it. A few blocks from our cramped attic, almost in the shade of the tower itself, we passed through a short and seemingly unremarkable street called Faraday Road. Here Mum stopped, glanced around, and then announced that this was the street where she and Dad had lived over the summer of 1969. This was long before the area mortgaged its soul to gentrification, and they had rented a room from a psychedelic rock band. Dad had taken a nightshift job vacuuming hotels whilst Mum, nineteen years old and straight off the train from Scotland, locked her bedroom door against the wailing sirens outside.

Thus fell apart my carefully laid plans: Mum had not only seen the Trellick Tower before, but had actually watched it being built. Adjusting our course, we now headed west instead of north, and found ourselves wandering around the grid of shopping streets behind Portobello Road. Here Mum stopped again, this time to point at a nearby shop.

'I think we have a photograph of Dominic standing there,' she said.

Dominic had never visited me in Ladbroke Grove and I began to tell Mum that she was mistaken, that two such coincidences in one morning were not possible. I fell silent when I saw the yellow façade that she was pointing at. It belonged to a distinctive wooden toy shop, and we did indeed have a photograph of Dominic in front of it.

This is one of the unanticipated things that happens when somebody dies: you come to know all the photographs by heart. You pore over them, stare at them, attempt to interrogate and decipher them as if their hidden details might reveal some kind of cosmic rabbit hole back to the person who is no longer there: where and when the picture was taken and by whom; whose arm that is poking into the edge of the frame, and whose shadow is there cast upon the wall; what happened immediately before this moment, and what happened directly after. You gather this information in your mind, collate it, edit it, and at a certain point each picture does indeed become something more than an image: it becomes a moment, an anecdote, an inarguable piece of the official life story of the deceased. In this way an entire human life can be rapidly reduced to a series of easily comprehended vignettes: the time we flew kites, the day she graduated, the afternoon we got caught in the rain.

I had not wanted this to happen, and right up until Dominic's funeral I had studiously avoided looking at any photographs of him. I had wanted to remember him as the human being he was, not as a two-dimensional image trapped in a series of random and transient moments. Similarly, I did not dare write about him for a long time, lest what I wrote – these stories that the very act of putting down might inevitably shape, polish and sheen – ever became more real to me than the memory of the person he actually was.

But I was wrong about the photographs, so perhaps I can

72

hope that I will be proven wrong regarding these stories too. I was wrong about the photographs because the picture Mum was recalling that day is no mere two-dimensional image, but is itself utterly alive. It was taken at the Notting Hill Carnival, a bank holiday weekend in August when the streets of Ladbroke Grove are commandeered by troupes of carnival dancers and booming reggae sound systems. Somehow I had forgotten that Dominic made an almost annual pilgrimage, and I now remembered that he had once asked me if the house Paul and I lived in was one of those huge Georgian affairs with white pillars flanking the entranceway. Sort of, I had replied, because we at least reached the staircase to our attic by going through such a door.

In the photograph, Dominic is in a state of bliss, arms aloft and dancing in the road as, somewhere in the far distance, the evening sun sets behind a terrace of white mansion houses. The picture does not capture any mere moment but distils his essence, and to look on it is to see him more or less exactly as he was: a young man who would not hesitate to travel five hundred miles if there was a good time with friends to be had at journey's end. In later years, when I begin to undertake my own pilgrimages to the Notting Hill Carnival and stand in this same spot with today's quiet streets turned to transient festival, I will look around me and fully expect to spot him amongst the crowd.

Mum returns to Edinburgh and a few days later I find myself sitting in a corner meeting room on the sixteenth floor of a skyscraper on the South Bank. The room's glass window runs from floor to ceiling, and the view is straight out of central casting, the city's storied landmarks – Waterloo Bridge, the Houses of Parliament, Buckingham Palace – unfolding beneath the windows like models in a child's pop-up book.

I am in this room because I have been asked to write a ninety-minute episode and polish three other scripts for a new ITV television drama, *Eleventh Hour*. Also around the table are the show's script editor, producers, director and leading man, the actor Patrick Stewart.

If it is not *Hamlet*, *Eleventh Hour* is far and away the biggest writing project I have ever worked on. In persuading Patrick Stewart to appear on British television for the first time in a decade, the producers have achieved a major coup and accordingly have raised a vertiginous million-pound-per-episode budget. The show's premise – the creation of a science fiction writer who has now departed the show – is suitably telegenic: the central character, Professor Hood, is a government scientist with a brief to stop malfeasance wherever he finds it; his past exploits mean that he must now travel everywhere with a Special Branch bodyguard, the inevitably beautiful but feisty Rachel. Due to Patrick Stewart's commitments on an upcoming X-Men movie, filming on my own episode – as yet entirely unwritten and little developed from the two-sentence pitch I gave the producers early last December – must commence in four short weeks. We are already more than living up to the show's nervy title, but this is the kind of chance I have been dreaming of for years.

But five minutes into the meeting, the uneasy realisation that I am entirely unmoved by the prospect begins to dawn. I try to reassure myself that I am simply star-struck: sitting across the table from me, after all, is Professor Xavier. This does not work, for really I know that what I am suffering from is not any surfeit of excitement but rather its polar opposite. I tell myself that the apparent apathy I am feeling must be due to a lack of confidence: in the last four months I have written only eulogies and obituaries, and here I am about to discuss script notes with a man who has served his

74

time on both the battlements of Elsinore and the bridge of the USS *Enterprise*.

As we get down to the scripts, however, I find I can still do it. I can still hear the dialogue, still see the characters walk around, Professor Hood perturb and deduct and Rachel fire her gun; most importantly, I can still manoeuvre the internal beams and joists that hold up each story without bringing the whole narrative house crashing down. I spent a long time trying to get to this room, and now that I am here I am not going to let myself down.

And yet, despite this – despite the fact that I am not starstruck and know that I am capable of doing a good job – I still cannot take any pleasure in the experience. If it is natural that I should still carry my sadness, it seems that there ought also to be a small part of me that is, if nothing else, at least relieved to have finally reached this stage, to be sitting here on the sixteenth floor, looking out over storybook London and about to write a script for Captain Jean-Luc Picard.

When we adjourn for the day, a broken elevator sends me around the far side of the building in search of a staircase. The view from here is different from the one I have been staring out on all day, and arrestingly so: extending to the east, this aspect is dominated by the dome of St Paul's Cathedral. Looking out at it, I begin to realise what it is that I have been missing all afternoon.

Down on the street I take out my phone and press the speed-dial button that will call Dominic. It connects, as it has done since that very first morning, to an error message, a computer-generated woman's voice telling me to please check the number and dial again. This, I understand now, is what has been the matter with me today: I have wanted to tell him.

I have wanted to tell him that I am writing a script for

Captain Jean-Luc Picard, that in this great big city of London my dreams are starting to come true. I have wanted to tell him to pack his own dreams and come here too. I have wanted to tell him to bring Eileen and get on a plane or a train or an overnight coach, because in this place so monstrous that after ten years our uncle still needed to rely on a map to find his way around, dreams can quickly be made to come true.

The dome of St Paul's Cathedral rises amongst the City's financial towers incongruous as a circus tent in midwinter. Emerging from the nearby underground station in the spring rain, we caught our first glimpses of a building at once exotic and somehow curiously familiar through a shifting canopy of umbrellas.

'What is it?' Dominic asked me, his voice quiet at the majesty of the place.

'The Old Bailey,' I answered, confidently naming a building we regularly heard mentioned on the six o'clock news.

Busy searching for the family entrance, neither Mum nor Grandma corrected me. Aware that the Old Bailey was reserved for the most serious crimes, Dominic and I muttered darkly and hopefully to each other that we might get to see a real-life murderer.

But it was not the Old Bailey and we were not there to look at murderers. It was St Paul's Cathedral and we were there to climb the narrow steps of the tower atop the dome in order to take in the nearest thing you can get to the view from a sixteenth-floor office when you are seven years old. Maybe we had also been brought there so that the seeds of grandeur might be sown in our young minds, and maybe this even worked, or at least half did, for one of us grew up to be an architect.

The highlight of our visit to St Paul's, however, was the whispering gallery, a chamber in the house of God given over to mischief and magic. High in the rotunda, a catwalk of a balcony circles the inside of the dome, the walls of which are hewn of telegraphic stone. If you stand and whisper a message into the wall, your confidant, diametrically opposite you with his ear against the wall, is supposed to be able to hear it. Here, for centuries, forbidden lovers and spies had met to exchange their secrets.

Love made us sick, but we adored spies. At home, a manual that professed to reveal the secret techniques of modern spying had long since become our bible. Studiously following its step-by-step lessons, we regularly used talcum powder to turn our mousy brown hair grey, brewed invisible inks from vinegar, and scouted out any number of dead-letter drop sites around our suburb.

Dedicated as we were to our espionage careers, we also knew it was all a kind of child's play, as imaginary as Oddjob or Auric Goldfinger in the James Bond films that we watched on bank holidays. There were no spy rings in suburban Edinburgh, our manual did not specify what a dead letter might actually say and, no matter how many lemons we squeezed, our invisible ink never reappeared.

This whispering gallery was different. Grandma assured us that it had once been frequented by bona fide secret agents who came here to exchange information about approaching armadas and treasonous plots. Better still, she lowered her voice to tell us that in these Cold War days of tapped telephones and poison-tipped umbrellas, it was the kind of place a modern spy might still have a use for. We did not need to hear any more than that, and rushed up the stairs ahead of her.

It was the perfect opportunity to finally put into practice

the skills we had spent months honing, but we fell at the very first hurdle. I see Dominic now, a boy of nine with a cow's lick in his hair, standing on the opposite balcony, signalling that he is about to tell me something. I move my ear close in to my section of wall and watch as he leans into his, a hand cupped against his mouth. He finishes speaking and stands back, but I have heard nothing. I move my ear a little closer to the wall, but still there is only silence. How fast does sound travel? At seven and nine we have no idea of such mysteries; across the rotunda, we shrug at each other and signal that he should try again.

Grandma, who has been discreetly observing us, now approaches to tell me that I need to move in closer to the wall, that my ear ought to be just shy of touching it. I am reluctant to heed her advice – we are the trained spies, not her – but I nevertheless try it, and the effect is as revelatory as the first time she held a seashell to my ear. Around the room's circumference, perhaps a dozen other people are whispering into the wall and I can hear them all: a quiet cacophony of code-names, midnight assignations and sailing times from distant ports. I look around the balcony in amazement: they have forgotten to speak in code, to don their raincoats and trilbies, to talcum-powder their hair grey, but every single person whispering into this wall is a spy.

Opposite me, Dominic is waiting for a sign that I have heard his message, but his was the only voice that I could not hear. He signals that he will try once more, but I shake my head; I have made an important discovery and I need to share it with him. He understands, and places his own ear against the wall.

'They're all spies!' I whisper. 'All of them!'

As my top-secret message travels the circumference to Dominic, I observe the spies for any sign of a reaction. None of them gives themselves away, but neither does any look of recognition appear on Dominic's face. I try again, more urgently this time, and speak so loudly that a few people standing nearby simply overhear and turn to look at me in mild puzzlement. Again, my message fails to reach Dominic. Grudgingly, I turn and ask Grandma what we are doing wrong. She smiles sympathetically and says that she thinks it is probably a matter of technique.

Technique. At seven years old I loathe technique. Technique is the word adults say to children when they are simply not good enough at something. Technique is why I cannot yet properly throw a frisbee, overarm bowl a cricket ball, or even progress beyond Grade Five at skiing, and Grade Five is the one you get just for turning up with a cheque from your parents for five lessons.

The next time I enter St Paul's I am no longer a tourist child visiting London on a family railcard at half term, but a citizen and a mourner both. It is May, a month after I returned, two months after Dominic's funeral, and a service of remembrance for the victims of the Indian Ocean tsunami is held in the cathedral.

It is a service that sings of connections, connections across the world and down through the years, maybe even between worlds. A lament is played on a Thai fiddle – perhaps the saddest sound man has ever learned to engineer – and a procession of the bereaved, who include Mum amongst their number, lay flowers at the altar. As the starting point of his centrepiece sermon, the Archbishop of Canterbury takes a line from 'An Arundel Tomb' by Philip Larkin: 'What will survive of us is love'.

I had no intention of being moved today, but the homily hits me surely as if it were a precision-tipped bullet fired from the gun of one of Rachel's Special Branch colleagues currently manning the cathedral doors. I had no intention of being moved because I have already been to Dominic's funeral, have let a velvet cord run through my hands to lower his coffin into the ground, have delivered his eulogy in front of a photograph of the two of us in our primary school uniforms. Today is not a day for getting upset. It is a day for the further paying of respects, a chance for Mum to meet with some of the other bereaved parents, for Grandma to perhaps meet the Queen.

It is largely on Grandma's account that the archbishop's line from Larkin has such an effect on me. It is an apposite quotation for an event that in many places took everything but memory, but on a personal level it is also a sucker punch that packs a power I had not expected from a fifty-something man in a white dress.

Not until my mid-teens did I properly notice the books on the shelf in the back bedroom of Grandma's house. Having recently become enamoured with Larkin at school – enticed initially by the swear words that seemed to be yelled from every second page – I had been taken aback to discover that almost all the books on Grandma's shelf were by Hull's poet-librarian. If it would have been a treasure trove anywhere, it was a bonanza all the sweeter for the seeming incongruity of its setting.

There were early editions with blank spaces where the censor had excised the precious swear words, there were entire volumes I had never heard of, and on every page of every book there were annotations pencilled in the margins by a reader who had clearly been as spellbound by these poems as I was. I spent an hour leafing through them, gorging on the yellowed paper, the old-fashioned fonts, the strangely delicious knowledge that someone in the family shared my secret passion. Sated, I went downstairs and asked Grandma which of my uncles the books had belonged to.

'Those are mine, dear,' she said.

My grandmother was born in 1922. During the war she enlisted in the Women's Royal Naval Service, and later was a teacher of children and raised a family of four strong-headed children of her own. Last summer, she celebrated her sixtieth year of marriage to a man who served in a rifle company in Greece, Italy and the Middle East and knows enough about history, language and art to complete the cryptic crossword in his newspaper every day of the week. As with Mum and her house of psychedelic hippies in the summer of love, Grandma is far more worldly than I can ever dream of being, and in her mid-eighties still takes the train up to London once a month to lunch with a friend and visit the galleries.

This, then, is what the archbishop's line sets me thinking of: what an amazing thing a properly lived human life can be, and how wrong it should be that anyone's should be cut short, that they should be deprived of the chance to surprise their presumptuous grandchildren with their taste in literature. It sets me thinking about that little upstairs back bedroom in Grandma's house where Dominic once gave me my best ever birthday present, and it sets me thinking, of course, about the last time we had all been together at St Paul's.

Still, the archbishop may have succeeded in moving me, but I am determined I am not going to cry. And I tell myself that as long as I do not look up, as long as I do not have to see the rotunda where Dominic and I once tried to whisper our secrets to each other, I will probably be all right.

But at the end of the service the Archbishop of Canterbury thwarts me. Two hundred and twenty-five thousand rose petals are dropped from the whispering gallery and I weep as I have not done in months. They fall from the rotunda, down amongst us and we stand silent in our pews and wonder if the dead can hear the messages we are sending them, if they can know that Larkin and even the archbishop actually have it only half right, that love is not merely what survives of the dead, but also what survives *for* them.

And as these petals fall among us like the tears now streaming down everybody's face, I again start to think that perhaps it is not impossible that the dead can hear us if we gather two or three in their name. The last time I visited this whispering gallery I heard what I wanted to hear: wound up on underground trains and the excitement of being in the big city, wrapped in the espionage daydreams my brother and I shared, I heard the voices of spies confessing state secrets when really all I had done was put a shell to my ear. And if such a thing is possible, if sometimes we can indeed genuinely hear what we want to hear, is it not just also possible that other people – even the dead ones – might occasionally hear what we want them to hear too, if only we can just somehow learn to master the technique?

After the service at St Paul's there is a reception in a nearby marquee. Under a pristine white canopy, waitresses wearing ties pirouette trays of fruit juice and slices of cake through crowds of the bereaved. It is the strangest wedding I have ever been to and, dizzy with the levity that comes after a bout of crying, it takes me a few moments to realise that the man being led towards my mum by a young aide with a clipboard is the Chancellor of the Exchequer, Gordon Brown.

Now, this is a man we have always held in high regard in our house – he is a Scot and Labour and therefore one of our own twice over – and in any normal year we would be thrilled to meet him, but this is not any normal year and I am apprehensive about him speaking to Mum this afternoon. If the popular caricature of him is to be believed, he is not generally perceived – and certainly not by comparison to his next-door neighbour, currently working the far side of the room – to be a people person. What will he say to her? What *can* he say to her? There have already been any number of occasions this year when I, her own son, have not known what to say to her, so what chance can any politician have?

Instantly, though, he puts her at ease. I cannot say what devilment of filters the television cameramen and newspaper photographers have conspired to use on him for the past two decades, because he does this with nothing more than a smile that is as genuine as it is sympathetic. Even Grandma – a life-long member of the Conservative Party, who lives in one of the safest Tory seats in the country but still regularly spends election day shepherding confused but pliable elderly ladies to and from the polls – is immediately and utterly taken with him.

The aide introduces everyone – the Chancellor is accompanied by his wife, Sarah, and we are a large and complicated family – and then quietly retreats. Sarah Brown is standing nearest to me; she offers me her condolences and we talk about the service. As always these days, I have one wary ear tuned to Mum's conversation, and that is how I overhear Gordon Brown say to her that there is no feeling in the world that can ever compare with that of the loss of a child.

He knows of what he speaks, because the Browns lost their own daughter a few days after her birth two years previously. I had not forgotten this – their tragedy played out in the media too – but somehow I had dissociated this private heart-break from the couple being ushered around the marquee, as if the Chancellor of the Exchequer and his partner could be separate people from the Gordon and Sarah Brown who lost

83

their own beloved child. They are, of course, exactly the same people and when this countryman of ours speaks to my mum, he gives her the purest and most human thing possible. Far beyond sympathy, beyond consolation, beyond empty promises that in time things will be better, he gives her the thing that most of us, no matter how well-meaning, have been utterly unable to offer her: empathy. Empathy, in the first and true meaning of the word: understanding. Together, they understand suffering in a way that most of us hope we will never have to.

The man who will soon be our Prime Minister tells Mum that he remembers hearing about Dominic and Eileen and asks her to tell him something about them, their lives and their work. Mum is pleased to do so, and soon they are chatting away, comparing notes on Marchmont, the area of Edinburgh where we lived as teenagers and the Chancellor resided as a student. He asks Mum where she lives now, and when she tells him that she is in Bruntsfield, he responds that he is in North Queensferry, 'Just up the road and across the water'. Geographically a stretch, perhaps, but his answer renders them neighbours and is an endearingly humble response from a man whose primary address these days is Number 11, Downing Street. For this moment, though, shorn of the white noise of high office and of personal tragedy as headline news, neighbours is exactly what they are: two bereaved parents who know something of each other's quiet and unbearable suffering.

The aide approaches and apologises that they must keep moving on, but before they go Gordon Brown asks me how long my family will be in London for, and if there is a telephone number on which we can be contacted. The aide passes him a pen and we all watch as the Chancellor of the Exchequer takes a piece of paper from his pocket and carefully writes down my mobile phone number. I manage to resist suggesting he gives me a missed call, but only just.

In truth, our favourite childhood experience of London did not take place at St Paul's, but at a cathedral of a different kind altogether: the old Wembley Stadium.

After our inaugural trip with Mum and Grandma, our Easter journey to London became an annual pilgrimage; the year we were eleven and newly thirteen, Dominic and I abruptly found ourselves deemed old enough to make the long rail journey south unaccompanied. We spent a few proud days with our grandparents on the south coast, revelling in what we took to be our new-found status as young adults, and then caught a train up to London, where Uncle John's girlfriend, Kate, met us at King's Cross Station.

Girlfriend. That John and Kate should live together but not actually be married was impossibly glamorous and bohemian to our young suburban minds, but then everything about their lives was impossibly glamorous and bohemian to our young suburban minds. They lived in a tumbledown townhouse where the single recognisable piece of furniture was an aluminium jukebox that played only one record, Debbie Harry's 'French Kissin' in the USA'. They owned a red Italian sports car that they could never start, and so instead drove around London in a rusted white Mini through the holes in whose floor you could see the road passing beneath. They ate out in restaurants when it was nobody's birthday. More than anything, though, they had each been to America several times.

When had Dominic and I fallen so deeply and helplessly in love with America and, moreover, why? We knew no Americans, had never been there, and, excepting John and Kate, had encountered nobody who had. And yet our hearts

burned with a singular passion for the place, and we understood exactly what Debbie Harry meant when she sang about
'French Kissin' in the USA'. Actually that is not entirely true,
because we had no first-hand experience whatsoever of
French kissing, but what I mean to say is that we intuitively
knew that, like everything else, French kissing would no
doubt be particularly special when conducted in America.

It was the movies that did for us, of course it was. It was all
those yellow school buses, those cellophane-wrapped newspapers tossed from bicycles. It was Marty McFly's DeLorean
and Ferris Bueller's life-affirming day off. We never had the
slightest chance.

We never had the slightest chance, and neither did any
other kid we knew, nor their parents. We daily pestered
any adult in sight to take us to Wimpy, for years Edinburgh's
only hamburger bar, and when a Burger King finally appeared
on Princes Street, it was an event of greater cultural significance to us than the first branch of McDonald's opening in
Moscow. When John posted us up two pairs of Nike shoes
he had bought on one of his work trips to America, they
might as well have been spun from a thread of pure gold.

But I put this down not to convey how deeply the stamps
in John and Kate's passports impressed us. Instead, I do it so
that when I write that, that Easter time in London, they took
us to an actual American football game, some measure of just
what this meant to us might come through here.

But already the recalled excitement has me getting ahead
of myself, for the day in question did not start with American
football but something almost equally alluring: gambling.
The first Saturday in April is Grand National day; John and
Kate had us each pick a horse from the spread in the paper
and placed an extravagant five pound bet on them for us.
Dominic's horse, chosen for the St Andrew's cross uniform

her jockey wore, came in at eleven to one and made us pocket money millionaires.

Far beyond monetary riches, though, was that evening's American football. In a match being contested as part of what would prove to be the short-lived European league, the London Monarchs were taking on Frankfurt Galaxy. Like the sport itself, the players, referees, even the cheerleaders had all been imported wholesale from America; to our minds, this only further increased the glamour of the occasion.

The London Monarchs wore white shirts and helmets of a regally golden hue. Frankfurt Galaxy, like the cinematic villains that they were, wore a slickly sinister black and silver strip, and we booed ourselves breathless every time they approached the ball. The floodlights shone halogen-white, the rain-polished grass was a technicolour dream of green, and the immaculate blonde cheerleaders were a fantasy of what we hoped high school might be like.

The internet tells me that the London Monarchs won by twenty-seven points and I will have to take its word for it, for the match play was stop-start and the rules anyway impossible to follow. It did not matter then, though, and it does not matter now, because we sat there high in the stands with our uncle and aunt, rich from gambling, sated on hotdogs, drunk on the infectious enthusiasm of genuine American cheerleaders, and were as happy as it is possible for two boys to be.

And then sitting in the back of the rusted white Mini, flying along the North Circular with the lights of the city rushing past us; the cold night air seeps in through the holes in the floor, but we are warm in the knowledge that we had seen a real-life American football match and when we go back to school and tell the others we shall be like kings in the world of boys. And filled with so much stadium Coca-Cola that we were laughing, laughing so hard every time we looked at each other because we were desperate to piss but did not want to tell them, for to do so would have rendered us children and, for this trip at least, we were now adults. And then Kate taking the *A–Z* from the glove compartment, and us whispering urgently to each other, asking if it was really possible that a single city might be so big that even our uncle could not find his own way home?

At nine o'clock on the morning after the ceremony at St Paul's, my phone starts to ring. I should be up by now, but our long day yesterday culminated in a late dinner and on the way home I took a detour so that I could pass by the Trellick Tower. Assuming that the phone call will be from someone on the production team of *Eleventh Hour*, which is now only days from filming, I decide that I had better answer it.

'Hello?' I say, my voice early morning thick.

'Good morning, Simon. It's Nigel Griffiths.'

'Nigel. Sorry, remind me what you do again?'

'I'm the Member of Parliament for Edinburgh South. Your mother's constituency.'

'Oh,' I say, fully awake now. 'Hello.'

'Listen, Gordon Brown mentioned your family were in London, and I was wondering if you might have the time to come and look around the House of Commons today?'

Dad is returning to France this morning, but I call Mum at the hotel where she and Rob are staying. I make arrangements to meet them in Parliament Square and hurry into our cold shower.

Summer comes early in London and the streets around Westminster are buzzing with tourists dangling expensive Nikons from their necks. They take turns snapping each other in front of Big Ben, and the pages of their guidebooks flutter back and forth in the breeze like flocks of pocket doves.

Inside the Houses of Parliament, the atmosphere is no less excitable. Today is swearing-in day, and a large number of Labour Members are celebrating retaining closely fought seats in the general election that was held a week ago. As our MP and his aide escort us along the corridors, reprieved Members congratulate each other in the hallways, shake hands, share war stories and compete over who was returned by the narrowest margin; some of our more youthful elected representatives even go as far as to high-five each other. The day has the atmosphere not so much of the beginning of a term as the end of one, and it is true that following today's swearing-in, little legislative work will be done until after the summer recess.

We are given the entire tour: through the 'Aye' and the 'Nay' arches, down regally carpeted corridors of Members' offices, and up to the public gallery where we can see into the racing-green lower chamber, inside which MPs are nervously lining up to be sworn in like fourth-formers awaiting their BCG jab. Not for a moment do we forget what awful thing has granted us such strange privilege today, and we talk of Dominic as we go, asking ourselves what his opinion of every vestibule or portico would have been, reminding each other how much more beautifully such things were always rendered when seen through his appreciative eyes.

As always, there are unexpected moments when he comes closer still. Much of the Palace of Westminster was designed by the architect Augustus Pugin, and his distinctive brand of gothic revival had a profound effect on many of his peers; George Gilbert Scott, who subsequently designed the main building at the University of Glasgow, even imagined Pugin to be his 'guardian angel'. When we descend to the basement of the palace to view the Speaker's gilt carriage, we could easily be in the cloisters of my alma mater; I could be nineteen years old and hurrying off to meet up with Dominic for a happy-hour pint.

Above our guilty protests that we have already taken up too much of their time, our hosts insist on taking us to lunch. Afterwards, we thank them and start to take our leave, but they have a surprise for us.

'They unfortunately can't be there themselves,' the aide says, 'but Gordon and Sarah Brown have invited you to look around Number Eleven this afternoon.'

We are ushered past tourists and policemen, down an eerily quiet street and through a black door, and before we know it find ourselves stood in the official residence of the Chancellor of the Exchequer. Here, on these surprisingly threadbare chairs, budgets are set and major decisions taken. But not on this particular afternoon: today the place is devoid of life, and we have the anticlimactic feeling that we are in a museum mock-up of Number 11 rather than the prestigious house itself. Much like its current tenant, we cannot help but wonder what it would feel like to step next door.

No doubt used to this reaction, the housekeeper tasked with showing us round has a question for us: do we know what happens at Number 12? We shrug that we do not. Number 12, she informs us with a twinkle in her eye, is the press office for Number 10 and the internal doors between all three buildings are therefore constantly kept open. If we wanted to, she says, it would be an easy thing to pop through from here to Number 12. Or, for that matter, to Number 10.

It is all there: the iconic mantelpiece, the chessboard floor, the portraits of previous Prime Ministers. Through a back window, the housekeeper points out where the present incumbent is meeting with his advisers in the garden. She asks us if we would like to take our picture by the fireplace, but we do not have a camera, and perhaps we are glad of it. It is intriguing and distracting to be here, but we did not arrive in London this time as tourists, not entirely.

What, then, does it mean to be here? In one way, it does not mean anything: nothing means anything any more because, short of miracles or time travel, nobody can fix the thing that is wrong with us. But in another way, it means almost as much as anything now can: in a year full of hollow and empty days, it means at least a slightly different sort of day from all those others that we have become so used to, and such a thing is priceless. A bittersweet, end-of-term kind of day, no doubt, but a day that means that when Mum returns to her own school on Monday she will not have to answer her pupils' well-intentioned enquiries by saying that she went to London to attend another kind of funeral service, but can instead say that she met the Chancellor of the Exchequer, and saw the Prime Minister sitting taking tea in his garden. Perhaps more than anything else, it means that a couple of fellow parents who lost their own child understood what for once not having to talk about it would mean to her.

A few weeks later, I am in Edinburgh Airport early on a Monday morning, assaulting the self check-in kiosk. I am theoretically en route to Manchester, where *Eleventh Hour* is fast filming itself into all kinds of narrative corners, but the machine has swallowed the bank card it promised it only needed to identify me. The screen has been frozen for what might only have been five minutes, but this still means that it will not now be possible for me to get to the gate before it closes. I force myself to take a few deep breaths and consider my predicament a little more rationally.

That done, I begin to hit the machine again. If this is undeniably bad behaviour, there are at least some extenuating circumstances for my conduct today. For one thing, I was not cutting it so fine because I got up too late this morning, but because I got up too early.

I got up too early because before emailing them to the production office in Manchester, I needed to proofread the redrafted script pages I had stayed up working on until the small hours. At seven o'clock this morning, though, somewhere between pressing 'send' and logging off, I fell asleep. When Mum found me with my head on the keyboard, I was almost an hour behind schedule.

Partly I am also so fractious because, despite all my best efforts, my big screenwriting break is not going anything like according to plan. In my bag I have a DVD of the rushes of the latest episode, but I have been forewarned that they will bear scant resemblance to the agreed script, for one of our directors has developed an inexplicable penchant for improvisation. Our actors are all consummate professionals who will try whatever is reasonably asked of them, but improvisation is an imprecise tool if what you are making is intended as a taut scientific thriller: if the script says a gun must be found in a drawer in scene fifteen, then this is generally how it needs to be. If a gun is not found, then in the climactic scene seventy-two, where your hero is supposed to shoot the bad guy with the gun he earlier found in the drawer, he will be left to pretend he has a gun in his pocket and hope that the bad guy is kind enough to play along.

Since the service at St Paul's, I have also become concerned about the character of Rachel and her entire role in the piece. As a classic detective's sidekick, Rachel functions as a Watson to whom our cerebral Holmes can explain his deductive leaps. The question troubling me is whether our esteemed Professor Hood would ever have been assigned Special Branch protection. At St Paul's I was distracted by the Thai fiddle and the archbishop's attempts to make me cry, but as far as I could see only the Queen and the Prime Minister arrived with their own Special Branch officers. If in reality neither the Foreign nor Home Secretaries are afforded such protection, does it therefore take more than a willing suspension of disbelief to think that a scientist might be granted it, no matter how cantankerous a maverick he may be?

But it is not merely that the dream writing assignment seems on the verge of turning into a nightmare, nor that the bank card in the check-in machine is the only one I have and that the way things are going I might be in Manchester for weeks. Edinburgh Airport itself remains bound up in memory, and my journey there inevitably takes me through Colinton village and within a few hundred yards of the churchyard where Dominic lies. If today it is no sadder a place than it always is, on this particular morning there has been something else too: angst, and not a little guilt with it.

Angst and guilt for the fact that I have not yet organised a headstone, that Dominic's resting place remains unmarked, that people take flowers out to Colinton and call me from the churchyard, embarrassed that they do not know where to lay them. Angst and guilt because I still have not written to thank the people who spoke at his services and tell them how we will always treasure their words, that I have not written to the Chancellor and his wife to thank them for our visit to Downing Street, that I have not written to Mum's MP to thank him for our tour of the House of Commons, that I have not done enough to sort out Dominic's estate. Angst and guilt that instead of doing such things I have leapt a little too wholeheartedly, a little too headlong, into trying to ensure my own life picked up precisely where it left off last December.

The screen on the check-in machine turns momentarily blank. I think I am reprieved, that my ticket is about to be printed, my card returned. Instead, the display reverts to the 'Welcome' screen.

I start to kick the machine in the area where its shins would be were it a person. As I am doing this, I become vaguely aware of another passenger waiting behind me, but I ignore them and continue with my assault. Only when two patrolling police officers begin to take an interest in me do I decide that it is time to cut my losses and make for the assistance desk.

As I turn to go, I glance at the person who has been waiting behind me. A smartly dressed woman in her early forties, she seems alarmed by what she has witnessed. I initially assume she is merely surprised by such a public display of violence so early in the morning, but she holds my gaze and I realise with horror that she seems to think that we know one another.

Strung out from stress and exhaustion, I am not at all certain that we do know each other; even if we do, I have no idea where from. She keeps looking at me, though, and seems to be considering whether it would be physically safe to say hello. This only makes me keener to flee the scene and I hurry away, telling myself as I go that she is probably a colleague of Mum's or at worst somebody I know from one of the hospitals. Whoever she might be, she is hopefully flying far away today; perhaps by the time she returns to Edinburgh she will have forgotten all about my moment of airport madness.

The assistance queue turns out to be mercifully swift-moving, and the man at the counter retrieves my card for me.

94

Better yet, he informs me that the late arrival of the inbound plane has delayed boarding of my flight. I will be able to make good my escape.

Or so I think. As we taxi out on to the runway, I am struck by a terrible realisation about the woman at the check-in kiosk. She was not a colleague of Mum's, nor somebody I knew from any hospital, and she was almost certainly travelling only as far as London. She was Sarah Brown, the wife of the Chancellor of the Exchequer, to whom I have not yet written a thank-you letter. Perhaps worst of all, she most assuredly did not have any Special Branch protection officer with her.

I spend the flight not watching the rushes, but writing a belated thank-you letter for the good care taken of us in London. I make no mention of the airport incident, and somehow even manage to refrain from asking whether the Browns might be able to let me know by return what they know regarding the assignment of Special Branch protection officers.

In December, as the first anniversary of the tsunami approaches, a letter arrives for Mum sealed in a House of Commons envelope. It is from Gordon Brown, several handwritten sides of A4 telling her how much we are all in his thoughts at this time of year. It is an incredible gesture, and we picture him, sitting down on one of the threadbare chairs, pushing away the budget papers, the trade agreements and the constituency work, taking out a fountain pen and starting to write. This time, I vow, we will send our thanks by return of post.

Instead, we go to Thailand for the one-year anniversary. A few days after our return in January, I ask Mum if she has responded to the Chancellor's letter. She says that her reply is on the hall table, waiting to be posted, and I ask if I can per-haps read it.

'You already have,' she says. 'It's the Christmas round-robin letter.'

Though she is puzzled as to why such a thing would be necessary, Mum agrees that I can write a covering note to go along with it, and that she will refrain from posting the round-robin letter until I do.

I do not get around to writing it. January slips into February, and by the time March rolls around it is too late to write at all, because how do you start a letter to the Chancellor of the Exchequer with an apology that you would have writ-ten sooner, only life has been busy lately?

When *Eleventh Hour* airs the following spring, it does so to decidedly mixed reviews. The critics are enamoured with Rachel but several find the character of Professor Hood too cold, too Spock-logical to be a hero they can take to their hearts. The plots, thankfully, seem to just about hold water, and nobody questions the fact that Hood has his own Special Branch bodyguard. The consensus, then, seems to be merely that people expected more from the show, and with the cast and budget we had at our disposal, they were perhaps entitled to. Still, it is by no means a disaster, and that in itself is a minor victory: I was not told at the time, but at the point at which I got involved, the expectation was that the show would likely turn out to be unscreenable, an eventuality that occurs in television drama more frequently than people prob-ably think.

And then our ratings come in. The one person I really wanted to see it could not, but four and a half million other people watch the opening episode. It might sound a lot – it did to me, as I naïvely waited for the congratulatory telegrams to start flooding in – but it is not enough for a major drama, and in fact not even close to enough. We have been soundly beaten by the launch of a rival BBC show, and, more embarrassingly, an episode of *Celebrity Big Brother* in which a Member of Parliament pretended to be a cat. The following Sunday, the *Observer* newspaper publishes a still photograph of Professor Hood and Rachel under the banner headline, IS THIS THE DEATH OF ITV?. I keep it pinned above my desk still; not many people, in their first major writing assignment, can claim to have murdered an entire television channel.

Perhaps it was not the career for me anyway. Television demands neat stories, three-act affairs where in the last scene the good guy reluctantly shoots the bad guy with a gun he found in the drawer in the bad guy's house before the commercial break at the end of act one. I can still write such stories – I never did get my Grade Four at skiing, nor properly learn to overarm bowl, so it is one of the few pieces of technique I can genuinely claim to have ever got something of the hang of – but increasingly I do not know if I want to write them, because I do not know if I believe in them any more.

Manuals of screenwriting insist that there can be no such thing as simple coincidence. Even in the most poorly scripted Hollywood disaster movie there is foreshadowing and harbinger, set-up and pay-off: people do not go to bed full of youthful vigour and happiness one night and die the next day. If this does ever happen on television or in the movies we feel cheated, perhaps even ask for our money back, and yet this random chance is the true fabric from which life is woven: if there is no such thing as simple bad luck how else to explain, how to even begin to comprehend, that Dominic and Eileen's three days on Phi Phi would coincide with the second largest earthquake since records began?

An everyday piece of happenstance: a year after I returned to London, I discovered that not only was the architect responsible for the Trellick Tower a man called Goldfinger, but that James Bond's nemesis had actually been named for him. As young spies we had wished only that villains like Auric Goldfinger existed, and yet in the months after Dominic died I had unknowingly become obsessed with a building designed by the man himself. It is a coincidence that still makes me smile, but written in a screenplay such serendipity would never survive beyond the first draft.

Equally, things that are made to seem inevitable on the screen often prove unlikely in life. Last Grand National day, my cousin Matthew called me to say that one of the runners was a horse called Simon with a last-minute substitute jockey called Dominic. In the Hollywood version this horse would have come from the back of the field to win by a nose, but I put a hundred pounds on this eleven-to-one outsider and he fell six fences from home after leading the pack all the way round.

Four and a half million people – likely more than will ever know that my gentle brother once walked this earth – tuned in to watch an episode of a television programme in which a government scientist battles an unscrupulous geneticist's attempts to clone a child to replace the dead son of a grief-stricken billionaire. In that story, the good guy chases the bad guy, the girl-in-jeopardy is saved with minutes to spare, and everybody lives happily ever after. How in ninety minutes minus advertisements do you even begin to tell a more honest story: a story that has no such resolution, a story that had no neat beginning but now will never end?

When we reached the end of filming on *Eleventh Hour*, I decided that I could not stay in London and try to write another three-act script where every set-up was paid off and everything ended happily. Whatever promises the Trellick Tower may have once made me, I had been naïve to think that I could simply insist my old life start up again, perhaps even more so to believe that I might actually want it to.

When he was eleven and I was still nine, my parents enrolled Dominic in a school near the city centre. Initially it all seemed a great adventure: Dominic would travel to and from this new school on the bus, he would study foreign languages and learn to play rugby in winter and cricket in summer. Initially it all seemed a great adventure, and then we learned that Dominic's teacher there was to be Miss Park.

We had known of Miss Park for years, for wild rumours about her disciplinarian ways circulated the suburbs. Brother Boy Scouts, teenaged babysitters, even the prefect who had shown us around Dominic's new school at open day: they had all warned us to avoid Miss Park's class.

When Dominic set off on his first morning we shook hands solemnly, as if he were a prisoner being led to the gallows. All day I waited with fretful anticipation, but the story he brought home that night seemed anticlimactic at best: Miss Park was every bit as fierce as we had heard, but the most noteworthy part of his day was that he had made a friend, a fellow new boy called Neil.

If I can still remember that first time I heard Neil's name, I can hardly recollect a time when we did not know him: rock-steady Neil, who could have grown a full beard by the age of thirteen, who was good at golf and better at rugby, who took Dominic on his holidays and sometimes came on ours. They chivvied each other through that first year at the new school, weathering their portion of the collective reprisals whilst always being careful not to draw such dangerous attention on themselves as another new boy, Michael Jones, was foolhardy enough to do.

The class had a homework assignment due and when Michael Jones failed to pass his forward, Miss Park click-clacked her way down the rows to loom over him.

'I didn't do the homework,' he shrugged.

'And why not?' she asked, her voice already tremulous with brewing rage.

'Because my sister died.'

Miss Park whispered that she was sorry to hear such sad news and returned to her desk.

I had Dominic and Neil recount this exchange to me so many times that I can still hear the collective gasp that Michael Jones's bold statement drew. The entire class knew that his sister was not dead but in the first year at the attached high school; they had seen her only that morning, carrying her hockey things and entirely alive.

Weeks pass. Each afternoon I rush home from school to ask Dominic if the elder Jones has been resurrected; each afternoon he tells me that she has not. The revelation finally occurs at a parents' night several months later. Mrs Jones sits down, eager to hear about her son's progress, and instead Miss Park tells her that she was very sorry to hear about her daughter.

The tale ends with a second anticlimax, a referral to an educational psychologist rather than a public hanging. Still, we continued to repeat the story to one another, for even at nine and eleven we knew how audacious the lie was, and not merely because Miss Park was such a crone: life was sacred, bereaved mothers even more so, and these were things you did not mess around with.

It was not yet eleven o'clock as we made our way from the ferry, but already it was a day hotter than any that Neil or I had known.

If we had been surprised by how workaday the little town at Tonsai had seemed – a post office, a pharmacy, pancake stalls – this Loh Dahlum side of the island remained apocalyptic. Here stood the petrified skeletons of a few vanished structures and here lay the bones of a filleted road, but mostly there was only absence, an eerie flatness to the land the sole evidence that this empty landscape had until recently teemed with life. The dead coconut trees provided no meaningful shade, and the broiling sun reflected, white-hot, off the thin dusting of sand that covered everything in sight.

On a barren patch of this ground at the far north-east of the bay, half a dozen people were labouring in the heat. They appeared to be digging a trench in the deep dry sand, or anyway trying to: for every spadeful they extracted, an almost equal amount seemed to rush back in. It looked absurd toil, and yet they kept diligently at it. Later, we would discover that they had no choice but to keep at it: they were constructing a memorial garden and had only four months in which to complete their task.

Piers, water mains and clinics: infrastructure had been repaired first and rightly so. As we planned our trip to Thailand, Neil and I had initially hoped to assist with these efforts, but by the time we reached Phi Phi such work was already all but complete. Under the umbrella of an organisation called Help International Phi Phi – abbreviated everywhere to 'Hi Phi Phi' – local people and international volunteers had spent the months after the tsunami labouring together to restore the island to the state in which we now found it.

Pulling on whatever gloves and boots were available – and simply going without if there were none – the Hi Phi Phi workers had carted untold tonnes of debris from the Front Street and dug a half-mile trench to drain the water from the spoiled reservoir. Later, they had progressed to rebuilding and restoration projects and to this day you will pass their handiwork at every corner and perhaps never realise it. *Time Asia* subsequently named the organisation among their Heroes of the Year, and nobody who knows even a little of what they achieved can doubt that the magazine was right to do so. From an entirely selfish point of view, it was also thanks to the labours of all those who had cleared the streets and patched up the buildings that Neil and I found ourselves free to join the people working on the memorial garden project.

On our second day on the island, we take our places amongst them. At a little after nine o'clock on a bright morning towards the end of August, they are a trio of young travellers from Ireland; a sun-bleached Portuguese surfer; an English couple at the beginning of a year out; and Toy and Carol, a Thai and Australian couple who have lived on the island for several years and lost both their three-year-old daughter and Carol's sister in the tsunami.

Toy and Carol, then, are the brains behind the garden, but they are also the heart. The people who had the initial inspiration, who obtained permission from the landowner and who each day direct the enthusiastic volunteers, it is within them that the desire to commemorate last December's dead burns brightest.

The memorial garden they have in mind is a democracy of a green and flowered space, a focal point on the island for all the relatives and friends of the deceased. It is to be a place for those who live here year round, for those who visit when they can, and for those who cannot travel here but might find comfort even in the idea of a garden.

In the heat of late August, this idea of a garden is all that we have. Our daydreams may have immediately populated themselves with shading trees and fragrant petals, but the reality is a rectangular patch of saltwater scrubland that is littered with rocks and broken glass. A hundred feet long by fifty feet wide, its two long boundaries are demarcated by the beach edge and the roughly parallel ruined road, its shorter ones by a thatched-roof beach bar, Sunflower Bar, and the trench we are today employed digging.

If from the safety of the road yesterday the labour had looked like absurd toil, up close it is immediately the hardest work that I have ever done. We stop for rest and water breaks as often as we like and yet on the first morning alone I quickly lose count of the number of times I come close to passing out.

Worse, all through that first day, I am dimly aware that we seem to be making scant progress. Towards evening, I learn a humbling truth from my co-workers: though I had assumed operations had commenced the previous morning, work on the garden had already been going on for weeks.

Beneath the beach boundary, a wall of sandbags has been discreetly stacked to raise the garden's edge some five feet above the sea that necessitated it in the first place. It would have taken a Herculean effort to fill and manoeuvre so many heavy bags into position, and on this first day of work I wonder aloud to my new colleagues if the mechanical digger I had seen elsewhere on the island might not have been borrowed for the task. My query was met only with silence; though everybody was too polite to say it out loud, I had the sense that they believed I had not quite grasped what was going on here.

The days quickly start to fall into one another. Each morning we convene at nine, and each evening we break at six. In between these times we dig and we barrow, we haul and we rake; when the sun is at its highest we try to find work that we can do in the shade, but often there is none, and we all know the schedule we are working to.

We go to bed each night filthy, sunburned and exhausted, and yet every morning the volunteers return. Individual travellers arrive and depart, but the communal dedication never lapses. Very few of these souls have any personal grief to work through in these endless shovels, and to begin with I try to explain to some of them just what their presence each day means to me. Quickly realising this is far beyond the reach of the words of any of the languages we collectively speak, I instead one-two my spade and pick-axe strokes with theirs and hope that the rhythm of the music of our work together will somehow convey to them these unutterable things.

If such unspoken empathy makes our labour a little easier, our Thai contingent also have a potent secret to share with us. Called *sanuk*, it is an aspect of Thai culture that has traditionally fascinated outsiders: the pre-eminent importance placed upon the notion of fun. Guidebooks to Thailand gleefully detail what they consider to be the incongruous situation whereby individuals select their occupation not on the basis of prestige or salary but on how much fun the job entails, as if Thailand were awash with accountants and lawyers desperately trying to break into full-time clowning or professional ice-cream tasting. In practice, what sanuk actually equates to is an enviable ability to render even the most wearisome task at least a little enjoyable: the bartender making his millionth pina colada of the night turns the act into a piece of performance art; the girls who clean the rooms in the resorts twist beach towels into the likenesses of animals not because anybody has told them they must, but because it makes the time go a little quicker.

As we worked together in the garden we learned not only how to dig and barrow efficiently, but also how to invest these acts with fun, how to perform this ancient Thai conjuring trick of sanuk: a human chain formed to unload heavy bags of peat metamorphoses into a game of pass the parcel played to the music on the Sunflower Bar stereo; two large boulders requiring to be carried from the land become a contest worthy of an episode of *The World's Strongest Man*.

On another day we push cartloads of rubbish so heavy that when our convoy reaches the square that currently serves as the town's dump it is all that most of us can do not to lay ourselves down among the debris. Mon, however – a man from the north of Thailand who has quickly become both a firm friend and attentive local guide to me – invites one of the volunteers to relax inside his empty cart for the return journey. As we pass back through town, Mon seems to have some business with every shopkeeper we encounter, and each of them finds it hilarious. After half a dozen such encounters, I eventually summon the breath and energy to ask him what he is saying.

'One foreigner for sale!' He grins. 'For ten baht this one in my cart will do anything!'

Yet this sanuk and the quiet solidarity of the volunteers were not the only things that carried me through these first weeks. I had arrived in Thailand a virtual stranger to physical work, but Dominic had always relished it, labouring alongside Neil on building sites around Edinburgh in the holidays when there were any number of easier positions available. He would return home shattered, his clothes dirty, his hands cracked with cement burns, and yet he would invariably be radiating weary contentment. I had never understood the attraction, but I thought of him now as I lifted a shovel, pushed the cart or collapsed under the shade of the banyan tree. And as I did this, I slowly began to understand a little of what had eluded me on that first day when I had looked at all the sandbags and wondered aloud whether the job might have been more easily achieved: whatever it was that we were attempting to do here, 'more easily' ought not be any part of it.

O ut for dinner on Phi Phi one night, Neil and I find ourselves reminiscing about the tenement flat in Marchmont where Dominic and I lived with Mum. Neil had helped us carry our furniture on the day that we moved in and had barely seemed to leave the place in the years that followed.

The door that led off from the street below was lilac; lilac like the amethyst in Dominic's birthstone, lilac like the one that adorns the locket Mum now wears around her neck each day. We loved that lilac door: you turned your key and then you walked in through a high, narrow and dusty entranceway – the communal stairway known in Scotland as a close – and then you were home.

The bright autumn Saturday we moved in Dominic and I were fourteen and thirteen years old, and the learning curve for children sheltered and suburban as we were was steep indeed. Taking this new close of ours for an urban version of the carports and garages we had that morning left behind, we decided that it would be a good place to store our bicycles. Dominic's did not last the first evening in our new home.

When the police arrived, they seemed incredulous that anybody could consider leaving a bicycle unlocked in a communal stair. Instead of accepting the implied rebuke, we simply took it as proof that we had at long last arrived in the big time.

The fact that Marchmont, fifteen minutes' walk south of Princes Street, was primarily a student district of only very mildly dilapidated tenement buildings mattered not to us.

NWA, a hip-hop group we liked who rapped about selling crack and performing drive-by shootings, made frequent mention of the fact that Compton, the infamous ghetto they hailed from, was located in South Central Los Angeles. When people we met asked us where we lived we now proudly told them that we were in South Central Edinburgh.

We tended not to mention that we had a turret. Our tenement had been built during the gothic revival and the flat came complete with an actual turret in the corner of the living room; stand inside its circle and look north and you could see – perfectly framed in a cracked window pane – the city's medieval castle perched atop its rock.

What wonder, then, if I look back now on that time as a sort of fairy tale? We were new teenagers, with the promise of long lives stretching in front of us. We lived in a home with a turret, and my own bedroom overlooked the Meadows, a sprawling city park that we quickly came to think of as a front garden through which we graciously permitted others to pass. Dominic's bedroom looked out on a street of shops, and here there were any number of businesses on whose behalf we could order pizzas.

If we did not sell drugs or shoot rival gang members, we still behaved pretty badly when we lived in our storybook flat. If I were one of the educational psychologists it was now our turn to regularly be threatened with being sent to, I might have been tempted to infer that this decline had something to do with our parents' recent separation. Maybe I would have even been partly right, but I would also have been entirely missing our real motivation: the exuberant, testosterone-boiling joy of being teenage boys together.

The telephone – a conduit of temptation between the worlds of childhood and adulthood – provided for much of our fun. At this distance it is hard to feel much remorse about all the pizzas, even if there might have been quite a lot of them: nobody got hurt, and a hungry worker perhaps even got a free dinner. Certainly if I worked in a pizza shop and a boy with a familiar voice called in to request five extra large pepperoni feasts but had to get his older brother to finish the order because he was giggling so much, I would like to think that I might at least ask for a number and call him back.

Later, when Edinburgh's first talk radio station launched we spent endless evenings attempting to get through. One night Graham succeeded.

'Caller, you are live on air,' said the DJ. 'What would you like to talk about tonight?'

'Well, my name is Neil,' Graham said. 'And I've got this really big problem.'

'Go on,' said the DJ.

'I want to be a woman. I live at—'

The DJ cut Graham off before he could announce Neil's home address, but it provided weeks of amusement.

Some of it was less forgivable. A few of Dominic's friends already had the voices of men and, with the rest of us listening in on an extension, we would have them phone the chatlines advertised on late-night television. At a certain point our stooge would drop in a casual remark about having maths first period Monday, and some poor lonely woman would realise she was on the point of arranging a date with a schoolboy. Had somebody only told us how much worse this was than dousing unwary pedestrians with water or playing our music loud as Dominic's stereo would go – the two crimes that most regularly brought the weary local constables to the door for another firm word – we would have ceased instantly.

Worth far more to us than any mischief, though, were the Meadows. So many of my best memories of Dominic are tied up in that wide parkland that sweeps up from Marchmont to the cobbled streets of the old town, to the pubs that we would soon enough be finding our way to. The Meadows were home to our endless frisbee nights, but they were everything else in our lives at that point besides. To get anywhere from our flat we had to traverse some part or other of them, and to walk across them today is to instantly be thirteen or fourteen years old again.

For the years that we lived in Marchmont, Dominic and the group of friends he was at the centre of had an unbreakable Saturday routine: over the Meadows and into town for a number three haircut at Mr Woods's barber shop and a cruise around the arcades, home for an epic game of football and then out in the early evening to Resurrection, a nightclub for under-seventeens held at a local disco.

It ran between seven and ten thirty and apart from the name there was very little holy about it. You entered the club's dingy cavern through a door of reinforced steel and immediately smelled the menace, and the smell of menace was cigarette smoke mixed with cheap aftershave. No alcohol could be purchased inside, and many of the young revellers had compensated for this by downing quarter-bottles of spirits and snorting cheap amphetamines in the alleyways around the club. Inside, they stumbled around and challenged anybody who dared to glance at them to a fight; as the dance floor featured a wall of full-length mirrors, the offending parties fortunately often proved to be their own reflections. All the same, some of these kids were genuinely to be feared: where we ordered hoax pizzas and made prank calls to radio stations, they went joyriding and housebreaking.

At thirteen I was afraid of almost everything else in life, but I was paradoxically never afraid to go there. I loved to walk across the Meadows with Dominic and his friends in the fading summer sunlight; more than anything I loved to have people know that Dominic, eighteen months and a seeming lifetime older than me, was my brother.

He wore Brylcreem in his hair, Levi Strauss jeans, a Los Angeles Raiders T-shirt and a Los Angeles Raiders jacket that Uncle John had brought for him from America. Sometimes he even topped off this outfit with a Los Angeles Raiders hat; if today that sounds like it may have been over-kill, it was the way that NWA dressed and in early nineties teenage Edinburgh it was the height of sartorial elegance.

He would wear this same outfit to the Meadows fair, which was more or less another kind of nightclub, albeit an open-air one: the same incessant music, the same flashing lights, even the same dangerous teenagers. It came only two weekends a summer, but from May onwards our shared first act on waking would be to look out my bedroom window for the solitary caravan of the advance man.

It took them several days to rig the fair, for the articulated lorries to arrive and give precipitous birth to their litters of dodgems, for the bow and stern of the pirate ship to be bolted together, for the air rifles to be precisely adjusted to ensure that they always just missed. The fair opened on a Thursday night, with every ride half price whilst they set the calibration and saw how far the outriders would this year sink into the muddy ground. On one such evening we saw a skinny girl we knew slip out of her seat on an attraction called the Terminator; the crowd screamed, and the operator, whose view had been obscured by a lady eating candy-floss, natur-ally only turned the thing up faster. The girl managed to hang on to a safety bar until the candy-floss lady wandered away towards the horse game, but only just; as compensation for her troubles she was given three free ride tokens, redeemable anywhere at the fair, and we were all jealous of her supreme good fortune.

On Friday night the fair is busier and by Saturday morning they are already putting down duckboards so you can still walk between the Wall of Death and the Ghost Train without losing your shoes. Business grows steadily brisker all through that day and come Saturday night everything is at full price and everywhere there is loud dance music punctuated only by the rising thrum of the diesel generators and the occasional silvery tumult of the ten pence waterfalls.

I am now five years older than Dominic was when he died, already eighteen years and another lifetime removed from the last of those long-ago evenings. I once read that time genuinely does speed up as you get older, for the human brain experiences it not as an even procession of days and weeks, but as a percentage of the time it has already known. Perhaps that is true enough, because already life sometimes seems a fairground waltzer overseen by a maniacal gypsy. Its colourful lights call to you and you enthusiastically climb aboard, certain of adventure and perhaps more besides. It starts to spin and you are excited to be there, to be moving so quickly, always seeming set to crash catastrophically into something, never quite doing so. But the thing keeps spinning faster, and at a certain point you look around and realise that those who boarded with you are no longer all there. You try to call out, but the music is now so loud that the only person who can hear you is the gypsy, and he responds only by spinning your car ever faster; the music keeps getting louder and now you feel sicker and sicker and you swear you would never, ever do this again. But suddenly your ride is over and they are hustling you off, and your only question is, can I stay on for another turn, can I please just go round once again?

It was Dominic who left our waltzer early, not me, but almost as much as anything else in this world, I would like to reminisce with him about what the Meadows mean to me, for they would mean the same to him. Many of these memories I am privileged to share with Neil and our other friends from that time, but Dominic and Dominic alone would remember the sight of the advance man's caravan on a weekday morning before school, the names of all the girls who lived in our street, and the sudden sadnesses that descended on a Sunday night after a weekend of teenage boy chaos. He would remember the handwritten addresses on the newspapers we delivered in the dark mornings before school and he would remember the strange programmes we watched on the illicit satellite television Uncle John rigged up for us. He would recall all these things, and on the telephone or on a car journey somewhere, we would laugh about how silly, how innocent, how young we were.

I cannot write about Phi Phi without writing of Ben, and yet that may be an impossible task, for Ben is as mercurial as a leaping shoal of rainbow fish and as soaringly elusive as a sea eagle on the wing. Moreover, he might not much care to be written about.

In the months that followed the tsunami, occasional journalists would track Ben down to his Sunflower Bar to enquire if they might do a piece on him. Ben would always politely agree, but with two immutable conditions: the journalist's name – as printed in his passport – must be 'The Right Honourable Tony Blair, MP', and he had to pay Ben the upfront sum of one million pounds for the privilege of writing about him.

Of course, Ben was no more interested in being paid a million pounds than he was in being elected Prime Minister of Britain, and his impossible caveats were merely a polite way of declining to be written about. Ben has seen my passport, knows both that my name is not Tony Blair and that I have no million pounds to offer, but all the same I hope that he will forgive my writing about him, for our stories are entwined and he is my friend and, more than that, my family.

In the bare feet in which he patrols his Sunflower Bar fiefdom, Ben stands somewhere a little to the north of five and a half feet tall, yet on account of the overwhelming force of his personality, people invariably recall him as a man of uncommon height. He dresses mostly in the locally de rigueur board shorts and faded football shirt, his jet-black hair hangs down his back to his waist and he sports a goatee beard on the boyishly handsome face that belies the troubles he has already known in his thirty-three years. His skin has been so long kissed by the south of Thailand sun that once when we went out to dinner his countryman waiter took him to be African and asked if I could translate the menu into his language for him; Ben's reply – in the English and Thai he switches between with the fluent carelessness with which you or I might change television channels – is unprintable here.

Like 'Bangkok', the proper Thai name for which runs several lines long, 'Ben' is also but an abbreviation: my friend's full name begins with the word 'Jaiben', a mountain of Mecca, and is more of a mouthful even than that which the capital city of his adored homeland is properly known by. Perhaps this is appropriate, because Ben is a man more complex than any single syllable might convey, and he is indeed a mountain and perhaps something more than that still: some days he will declare that he is the son of God, and some days it is hard to argue with him on this matter.

Ben is the scion of a family that has lived on Phi Phi for generations, a first son of a first son who knew the island before the tourists came. He sometimes says that he has done every job there is on Phi Phi, and if that may be only almost true then he has certainly kept his eyes open along the way, for he can fashion you a bouquet of carnations from a drinking straw, pilot a longtail through the mid-morning traffic in Tonsai, show you where to catch a prize kingfish, and double the eight ball into the corner pocket with his eyes closed and one hand held behind his back.

Ben's dexterity is perhaps most obviously visible in the home he began building in the aftermath of the tsunami, a landlocked tugboat fashioned from tsunami-felled trees and the remains of broken longtail boats. If this construction might initially seem an idiosyncratic prayer, its design is entirely pragmatic: Ben's wheelhouse sleeping quarters are raised fifteen feet above ground and if his new home is indeed a boat that will never go to sea, he has built it high enough that, even if the worst were to happen again, it shall hopefully never need to.

If Ben is a man of his hands, however, then he is equally a man of deep and complex thought, a man who can tell you the complete and unabridged history of Thailand and the gospel-true story behind the composition of every Bob Marley song. If occasionally his candlelit tales might strike you as a little far-fetched – if it seems slightly credulous, for instance, to believe that Bob Marley wrote the song 'No Woman, No Cry' because his wife's incessant crying was disrupting his efforts to write an entirely different and upbeat song – then beware that you doubt the veracity of anything Ben tells you at your own peril.

When late one night Ben declared to me that the First World War had been fought between the Kaiser on one side and Thailand and Britain on the other, I did not disagree with him but took it with a quiet pinch of salt; Thailand, I was reasonably certain, would not have been involved in what was essentially a European war. Wandering through the National Museum in Bangkok two years later, I came across a display case containing the artefacts of some of the dozen Thai soldiers who had perished on the Western Front in 1916.

Yet as much as he is anything else, Ben is a man of humour: leaping shoal of rainbow fish and soaring sea eagle he might well be, but he is simultaneously mischievous as a sackful of kittens. Mum likes to tell the story of how the first time she met Ben he was sitting in the middle of his bar with a football shirt draped over his head; when Mum enquired what he was doing, Ben's muffled response came through the shirt that he was hiding from Carol. Two truths are revealed in this story: one is that Ben is an old-fashioned showman, and the other is that he has long since elevated the art of arguing with Carol to something approaching the level of an Olympic sport.

Exasperating Carol is one of Ben's favourite pastimes. He likes to borrow her bicycle for days on end, to stand outside her house at dawn and make just enough noise to wake her and Toy up but still be able to claim innocence, to give away all the water from her well and deny all knowledge when the bill comes in, and then to gleefully tell anybody who will listen that Carol is indeed a naughty one. It is all done in the best spirit of friendship, though, and even if Carol would undoubtedly deny it, she enjoys this badinage almost as much as we onlookers do.

Of course, when the magazine journalists asked Ben if they could do a piece on him, they had no interest in hearing about any of this, did not want to write that Ben was talented, that he was funny, that he was smart. What they wanted to write about was overwhelming grief, and they came down to the bar because they had heard that, on an island of loss, Ben had suffered as much as anybody and more than most. On the twenty-sixth of December, Ben lost his wife and his two young daughters, his closest sister, a dozen cousins and innumerable friends; amidst this, the mere loss of his home, his livelihood and the physical pain of a leg broken in three separate places barely even registered.

Even knowing Ben as I do now, the truth is that there is almost nothing to write about what happened to him beyond the above simple repetition of facts. Similarly, there is nothing even to say to him about these events: you cannot tell a man in Ben's position that you understand what he is going through, because you do not; nor can you ask him how he feels, for he cannot possibly tell you. Even well-meant condolences have little place; this last I know only too well, because the first time I met Ben I made precisely this mistake.

It was our third day working in the garden and I had gone into Sunflower Bar to get some water. Finding it empty, I had taken a couple of bottles from the cooler and left some money in the drawer as I'd been assured was the practice. On the way out, I had literally bumped into Ben.

We had never been introduced and it felt a little awkward now, to be leaving his bar clutching these bottles I had not visibly paid for. I started to mumble about having left the money inside, but as I spoke I saw that Ben could not have cared less; later I would learn that he would have been just as disinterested if he had found me leaving with the battered wooden takings drawer itself.

Having heard about Ben's loss, I wanted to say something to him about it; in my own life I had quickly understood that I preferred it when people acknowledged the tsunami rather than attempted to tiptoe around it out of a misguided fear of upsetting me. I told him that I had heard about his family, and that I was sorry.

Ben smiled at me and nodded graciously, but I can still remember the look his instinctive politeness only partly managed to mask that morning. He was not upset nor offended, but simply uncomprehending. The sheer meaninglessness of my words had been unfathomable to him: whatever I might say could not change anything that had already happened, and I might as well have just told him my favourite colour or the name of my first teacher at primary school.

As the days and weeks pass, Ben and I gradually become friends. It happens slowly, seemingly by chance, and yet with hindsight each development is heavy with symbolism and occasionally a little magic besides.

I lose the Swiss Army knife that Barney gave me before I left Edinburgh, a talisman of good hope that is a spiritual heir to one I gave Dominic before his own first trip to Thailand. I dig over the entire nascent garden without finding it, and when night falls I leave empty-handed and more than a little distraught. Ben has quietly witnessed my search and the next morning tells me to look atop the bar and there it sits, the mud scraped from it, the red enamel and the silver steel polished back to a shine.

One night we discover that the area where Ben once lived with his late wife in London is not far from Ladbroke Grove, and we know the same streets, the same tube stations, are even acquainted with the same lady who sells Thai food at Portobello Road Market on a Saturday. A week later Ben comes to me with a small medical problem, and I perform some minor first aid in Carol's kitchen. Another day we catch each other crying and he tells me an old saying of his grandmother's, that the sky is always much brighter after the rain.

The deal is sealed when one evening I bring a photograph of Dominic and Eileen down to the bar and receive a reaction that I had not allowed myself to hope for. I had always suspected that Dominic and Ben would have got on well – these two superstitious first-born sons who shared a love of reggae – but at that time a score of bars lined Loh Dahlum Bay; for Dominic and Eileen to have somehow found their way along to Sunflower Bar during their two nights on Phi Phi seemed an unlikely dream.

But Ben looks up from my photograph and says that he recognises them. Urgently, he summons the boys from the bar to show them my picture. They talk rapidly and excitedly in Thai, and Ben then translates for me: a few of the others think they might recognise Dominic and Eileen too, but nobody can say for certain where they have seen them before. For tonight this detail does not matter: it feels good simply to think that there is a connection. When months later it transpires that Uncle Bob met Ben and his relatives in Krabi in the desperate aftermath – and Ben likely recognises Dominic and Eileen from the photographs he would have seen at that time – it only strengthens the bond I feel.

Our evening with the photograph aside, Ben and I rarely speak of the tsunami. There is little need to when there is still so much evidence of it all around: the broken longtail boats we sit on to drink our beer, a water-damaged Tellytubby that hangs behind the bar, the beginnings of a memorial garden next door. Instead, I listen each evening as Ben tells me about his country's history, about the cultural significance of reggae music, about pirates, about the Second World War in which Thailand once again defeated Germany. Ben says he can tell where every plane that passes overhead is going to, and nightly we play this game: Kuala Lumpur, Los Angeles, Edinburgh. It does not take me long to fathom that the destinations tend to relate to the nationalities of the people in the bar or the countries that have come up in conversation that day, but still I keep asking. We are marking time, finding our way through the days in whatever way we can.

As the rainy season arrives, Ben starts to refer to me as his 'nong chai'. I don't properly notice at first, and when I do it is a term I have not heard before, so I have to seek out Carol to ask her what it means. She tells me that it is Thai for 'little brother'.

But we worry about him. By the middle of October, Ben has all but abandoned work on his boat and has started to spend more and more time in the unknowable jungle places he goes to when he feels the need for solitude. He stops eating, starts to drink shots of tequila for breakfast, and sometimes shouts at the people passing in the street. He stays up for days and then sleeps for a week. When he declares that he is the son of God, it is no longer entirely clear that he is joking.

By far the worst of it is that he seems almost entirely unreachable, even the reliable delight of winding Carol up holding little pleasure for him now. I fetch plastic cartons of spaghetti from town and remind him about the sky after the rain, but to talk in detail of your feelings is a western conceit, and Ben has no interest in doing so. To attempt to force him into a conversation that he does not wish to have is to come up against one of three replies – 'Hungry now', 'Tired now', or 'Bored now' – all of which amount to the same thing, which is that the next time you turn away you will look back to find that Ben has vanished. Giving up trying to talk, I decide just to sit there beside him; he will still tell me where the planes are going to, and for days this is the only conversation we have.

And yet there remain plenty of people keen to ask Ben how he is feeling. Journalists are not the only ones drawn irresistibly to heartbreak, and since I have been here a steady stream of pretty backpacker girls have found their way down to the bar, keen to meet the man who has suffered so much in the tsunami and perhaps even offer him a little succour. They mean well but they are wasting their time, their gap-year dreadlocks, fresh tattoos and doe-eyed sympathy as entirely lost on Ben as the depth of his hell is on them. Yet even in his profound despair, Ben is a gentleman, and lets them down graciously.

When these girls fix his gaze and ask him how he feels, Ben's invariable reply is to ask them if they know about the buffalo and the two birds. Of course, they do not – how can they, when it is a fable of Ben's own creation? – and so Ben settles down, cross-legged on the bow of a broken longtail, to tell them the story. With his bare feet and his long hair Ben can do a good impression of having just emerged from the jungle, and if he lets his English run a little thicker than usual when he recounts his story of the buffalo and two birds, it is all in the service of the tale.

'So there is a very old water buffalo,' he begins. 'Grandfather water buffalo. And on the back of this buffalo there live two birds. Usually, these two birds they are the best of friends: they live together on the middle of the buffalo's back and all three of them are happy.

'One day, the buffalo he wakes up and the birds are flying around in the sky above him, twittering and calling out to each other. And the buffalo he looks up and he says, "Come on, birds! Why do you have to make so much noise? You have woken me up!"

'And the birds, they tell him they are fighting with each other, they are no longer friends. So the buffalo – he is old and a buffalo, so he is the boss of the birds – he tells the birds to come down and be quiet because he is tired now, he wants to sleep. The birds, they obey him, but when they land on him, they do not land together in the middle of his back any more: one bird he lands on the head of the buffalo, and the other one he lands on the tail.'

At this point, Ben turns to his rapt audience.

'So this is the question for you: where does the buffalo now feel heaviest?'

'In the middle.'

'At the back.'

'On his head.'

'In his heart.'

Eventually they run out of possible answers, fall quiet, and ask Ben to reveal where the buffalo feels heaviest. Ben's reply, delivered with a sanguine shrug of the shoulders as he climbs down from the boat to take his leave to the jungle, is always the same.

'Who am I to know what a buffalo feels?'

I have heard this story a dozen times, but every time it comes as a reminder to me as much as it does a revelation to them: you cannot offer condolences, intervene, make things better. Ben will go through what he must go through, and he will do so with the quiet dignity and stoicism of a grandfather water buffalo.

Perhaps it is not even for us to worry about him. One night I walk home from town after midnight, thinking to call in and see Ben for a nightcap. From a distance it seems that the bar is still open, but as I get closer I see that the light is coming not from the bar but from the boat Ben had seemed to abandon work on a month previously. Lamps have been jerry-rigged around its deck, and he and his brother are quietly working, sanding and planing, lifting and nailing. They nod me a hello but carry on with their work, and when I return in the morning an entire side of the hull has been framed and fitted.

In October, my visa expires and I make the long journey back to Edinburgh. It would have been far greener to travel across the Malaysian border for a renewal, but there is an ulterior motive to my going home: Mum has a week's half-term holiday from school coming up, and I want her to stretch it out to ten days and return to Thailand with me.

The night before I leave, Mon gives me an amulet of the Buddha that has been carved in a temple near his home town. He tells me that he does not know which next paradise I believe in, but that it does not matter anyway: if I wear the amulet each day, it will bring me happiness, good fortune and protection from danger. I say that I could certainly use all three, and he leans in close to tell me that the protection offered is not solely of the spiritual kind, for the hometown temple is particularly revered by Thai policemen; if ever I find myself in difficulty with the law, he whispers, sight of this amulet might just smooth things over. My eyebrows must rise at this, because Mon is quick to add that this would likely only work for the more minor crimes.

I hang the amulet around my neck and make it back to Edinburgh without committing any felonies. Mum collects me at the airport and in the car on the way home I explain my plan for us. Already booked to travel to Phi Phi for the first anniversary in December, she is initially reluctant to even consider the notion of an earlier trip: quite apart from any emotional trauma inherent in the journey, she rightly

125

points out that it is an absurd distance to go for what will amount at most to five or six days on the island.

But I keep at her, and after a few days she acquiesces. Perhaps I put her under more pressure than is fair, but for some time now I have had the feeling that by Christmas an important moment will have been lost.

Because I want her to witness what remains of the destruction. I want her to see first-hand that we were not alone in being broken that day, to feel for herself the empathy of the people and the land. I want her to work alongside the volunteers that come to the garden daily, and I want her to feel what it means to know that they will be there on the next day too.

At the root of all of this, another unvoiced hope: that these things might start to heal Mum in the same way that they seem to have been healing me. In Edinburgh she has been bravely going to her school each morning and returning home each evening, but this island, where it is understood that life need never be normal again, has proven a strange kind of homeopathy for me, and I want the same for her.

But really, what do I know about it? I am twenty-six years old and have lost my manual labour-loving older brother, not my firstborn son; maybe digging trenches is therapeutic for me in a way that it can never be for her. Besides, there is another consideration: Mum visited Phi Phi the year before the tsunami, and this has proven a heavy burden.

A self-styled silver backpacker, Mum had made her second trip to Thailand the previous summer. At the end of the month-long tour, the choice for her party's final week had come down to a picture-postcard island, or a visit to a remote Golden Triangle region that intrepid Uncle Bob had read about in one of his online newsgroups. After so many days on the road, they had not even needed to take a vote.

Even now, this remains impossibly difficult for Mum, the notion that she was on Phi Phi and later mentioned to Dominic that it might be a good place for him to visit on his next trip to Thailand. If I yet hold it in my power to talk Mum into a five thousand mile journey at a few days' remove, after years of trying there are still moments when I realise that I have not been entirely able to make her understand that this recommendation is genuinely not anything that she should feel any measure of guilt about. Half a dozen friends have told me that they also told Dominic that Phi Phi should not be missed; like Mum they all did so not in the knowledge that there was going to be a tsunami, but because Phi Phi was an island of absurd beauty whose lamplit streets came alive with magic at night. Most people who visit the beaches of Thailand spend at least a couple of days on Phi Phi, and the ones that do not are usually those that have not done their research.

A secret.

Not a cross-your-heart secret, but just something that for everybody except the people most intimately involved the passage of a quarter of a century has faded into history: Dominic was not the first son that my parents had lost.

We had another brother, Sebastian, who had been born with severe cerebral palsy. He was six years less six days younger than me, an interval forever fixed in my head because in my childhood album there is a photograph that was taken in a maternity ward side room on the occasion of my sixth birthday. Proudly wearing a birthday badge and dressed in denim dungarees identical to the ones Dominic has on, I am surrounded by new *Star Wars* figurines and torn wrapping paper. Sat on the bed with her arms around us, Mum is smiling for the camera that Dad is pointing at us;

127

only if you look closely can you see that she has not slept in days, that she is anaemic, that she is carrying herself carefully so as not to stretch the wound beneath her nightdress. The newest member of our family, cocooned in a special care incubator on another floor, is not well enough to join us in the picture.

Having previously conducted a cot-side vigil for Dominic, who had also been born prematurely, Mum and Dad are only too familiar with the endless heave of the mechanical ventilators and the flickering of the ultraviolet lamps. By now the science is seven years more advanced, but the real difference this time is that the odds are stacked far higher against than when it was Dominic lying inside the hermetically sealed world.

In these first days of touch and go, Dominic and I know nothing of any of this. Grandma arrives on the train and spoils us rotten, taking us to watch the penguin parade at the zoo and buying reinforcements for our figurine army, but life otherwise continues as normal. At some point Mum comes home from the hospital, but Sebastian is not well enough to accompany her; our baby things that have been brought down from the loft remain packed in their boxes.

On our plane to Bangkok I worry that Mum is a little too quiet, that the strains of our journey might already be getting to her. When I put this to her she agrees that she is quiet, but says that this is only because it is the middle of the night and everybody around us is trying to sleep. She is right: it is the middle of the night and everybody around us is indeed trying to sleep.

Arriving in Krabi too late to make the afternoon ferry, we check into a guesthouse and go out for dinner in a strip-lit place near the night market. Somewhere in the back, a television is playing an old episode of *Only Fools and Horses* that has been dubbed into Thai. We are the evening's only customers.

We make small talk about this and that, about fish sauce and how it feels when the aeroplane doors open to a hot country, but at a certain point I ask Mum if she is feeling apprehensive about the next day. She stirs her soup, smiles at me, shakes her head a little sadly and says no, whatever she is feeling at this point, it is not apprehension. Only later did I understand what she meant that night, and how she could have been facing her first trip back to the island with such equanimity: it did not matter. Whatever was going to happen tomorrow, whatever she might see on the next day, it would always be as nothing compared to the truths that she now lived with daily. Dominic was gone and no journey in the world could change that.

In the morning a tuk-tuk to the docks, and then the chaos of the about-to-depart ferry: the blaring of the horn, the good-fortune firecrackers of the nearby fishing boats, the excited chitter-chatter of the travellers basking on the deck and the cool, sleepy calm in the cabin beneath. Every five or ten minutes I ask Mum if she is okay, and every five or ten minutes she tells me that she is fine except for the fact that I keep asking if she is okay.

The two-hour journey to Phi Phi passes, as it forever will, with thoughts and daydreams of the one that we are retracing. The reverie slips in insidiously as the diesel fumes creeping up from the engine room below. To have been in your twenties, in love, and taking this boat on a busy Christmas Eve. To have known that you would be greeted at Tonsai pier and taken to a sea-view bungalow with an air conditioner and mini bar. To have known that in your rucksacks you carried the renovation plans for the flat you had just bought in the city that you had always been proud to call your home. Well, it must have felt good, and they surely would have been happy that day.

Twenty minutes out from the island, Mum and I go up and stand on deck. Tonsai Bay is now in plain sight and Mum reacts with the same disbelief that everybody who knew it before the tsunami does when they return for the first time. Disbelief that you can see clean through to Loh Dahlum Bay now; you could not do that before, for there used to be a town in the way.

His given name is Sebastian, but his middle name is Nicholas and he is always Nicky to Dominic and me, as he is to Mum whenever she talks to us about him. Sebastian is a name for grown-ups to know a little boy by, but Nicky is a name for children, a secret name for us to call our new baby brother.

But for all that we have our own name for him, still we rarely see him. He is too unwell, and there is a fear that we will leave him with some playground measles or chicken pox, or that his various tubes and wires will in return send us home with nightmares. We come to know him as an absence rather than a presence, a name to be spoken rather than a person to be seen.

Nicky was allowed home to our house in Colinton only once. He was obviously very sick – he had a feeding tube in his nose and even we could see that he was little more than half the size he should be – but the day was still a glory. The hospital had lent Mum a special swing for him, and our little brother Nicky loved it. He expressed himself best through laughing, and he did so to bring the house down when you pushed him in this chair of his. And when he laughed Mum laughed, and then we did too. At some point a friend called in for me and I went out to play, but not before proudly showing him my laughing little brother through the living room window.

On our first night on the island together, Mum and I walk down to the pier at Tonsai and continue along to the place where a resort called Cabana Bungalows had stood before the tsunami.

If the land around the memorial garden haunted by its bleak emptiness, on this other side of the island you sensed the missing from the things they left behind. Here the water arrived as a rising flood tide rather than a river; as everywhere, the bamboo bungalows have all vanished, but here signposts still direct you to their vacant plots, empty squares of ground forlornly linked by trellised walkways entwined with dead vines. A staff dormitory block still stands, too, and inside it has been left untouched: bunk beds upended, doors wrenched from their hinges, clothes scattered as if by ransacking burglars. Tonight packs of stray cats run through this desolation and brush against our ankles, mewling out will we please feed them, love them, remember them? Mum and I walk through all this in silence, our shared grief requiring no words, and I wonder again what on earth I thought I was doing by bringing her here.

If I am hoping things will seem better in the morning, I am to be disappointed. We wake to discover that the island's microclimate means that we are in the nearest thing Phi Phi has to a monsoon season. We spend our first morning watching the rain teeming down from inside Sunflower Bar, and indeed this is how much of Mum's trip will turn out.

But we talk and we talk, and in the evenings we walk around town. Mum gets to know all the local people I have met and they quickly take her to their collective heart. Everywhere we go people are keen to meet her, to ask her how she is, to do whatever they can for her. And when they speak to her, they call her 'Mum'.

On one level, it is simply a quirk of language. All women of a certain age in Thailand are 'Mum', just as all those a little older are 'Auntie'. And yet it is hard not to hear a significance in it, an acknowledgement of her loss and a quiet reassurance that she will for ever be Dominic's mum.

In late August, a fortnight after my sixth birthday, I moved into Miss Fell's Primary Two class and instantly fell hopelessly in love with her. Young and energetic, Miss Fell wore her hair in a neat black bob that with hindsight might have been rather similar to Mum's. When at our infant assemblies she led us in 'Who Put the Colours in the Rainbow?' she did so with first-hand knowledge, for her singing voice was that of an angel fallen to earth.

The education authority also understood something of how wonderful Miss Fell was, because despite her youth she already alternated as assistant head teacher of our infant school. On these days we had a different classroom teacher, a lady about whom almost all I noticed was that she was Not-Miss-Fell. As soon as I got to school in the morning and saw this lady sitting in Miss Fell's chair, I would know the day was already lost.

The day that Nicky died was one such day. Shortly after playtime the school secretary came in and whispered something in the ear of the Not-Miss-Fell teacher, who then came to my desk and told me to pack my things because my dad was coming to collect me.

It was the middle of the school day and even at six years old it made no sense. I kept returning to this Not-Miss-Fell's desk to tell her that there must have been some mistake, that if I had a dentist or doctor's appointment then my mum would surely have told me and, anyway, my dad would be at work conducting important meetings and could not possibly come here to the school during the day. Not-Miss-Fell only gently insisted that I pack my things and, though I eventually did so, it was with mounting indignation and welling tears. Such a mix-up, I hardly need say, would never have occurred on Miss Fell's watch.

At the children's hospital they had Nicky's body wrapped in bedclothes in a gently lit room. Dad and I must have collected Dominic from his school en route because he was there too, and Mum asked us if we wanted to hold Nicky. Dominic, always cautious in the company of adults, declined, but I did not: I held Nicky in my arms, one child cradling another, both of us decades too young to comprehend anything of what it meant.

At lunchtime on Mum's last day on the island she sits at the bar in Sunflower, chatting with Ben whilst I look out at the rain falling on the garden, convinced that I have dragged her a quarter of the way around the world for naught.

We have spent endless hours together, talking, reminiscing, sometimes even laughing, but when she boards her plane in Bangkok tomorrow night she will do so carrying the same weight of sadness with which she disembarked. I no longer even know what kind of epiphany I expected to provide for her, only that it has not happened. We have one small ritual left to perform this evening, but whatever comfort this might bring her, it surely will not atone for the journey that I have inflicted on her.

Six weeks ago, in front of the flat strip of land where Charlie's Resort once stood, Neil and I had lit two candles, listened to reggae music and waited for the sun to sink into the ocean. We had thought we were as close to the last place Dominic and Eileen had been as it was possible to get, a belief seemingly confirmed when the island's rocky western out-crop split the light of the setting sun into two brilliant shafts that reached to the clouds. Our plan for tonight is that Mum and I will perform a similar ceremony in the same spot, but she breaks off her conversation with Ben to come over and tell me that it appears we might be able to get a little closer yet.

In the first days after the tsunami, Dad had managed to obtain the number of the bungalow that Dominic and Eileen had been staying in. When it became clear that nothing remained of the resort, we had discarded the detail, but Ben has just informed Mum that his sister-in-law used to work at Charlie's Resort. If we meet her over there after lunch, he thinks that she might be able to lead us to the spot where bungalow A12 stood.

If it is not the epiphany I have been hoping for, it is still important. It will mean something to finally know a fact forensic and indisputable. Whatever other mysteries that day must for ever hold and whatever else we have failed to achieve on our trip, Mum and I can now at least together bear witness to the last spot where our two lost travellers slept.

It is a holy location for us, a station of the cross, but – as we always do now – we tell each other to prepare for disappoint-ment, for a little more heartbreak. Even if Ben's sister-in-law can find the correct place, we know that there will be noth-ing to see except weeds growing through dusty sand and possibly a few ceramic tiles where a bathroom once stood.

And yet what she leads us to after lunch is a shrine. A shrine fashioned from a driftwood tree, planted in the sand

and garlanded with orchids and lotus petals, with incense and candles. A shrine to protect us against disappointment and heartbreak. A shrine that Ben has built for us in the place where bungalow A12 once stood.

We return that evening to light the candles and the incense, to listen to our reggae music and to wait once again for the sun to go down.

On the day Mum is to leave Thailand we travel to Krabi with Carol and Toy. On the way in from the ferry, we stop off to visit a nursery school that Ben's English sister-in-law built for the evacuated children of Phi Phi.

The pupils are on holiday today, but their teacher is here and happy to show us around. The outside of the simple brick building has been painted with an invitingly colourful mural, and the interior entirely lives up to its promises. Boxes overflow with toys, shelves heave with books, and there are plump cushions to sit on at story-time and soft mats to lay on at nap-time. Here the walls are painted too, this time with life-sized renditions of beloved cartoon characters: Simba and Nala, Pooh and Piglet, Sylvester the Cat.

It is an enchanting space and the teacher proudly confirms that the children all adore it. Even as adults, the place arouses strong emotions, for to look around this nursery that has been built by a bereaved aunt for the traumatised playmates of her lost nieces is to understand for the second time in successive days what the minister at Dominic's funeral meant when he said that he has occasionally witnessed the divine moving in and amongst the people to whom terrible things have happened.

We spend Mum's last afternoon in Thailand shopping for supplies for the memorial garden. If I had been a little dismayed to discover that a country as ostensibly exotic as Thailand possesses institutions as mundane as garden centres, the term quickly proves a misnomer.

The place we visit is not so much a garden centre as an arboretum. There are avenues and groves, copses and orchards, rose bushes and lily-ponds. The borders seem slide-ruled, and you can wander the manicured walkways for miles and encounter only butterflies and lawn sprinklers. In the shade of a dalbergia tree you come upon a picnicking family, and a little further on pass a man selling ice cream from the back of his tricycle. The only way you ever know that you are in a place of commerce is that occasionally you will come upon a visitor wrestling a particularly handsome plant from a flowerbed, although in truth I have also seen that happen in the Botanical Gardens in Glasgow.

With so vast a park to explore, our party quickly gets separated. Mum and I find ourselves walking through a field of saplings that are fast outgrowing the poles of bamboo staking them to the ground. She asks me what my favourite kind of tree is, and I cannot bring myself to admit that they are essentially indistinguishable to me, for in this I am not her son. Mum has a kinship with trees, knows their names, the familial DNA of their bark and the distinctive fingerprints of their leaves; in those same Glasgow Botanics I once challenged her to see how many trees she could identify, and I ran out of specimens long before she ran out of names.

We continue through the nursery. We are far from the main pavilion now, and if it is an accident that we have stumbled upon these young trees, it is a fortunate one. Some of the money we are spending today has come from Mum, and Carol has asked her to choose a pair of trees with which to commemorate Dominic and Eileen.

In a field of endless eucalypti, we know our trees as soon

as we see them. They are another indigenous species and so for once Mum cannot give their precise name, though even I know something very close to it: Scots Pine. That is what they look like, these two shoulder-high trees with their branches lined with rows of dark green needles: Scots Pines, the trees that filled our Pentland forests at home, that lined our Sunday walks, that sat in the corners of our living rooms every December.

That night, Toy and I drive Mum out to the airport, the three of us up front in his truck. I am sad that she is going, heading back home to the coming winter and the routine that from this distance seems so melancholy. Moreover, I still cannot shake the feeling that I have let her down, that all the promises I made her about this trip have gone unfulfilled. Ben touched her soul with the shrine he built and we found the Scots Pine trees to plant, but there have been no great epiphanies; Dominic is still gone and we are both just one more week older, one more week further away from him.

At least, that is what I think has happened, what Mum's trip has meant. As she flies home, however, as her plane follows the long curve our diminished family are becoming so used to traversing, something starts to change. When I go to bed in the Krabi guesthouse that night I have a sense that things are somehow not quite still as desperate as I had imagined at the airport.

The revelation occurs a few days later and comes, ironically enough, as an epiphany. It is late evening on the island when Toy and I dig two large holes at the edge of the garden and fill them with alternating layers of peat and sawdust. We position the trees so that they stand perfectly vertical, pack them solid and then take a step back to admire our handi-work. Our two Scots Pines look suddenly small in front of the sea, and this is when I receive my epiphany: what, really, did I expect would happen?

A week on Phi Phi could not change anything and Mum would have known this when she agreed to come, would have known that you cannot speed up suffering. All through her trip I had been waiting for a breakthrough, a letting go, some catharsis that could somehow lead us to the permanent sky after the rain. But that, I realise as I look at our trees, is not what this is. This is a sadness that we live with; sometimes you carry it, and sometimes it even carries you. Mum, who lost a son before Dominic, knows better than anybody that this is not a television drama, that there is no closure, no third-act resolution, no end. There is only a living and a sharing, but – and here is the biggest catch – sometimes there can be a kind of comfort in this.

This comfort bit takes me even longer to comprehend. Years, in fact, and it is only latterly that I have begun to figure out this final part. Our trip that October was not about breakthroughs or epiphanies, and nor was it even about the absence or impossibility of them. What it was about was a mother and her son travelling together through the country of their grief; ours was a journey made not out of pilgrimage but out of simple companionship.

Recently I asked Mum what she remembered about the trip, whether it was a long way to go for nothing and if the fact that we did not ultimately do a lot of work in the memorial garden had mattered to her. She replied that it had felt good simply to be there with me, a mother and her son together remembering another son that was here no longer. Likewise, Mum, likewise. And something else: sometimes I think we are still there even now: sitting at our shrine, walking amongst the ruins, watching the rain fall in the monsoon season we find ourselves in.

In the late afternoon, girls with sun-bleached hair are making mosaics in the shade beneath the banyan tree, fashioning images and words from fragments of the broken tiles and mirrors that until recently littered this ground: a Chinese dragon, 'LOVE', a flower, 'KATHY'. Other volunteers, meanwhile, are mixing concrete, buckets of which they carefully pass down to Toy, who stands in a large, figure of eight-shaped hole in the ground. One day there will be a pond here, and the mosaics the girls are making will line it.

In months to come, people will sometimes ask me who designed the memorial garden, and my honest answer will be that nobody really did. This pond that we are making today is as good an example of this process as any that I can give.

Once the garden boundaries had all been dug out and the walls around them built, we naturally began to wonder what they might enclose. Carol suggested a pond, a tranquil centrepiece that could act as a focal point for quiet contemplation. It sounded a good idea, but when we began to talk about it – about the optimum shape, about liners and pumps – it took on a surprising complexity.

I dispatched myself to an internet café in town to find the answers, but an hour of scrolling through pond-enthusiast websites provided only more questions. Downhearted, I trudged back down the road to report my findings to Carol and Toy: a pond was far too complicated a thing for us to build, and the internet had not so much as known how to begin.

But Carol and Toy were not discouraged and in fact already knew how we would begin. We would begin in the way that we always did, by picking up our shovels and digging. We would dig a deep hole and as we did so it would gradually take the form of the pond we could not yet visualise; if it somehow failed to assume the mystical shape floating just out of the reach of collective consciousness, we would fill it in and start again, repeating the process as many times as it took to get it right. Moreover, by the time we had lighted upon the correct shape, we would somehow know whether we needed such things as liners and pumps, or whether old-fashioned concrete and good luck would work just as well.

This, then, is how the memorial garden develops: with several false starts and plenty of blind alleys, but always organically, always collectively and always with love. Much like the building of a boat that will never go to sea, perhaps this is actually the only way to perform such a task: you start digging, or hammering, follow what is in your heart and simply see where it takes you.

And yet there are still certain things that can never be approached in this way. Digging a pond is one thing, but raising a garden in saltwater ground is quite another. Unless you have unlimited credit at the Krabi garden centre and are happy to sacrifice any number of saplings on the altar of trial and error, you cannot simply guess which will perish in direct tropical sunlight and which will perish without it. Lucky for us, then, that we were blessed with Ko Hang.

One morning we arrive at the garden to find that Toy has been called away to Phuket. Standing in his place is his brother-in-law Ko Hang, a palm and rubber tree farmer from Krabi. Forty-three years old that November, Hang wears his black hair long like Ben's, carries the traditional farmer's knife-sharp axe in the back pocket of his jeans and understands the land with an intimacy that comes from having spent much of his adult life working it.

In the months and years that follow, Hang and I will become close friends and I will learn many things about him: that the 'Ko' part of his name is a singularly appropriate honorific that in this context means 'distinguished uncle'; that all children love him, and he them; that he once spent a year as a novice monk; that he has a degree in economics and was a bass player in a Bangkok bar band; that he is patient where I am hasty, humble where I am proud, and, frequently, wise where I am an idiot.

On this first day, though, as we work together to clear the tall grass from a patch of ground that is to become our own nursery – he with graceful strokes of his scythe, me with dangerously stabbing ones of mine – he tells me only a single thing, and it stays with me for ever. Ko Hang tells me that he wants this garden we are making to be a place where the living can meet the dead.

A place where the living can meet the dead. Thai people believe in ghosts in the same matter-of-fact way that Roman Catholics believe in transubstantiation or Episcopalians believe in two or three gathered in my name. They believe that the spirits of the people we loved watch over us and indeed occasionally visit us, encounters to which those born on a Saturday or Sunday are considered most prone.

On Phi Phi, the belief in ghosts is manifest most obviously in the fact that many Thai people still do not care to walk down the broken road to Sunflower Bar after dark. If it is indeed a superstition, it is one locally potentiated by language: 'ko' traditionally means 'island', 'phi' means 'ghost', and in Thai grammar duplication of a word signifies a large amount of it; the literal meaning of Ko Phi Phi, then, is 'Island of Many Ghosts'. I was born on a Wednesday but nevertheless still sometimes walk the road at night in yearning anticipation.

A place where the living can meet the dead. It is quite a hope to express, and yet when Hang spoke it aloud I realised that I shared in it, and had done since the very first day I saw those half-dozen people digging their hopeless trench in the sun.

I had shared in it because you work to build a memorial garden for the same reason that you lay flowers on a grave, gather two or three in somebody's name or light candles in an empty cathedral. Flowers are not placed on a grave to demonstrate to the municipal cemetery workers that a departed one has not been forgotten and nor do you dig holes and shovel concrete in the sun merely to ensure that the boys pushing a trolley back and forth to the resort at the end of the bay will know that somebody you loved is no longer here. No, you do it partly for the healing of the ritual of it, but inherent in such acts – unspoken, unexamined and perhaps even unconsidered – there must by definition be a belief that the soul to which you are paying tribute, the ghost you keep missing on the road because you were born on the wrong day of the week, will somehow know these things that you do in their name, will somehow hear the messages you are still trying to whisper to them all these months later.

Down at the bar on the night before Halloween, and Ben tells me a superstition of his own: Allah, he says, gives out the good luck early in the morning. On this island, such a notion is hard to argue with. On Boxing Day the waters arrived at ten thirty in the morning; those that were up and about early generally had a slightly better shot at luck than those who slept in.

But this is not Ben's point. Ben's point is that tomorrow morning he is going to the jungle to chop wood for his land-locked boat that now seems to grow nightly; if I would like to see the jungle, I am welcome to accompany him.

For a long time now, I have wanted to see the jungle. Not the verdant canopy of the tourist path to Viewpoint, but the jungle proper: the seething dark place that encroaches on the town from both sides, the secret place Ben returns from carrying fragile orchids, the mysterious place a few Thai friends live amidst. If I really want to know Phi Phi, then it is no use walking only the beaches and the town. I cannot ignore that which covers nine-tenths of the land.

The catch is that we must leave at first light, around five thirty in the morning. Neither of us says it out loud, but both Ben and I know that this is hours earlier than I have been up during my time here. I reassure him that I will be at the bar before the break of dawn. His response is to look at me sceptically and tell me that if I am late he will not be able to wait.

I sleep past the alarm and get down to the bar a little after six. Whilst there is still no actual sun yet, the world is now indisputably light and the bar and its environs deserted. I have missed Ben, but he gave me fair warning and I have only myself to blame.

Downhearted, I sit on the swing that hangs from the banyan tree at the edge of the garden and try to console myself with memories of other Halloweens. Quickly I find that I do not have much to draw on.

Sometimes this happens: the more you want to remember something – the location of a scar, the way a voice sounded, sometimes even what a person looked like – the harder it becomes to do so. My Halloween memories all seemed to be fleeting glimpses and anyway hopelessly generic: a classroom turned to a witch's grotto, the turnips all children in Scotland carve as lanterns because pumpkins are too precious, a television special that spooked us.

Even the family albums I now have by heart offer nothing, the sole concession to dressing-up being a photograph of Dominic made up as a soldier and me wearing his hand-me-down Superman costume, a picture I anyway know was taken at a summer birthday party. Still, this thought does at least remind me of something else that sets me drifting into happy slumbers: when Dominic was seven, he and another boy decided that not only was it a good idea for them to go to their class's after-school fancy-dress party as a pair of old ladies, but that it would be easiest all round if they arrived at school in the morning already wearing their costumes. Dropping them off, Mum saw that none of their classmates were dressed up and asked if they perhaps wanted to pop home and change into their uniforms. Indignantly they replied no, of course they did not, and blithely sat through that day's lessons wearing dresses and headscarves with their handbags slung over the backs of their chairs.

A noise from the wheelhouse of Ben's boat wakes me. A

Thai man emerges and rubs his eyes. He looks at me, sleepy and apparently confused that I should be here so early, and then waves a greeting. I – still sleepy and confused myself – wave back. Down on the shore crab fishermen are kicking through the shallow waters and a group of longtail captains are preparing their boats for the day's business. It must by now be coming up for seven and yet there is no sign of the sun; absent-mindedly I wonder why it is taking so long to rise.

Another man now emerges from the wheelhouse and somnambulantly descends the ladder. He is followed by another, then another, seven or eight of them in all. Some of them I recognise and some of them I have not seen before, but I know that if I later ask Ben about them he will tell me simply that they are all his cousins; most people at this end of the island are related to him in some way or other and, even when they are not, it is easier for him to say that they are his cousins.

One of these cousins walks down to the beach near to where I am sitting. We nod at each other, and then something occurs to me.

'Where's Ben?' I ask.

The man turns and points towards the wheelhouse.

As if he had been waiting for this cue, Ben now emerges and climbs down the ladder. At the bottom, he stretches and looks around; noticing me, he walks across to the swing and sits down beside me. We remain in silence for a few minutes and then Ben speaks.

'Simon, why are you here so early in the morning?'

If anything, he seems more perplexed by my presence than I am by his apparent amnesia.

'Weren't we supposed to go to the jungle today?' I ask.

'We are going to the jungle today,' he replies.

'But we were supposed to leave at dawn. So it doesn't get too hot.'

'Oh, come on, Simon,' Ben sighs, and I recognise the phrase he employs when he is exasperated with me for failing to grasp what he feels should be simple concepts to anybody with any semblance of sense, 'How can it get too hot when there is no sun today?'

He is right. The sun is not merely taking a long time to come up: there is no sun today, will be no sun today. What I had dozily imagined was a lingering dawn is actually a thick layer of grey cumulus that will not shift however strong the winds blow. Today is the rare day where the sun will not shine on Phi Phi, and how can I possibly be cross with Ben for knowing this in his sleep? Still, I have gotten up early for our jungle trip, and I am determined this will not go unrewarded.

'Allah gives out all the good luck early in the morning,' I remind him.

He shrugs. 'It's still early in the morning.'

The trail through the jungle is lined with jackfruit and spreading cashew trees. Ben, walking in front, is carrying an antiquated chainsaw over his shoulder; I follow behind with a length of rope and a bottle of fuel.

A quarter-hour's hike from the bar and we are already in a dense wilderness. Many people spent the first night following the tsunami in the jungle and it must have been another circle of hell for them. If I had to find my way back right now I already would not be able to and even in this daylight, and with Ben on hand as my expert guide, it is hard not to think of snakes.

We climb halfway up the mountainside before the trail levels out and then, imperceptibly at first, begins to descend back towards the sea. An hour after we set off, we emerge on the shore of a small cove where the trunks of two tsunami-felled trees lie on the beach. In the far distance around the headland, a longtail boat is putt-putting towards us.

The longtail, piloted by Ben's brother, is coming to drop his uncle and cousin with us. This is just as well, for the trees we are to cut are huge and waterlogged. Alone I would be no help whatsoever; even as part of a four-man team my main contribution seems to be to provide light relief by falling over in the shallows.

Once the logs have been manoeuvred into position, I am left to my own devices. For a while, I sit and watch Ben's uncle work his chainsaw – the wood's marinated pulp is rich as marrow, the spraying sawdust blood-red – and then wander off down the beach.

Like all of Phi Phi's beaches this cove would have been searched and cleaned up after the tsunami, but in the months since then the debris has re-accumulated, and as I walk along the beach I make a close study of it. As always, I am hoping for a sign from Dominic to tell me that he knows I am here. I am looking, as I do each day I dig the garden, for the Swiss Army knife I once gave him, for his engraved wristwatch or his silver digital camera, its lens smashed, its circuits shorted by salt water, yet its message-in-a-bottle memory card still miraculously intact. Of all things, I am looking most intently for his flip-flops.

On Loh Dahlum beach, another dozen appear at the high-tide line each morning. Separated from their partners and faded from months spent in water, they are the shoes of the tsunami, if not always the shoes of the dead; shoes are removed before entering a home or shop in Thailand, so even if you were safely on the second floor when the water came, you probably still lost your flip-flops. The ones I am eternally searching for are black, size nine, and have the single word 'Surfing' embroidered across them.

What I find instead is a bone.

It is down on the water's edge, nestled in seaweed and bleached by the sun, the tapering downstroke of a brilliant white exclamation mark. I pick it up and turn it over in my hand: three inches by one half inch, S-curved along its long axis and gently bowed across its short one, it is a perfect match for the clavicle of a young child.

I tell myself that there are a hundred other creatures this bone could have come from, and yet when it comes to it find that I can name at most three: a dog, a cow, perhaps a goat, though in truth I have never seen either of the latter on Phi Phi, where even dogs are a rarity. I run my finger along it, trying to think of reasons why it cannot be human, trying to recall my anatomy lectures from medical school, as if there were some fact that, if I could only remember it, would allow me to discard it.

I wish that I had not noticed it, wish I had not picked it up, wish that I could simply throw it back out to sea, but I cannot. It might be nothing, but there is a chance that even such a single small bone could yield all the information that a family ever gets. I wrap it in a tissue and put it in my pocket.

At noon, Ben's brother returns in the longtail. Once the wood has all been loaded, it becomes clear that there is not room for us all aboard too. It is agreed that Ben's uncle and I will walk back. This time we do not go through the jungle, but pick our way over the rocks around the edge of the bay.

Neither one of us is now carrying a chainsaw, but the journey back takes longer than our trek through the jungle did. The rocks rise in places to fifteen and twenty feet and are treacherously slippery. Any single misstep could have disastrous consequences, but Ben's uncle is determined to take good care of me.

'*Loong*, Simon,' he repeats as we face each new challenge, 'loong.'

Ben's uncle speaks no English and I have never heard this Thai word before, but I instinctively know what it means. It means 'be careful', it means 'take it slowly', it means 'we will surely get there if we are patient'. More than that, it means that even so far from home and amongst these people with no shortage of their own sadnesses, in this place where bones washed up on the beach may be the bones of young children, there are still those who will take care of me. Loong, Simon.

Years later, at a Thai evening class in London, I will be falteringly reading aloud when I come to a word with the phonetic sounds *law-eu-ng*. I will recognise the word instantly, and my teacher will tell me what it means: uncle. He was telling me that he was my Uncle.

A cartoon in a magazine that I framed for my Uncle Bob on his sixtieth birthday.

It is evening, and a hippyish couple are sharing a quiet moment on the sands of a deserted tropical beach. A gentle breeze is tickling the fronds of a solitary palm tree, and in front of the couple the sun has just set into the ocean. It would be paradise except for the fact that the sun has literally just set into the ocean, a fizzle of steam rising up from the place where it entered the water.

They must realise that they have just witnessed the beginning of the apocalypse, but the couple are not panicking. Rather, the man has merely half-turned towards his wife. An italicised caption informs us what he is saying: *That can't be a good sign*.

As far as I can know, the cartoonist who drew this picture

has never met my Uncle Bob, but he has captured his essence perfectly.

It is not that the figure in the picture looks sufficiently like Bob that you half expect him to reach out and embrace you in one of his famous bear hugs, nor that the kind of enthusiastically garish Hawaiian shirt he is wearing is a staple of Bob's travelling wardrobe. It is not that his serene companion resembles my Aunt Catriona, and nor is it even the fact that a deserted tropical beach at sunset is precisely the kind of place you would find them. No, it is rather what the man is saying and, even more than that, what he is about to say. From the first moment that I saw the cartoon and read the caption, I instantly knew what the very next words out of the man in the frame's mouth would be: Keep on trucking, brother.

Keep on trucking, brother. That is what Bob says when the end of the world is nigh. When the first internet rumours about the decimation of Phi Phi start to appear. Keep on trucking, brother. When two days have passed with no news. Keep on trucking, brother. When he is setting off for Thailand. Keep on trucking, brother. When he has visited the final hospital on his list and they were not amongst the last unidentified amnesiacs. Keep on trucking, brother. When he has spent the day looking at bodies in the mortuary, and they were not there either. Keep on trucking, brother. When he has hitched a ride on a newspaper speedboat to Phi Phi and had images of destruction burned into his eyes. Keep on trucking, brother. When a rescue worker has shown him Dominic's wallet and then his body. Keep on trucking, brother.

Keep on trucking, brother. It is a throwaway little phrase from an old blues song, but when my Uncle Bob speaks it, it means the world. It means that he is a man who has been around long enough to have seen good and bad days both. It means that he is a man who has travelled to faraway places and witnessed things that must be witnessed. Most of all, it means that he is your uncle, and he will surely see you through.

Both my parents have several siblings and thus in life I have been blessed with a wealth of uncles. Aunts too, of course, but when you lose your older brother at a time before you have really known death, there is something particular about having an uncle close by. If anybody else had died, you would have naturally looked to your older brother at this moment, but now you cannot. Uncles, though, are older boys too, and they have walked this road ahead of you, have known death several times over now that they are in their fifth and sixth decades: they have lost their mothers and fathers and innumerable friends along the way. In the first empty months, dozens of people told me that I would some-day reach a point where I could think of Dominic and smile, but I only started to believe this might be true when my Uncle John said it.

I am still to find an appropriate cartoon for my Uncle John but he too has something that he tells you in the moments when the end of the world seems nigh: keep on keeping on.

Keep on keeping on. When the news and the no news only ever seem to worsen. Keep on keeping on. When he has made the phone calls and looked at the pictures that you could not. Keep on keeping on. When you are sick of death and almost of life too. Keep on keeping on. When two months have passed and still they will not bring his body home. Keep on keeping on. When there is a funeral to organise and you have no earthly idea where to begin. Keep on keeping on.

Just as 'keep on trucking, brother' comes from the old blues song, this phrase of John's comes from a song, too: Bob

Dylan's 'Tangled up in Blue'. Each uncle is unaware of the other's mantra, and yet John's phrase means precisely the same thing that Bob's does. It means that when trouble comes down he will appear on the doorstep having driven through the dawn, and he will not leave until you tell him that you are sure you are going to make it. It means that he is your uncle, and he will surely see you through.

I do understand how blessed I have been, I really do, but even these thoughts can bring their own sadness too. A projected and anticipatory sadness, perhaps, but a heartfelt one all the same: all these incredible uncles Dominic and I have shared, but I will not now have the chance to try to emulate them as an uncle to Dominic's own boy children, nor he to mine. It should be hard to miss these imagined nephews – there are plenty of real griefs to be getting on with – but I still sometimes find that I do.

Back at the memorial garden, Hang informs me that one of the dive shops in town sends a regular package to the Disaster Victim Identification centre still in operation on Phuket. In the late afternoon I walk down there, clutching the bone in my pocket. One of the Front Street bars has arranged a Halloween party tonight, and already the tourists are running around in costume: there are witches and vampires, ghosts and goblins, even skeletons. It all seems a little too much, too soon, and as I make my way amongst them I find that I am repeating Uncle's phrase under my breath like another mantra: loong, Simon, loong.

The man at the dive shop accepts the bone without question, and I never hear anything more about it. Perhaps it was human, and perhaps it was not; people who properly recall their anatomy lectures will have looked down their microscopes and done whatever is necessary.

That evening, sitting on the balcony of my bungalow as the shouts and screams of the Halloween party drift up to me, it finally comes back to me, my Halloween memory: we once had our very own Halloween party.

When I was seven and Dominic was eight, I was not old enough to join the Cub Scout pack of which he was a member. I would not have minded quite so much, except several of my classmates whose birthdays fell earlier in the year had already been admitted. And then one night in October Dominic came home and told us about a Halloween party they had all just had, and I knew that I had missed the greatest Halloween party ever.

Or rather, I thought that I had missed it, but no son of Mum's was ever going to miss out on such a thing. And so, under Dominic's meticulous instruction, she recreated for us the very same party he had just been to: hung treacle-dripping scones from pieces of string, filled the red washing-up basin with water and apples, blindfolded us and placed peeled grapes in our hands and told us they were the eyeballs of witches. Treacle-chinned and laughing with my brother at a party I was too young to go to; I must have been up early indeed that morning.

In November, stories about Thailand again come to dominate the international news, the headlines I read each time I visit the internet shop detailing the steady march through Southeast Asia of a virulent new strain of avian influenza. Thailand is considered to be at particular risk; so far, two people have died in the north, and the experts have been falling over themselves to predict that a catastrophic epidemic will decimate the kingdom any day now.

Down at Sunflower Bar, we are terrified of bird flu, or at least often tell each other that we are. Really, I suspect, we remain terrified of something that happened ten months ago, but we call it 'bird flu', and for a while that makes it a little easier to talk about. After a few weeks of increasingly hysterical news coverage, however, even the phrase 'bird flu' starts to sound too foreboding, and Ben decrees that from now on the illness must be known as 'bird *nok*'. It is a typically ingenious idea: 'nok' is the Thai word for 'bird', and we quickly find that it is impossible to be too frightened of an illness whose name translates literally as 'bird bird'.

But it does not go away. It is there every time we check our email and every time one of us buys a newspaper; each time I walk through town, I overhear the word 'nok' in every second conversation.

One night, Carol, Ben and I go out to dinner and perched on our table is a black and white plastic toucan whose grinning beak dispenses a toothpick when pulled down. We try our best to ignore it, but by the time our food arrives the

154

wretched thing might as well be flapping its wings and squawking our names. When Carol slips the cursed creature off the table and puts it in her bag, Ben and I demonstrate our appreciation by not telling on her.

Later that night the toothpick toucan is carefully placed inside a wicker birdcage that has long hung unoccupied above the bar at Sunflower, and the door is firmly shut. We decide that this toothpick toucan will be our bird nok bird and agree that, as long as he stays firmly locked in his cage, we will be kept safe from bird nok and everything that may go along with it.

After another fortnight my visa expires and the time again comes to depart Thailand. The bird nok bird has remained locked in its cage and the memorial garden has finally started to properly look like one, but for weeks now the weight of all the other things that I ought to be doing has made every shovel of earth I have lifted feel heavier than it should. There is Dominic's estate to be sorted out, his grave that still remains unmarked and, though in our long-distance telephone calls she is forever insisting that I do not worry about her, Mum, who in the last few months I have spent only a single week with.

It is no sacrifice – in less than a month I will be returning to Phi Phi with Mum and the rest of the family for the one-year anniversary – but as I stand on the deck of my departing ferry, I feel an overwhelming urge to leap overboard and swim back to shore. More than just the fact that for the first time in almost a year I have lately been something close to happy, more than just the fact that I will miss my friends here over the next few weeks, I have an unshakeable feeling that if I do not immediately dive into the inviting green water, something awful will soon happen to me.

I am neither brave nor spontaneous enough to jump. Instead, I sit down on the deck in the sunshine and tell myself that I am simply sad to be leaving, that the voice urging me to jump is merely desire, that my fear is anxiety rather than intuition. It does not work: by the time we dock at the pier in Krabi the voice is shouting at me to stow away until the afternoon's return sailing. Instead, I dutifully pick my way through the crowds to the waiting minibus.

The journeys aboard the little minibuses from the ferry to the airport are always passed in silence and this one is no exception: a dozen passengers pressed too closely together, all of us full of stories of the things we have seen, the people we have come to know, and yet nobody uttering even a single word. The planes at Krabi Airport will take us home or anyway away, and nobody wants to go. I try to understand the silences of my companions as reassurance: I am not the only one who wishes he could stay here, and nothing too bad will happen to me if I leave.

On board the first plane I lay my head against the window and sleep for the hour north. I wake only as we touch down, but the rest has not cured me. At the airport in Bangkok I feel the familiar misgivings, the same desire to turn and run back to Phi Phi. I attempt to miss my onward connection with a hopeless act of procrastination, stopping to undertake some shopping long after the monitor has announced that my flight is closing. It does not work: I end up aboard the plane, clutching a pair of overpriced elephant-patterned silk boxer shorts.

The long plane journey is drowsy and confusing, scenes from the film they keep repeating on the overhead screen mixed in with the fractured dreams brought on by all the miniature bottles I could persuade the stewardess to leave. And always that feeling that I should not be going, that I am leaving behind something precious that I will never, ever regain.

Somewhere over Russia I wake with a start and the feeling that I have heard something snap. By the time they turn on the lights to serve breakfast prior to landing, I can hardly remember where it is that I am travelling to; when we disembark, I actually have to check my ticket to discover my final destination. As I walk through the airport in London with its make-up counters and seafood bars, I cannot shake the feeling that an essential part of me is indeed now missing, has been somehow and permanently lost on the way home. Whatever the terrible nameless thing is, it has happened.

Sitting on the plastic chairs in the domestic departure lounge, looking out at the winter rain and the landing planes as I await my last flight home, I recall a theory I once heard about the problem with air travel being that it is simply too fast: our souls cannot move at jet speed and need a few days to catch up with our bodies. I try to reassure myself that this is all that went wrong over Russia, that my soul has merely been travelling more slowly and, like a mishandled bag left behind on a runway, it will find its way back to me in due course.

But what if it does not? What if somewhere amidst all the back and forth across the oceans and continents, amidst the digging and the grief and the sunsets viewed from the deck of Ben's landlocked boat, what if something inside really has broken, and permanently? What if my soul never catches me up? What then?

Because something does feel very wrong. I have been jet-lagged before and I have been sleepless and I have certainly been sad, but never have I felt so completely and utterly disconnected from the world around me. The check-in girls, the travelling businessmen, the policemen with their machine guns; if any of them were to speak to me right now, I would not be able to utter any word of reply. I wrote my single notebook entry from that journey in the departure lounge and if it is pretentious it is also telling: 'I am an actor who did not receive his script when the screenwriter went on long-term sick leave.'

As my final flight starts boarding, I tell myself that I just need to get home. Back there, in the place that I come from, amidst familiar things and people, I will surely not feel so far removed from the world.

Edinburgh, where the smell of the brewery hops hits you when you step outside the airport at lunchtime on a foggy winter's day. Edinburgh, where the taxi drivers speak the way Dominic did and want to know what you make of the incredible season Hearts are having. Edinburgh, where the four o'clock dusk is this year laced with sadness; I light a candle in the empty cathedral then go to visit Barney and his wife.

As always, they cheer me up, but even in their living room that has been my sanctuary on so many occasions this year, I cannot shake the feeling that something has lately gone very badly wrong. I tell them about it, and we agree that it is probably just a kind of inverse culture shock: for all the awful things that happened on Phi Phi, you can still hear reggae music drifting out across the bay, still get a beer at three a.m., still stay out until the sun rises behind Phi Phi Leh; you can, in short, still avoid anything that remotely resembles a normal life. Back here at home, however, the illuminations have been strung along George Street, the tree on the Mound blossoms with bright baubles, and the Christmas parties nightly spill out on to the city's freezing pavements. We toast each other's best health and decide that I will probably feel at least a little more normal tomorrow.

But I don't. I wake early and feel only further removed from life. I drive out to the unmarked grave at the church-yard in Colinton and, even in that charged location, struggle to feel much of anything. Later, wandering Edinburgh's familiar streets, I make a point of walking across the Meadows to the hospital Dominic and I were both born in, but nothing helps; in fact, the more time passes, the more certain I become that my situation is uniquely irredeemable. By the time the few days it should take my soul to catch up have elapsed, I no longer feel like a foreigner but like an alien. I begin to give serious thought to how I might live the rest of my life devoid of a soul.

Saturday night comes around and I go out with Dominic's friends. They too are finding it difficult that there should ever be another Christmas, let alone that it should be beginning eight months after we buried him. We have grown close this year, but with me missing my soul, it is as if our words have to struggle through the thick lowland haar to even reach one another.

And so we drink. We start out on beer but quickly move to whisky; when we have had our fill of whisky, we toast its memory with gin, with tequila, with black sambuca, with whatever catches our eye. Desperate now to feel anything, I am already anticipating the peculiar brand of make-it-through-the-day clarity I have known the worst hangovers to bring; perhaps in such a state I will be able to work out where my soul went and, possibly, what I have to do to get it back.

It is a ridiculous plan and it does not work. I wake up at lunchtime on Sunday on a sofa in a stranger's flat. The only thing I feel is sick and it is a struggle to locate my shoes, let alone my soul. The headache stays with me all day and by the time I wake on the Monday morning it has become so bad that I cannot get out of bed. My sinuses feel heavy and, groggily diagnosing myself with some plane-acquired cold on top of a two-day hangover, I go back to sleep. Five minutes later, Mum shakes me awake. She claims that it is now six o'clock in the evening and she wants to know why I am still in bed.

I tell her that I am still in bed because I have a headache. She immediately wants to phone the doctor, but I remind her that I am actually a doctor and reassure her that there is nothing wrong with me apart from the fact that I am missing my soul. Agreeing that she will take no action, Mum goes downstairs and immediately phones the doctor.

As we wait for the out-of-hours GP to arrive, I think about the questions that she will ask and the answers that will get rid of her most swiftly. Undoubtedly, this doctor will be keen to know where my headache is located, what kind of pain it is, and when it started. The problem is that my headache is a throbbing ache felt directly behind the eyes and it has been going on now for thirty-six hours. Put like that, and taken with my recent return from Thailand, my simple triad of common cold, prolonged hangover and lost soul could easily be mistaken for dengue fever. I do not have dengue fever and, still lacking a soul, the last thing I need is to be carted off to hospital with a presumptive diagnosis of a serious tropical disease.

Endemic across Southeast Asia, dengue fever is caused by a virus spread by the bite of infected *aedes aegypti* mosquitoes, insects recognisable by a menacing white stripe across their thorax. There is no vaccine for dengue, and its management is conservative, which is another way of saying painkillers and fluids and the crossing of fingers that it does not transubstantiate; though dengue fever itself is unpleasant, it is only truly dangerous if it evolves into its feared older brother, dengue haemorrhagic fever. Of course, I do not need to worry about this complication, because I do not have dengue fever in the first place: it was named dengue *fever* for good reason, and I have not felt even so much as mildly flushed since my symptoms began.

When the doctor arrives, the first thing she does is take my temperature. It is forty degrees centigrade. I have dengue fever.

The doctor asks me if I have been experiencing any other symptoms. She does not expressly say so, but she is asking about bleeding: in dengue haemorrhagic fever, the blood thins and first leaks into the skin as rashes and bruises, before eventually trickling out through the gums, the stomach, even the eyeballs. Thankfully, I have only one other symptom worth mentioning, and it is a little more metaphysical than any mere haemorrhage. I tell her that I lost my soul – probably somewhere over the Russian steppes – and she hurries off to telephone the hospital.

I am admitted for painkillers and fluids and the crossing of fingers. A junior doctor takes a blood sample and reassures me that the consultant will be in to see me first thing in the morning. Of course he will, thinks my increasingly confused brain, of course he will come and see me first thing in the morning because dengue fever is a terrific illness and I am a fine specimen of it. Frankly, he will be grateful to me for bringing such a fascinating pathology before him.

I spend the night in an observation ward next door to the Accident and Emergency department. The lights are kept on to allow the staff to tend the heart attacks and head injuries, so I sleep with my thick winter coat over my head. Aside from the elephant-patterned boxer shorts that I am somehow now wearing, it seems to be the only item of clothing I have with me.

At ten o'clock the following morning I ask a nurse when the consultant will be coming to see me. She tells me that there is no longer any need for him to see me, for I am being discharged.

'With dengue fever?' I ask her, puzzled that medical practice can have changed so much in the short time I have been away.

'You don't have dengue fever,' she says. 'Your white cell count was normal.'

White blood cells fight infection and their numbers generally rise in the presence of one. Only as the nurse departs do I register the insinuation in her tone: they think I am a hypochondriac, here for the attention and the drugs, knowledgeable enough to fool the admitting GP with an esoteric but feared illness – perhaps even wily enough to warm a thermometer under a duvet – but exposed for the fraud that I am by the rigours of laboratory science.

Half an hour later I am still wondering how I might prove that I am genuinely unwell when I overhear the nurse ask a passing registrar to sign my discharge papers.

'But he doesn't look very well,' she says. 'What did he come in with?'

'Non-specific headache,' replies the nurse. 'His white cells were normal.'

The registrar comes and peers at me from the end of the bed.

'What's wrong with you?' she asks.

'I have dengue fever,' I say.

She looks down at my temperature chart and frowns. 'Christ,' she says. 'You actually do, don't you?'

I nod, suddenly acutely embarrassed that I had ever imagined anybody would be thanking me for bringing this illness before them. Quickly using a glove as a makeshift tourniquet, the registrar sticks a needle in my arm and extracts a tube full of maroon blood.

'Don't go anywhere,' she says and hurries away.

No sooner has the registrar departed than the nurse approaches and tells me that an inpatient bed is now urgently being prepared for me. Meantime, she says, they desperately require this observation bed back; if I could possibly wait in the day room for a few minutes, I would be doing her a very big favour.

Keen to show that I harbour no hard feelings about her baseless suspicions of hypochondria, I clamber out of bed. Handing me my winter coat, the nurse strides towards a door and I shuffle along behind her; ostensibly I am pushing my drip stand beside me, but really it is the only thing keeping me upright.

The nurse holds open the door – a heavy, fireproof affair, with a single window of reinforced glass set uncomfortably high into it – and smiles at me as I stumble through into the day room.

But it is not a day room. It is an interminable corridor out of Kafka: a single orange plastic chair, a loudly ticking clock on the wall above and, perched behind a desk at the vanishing-point end, an officious-looking receptionist. Hearing the door shut and lock behind me, I turn to see the nurse peering out at me from behind the reinforced glass. Stood on her tiptoes, she is pointing at the orange plastic chair. I sit down on it and pass out.

When I wake, the clock above me tells me it is noon. Mildly surprised to find that I am still alive, I struggle up the long corridor towards the receptionist.

Dengue fever can affect the optic nerves and only when I get close do I see that there is a large room recessed behind the receptionist. A sign on the wall proclaims this to be the 'Out of Hours Waiting Area'; despite this being the middle of a working weekday, it is full of red-nosed people coughing and sneezing. They are all staring at me in a way that suggests they have never seen a man wearing only an amulet of the Buddha, a heavy winter coat and elephant-patterned boxer shorts attached to an intravenous drip before.

The receptionist knows that I am there but keeps typing for fully five minutes before looking up.

'Yes?' she finally asks, making no effort to conceal her irritation.

Even in my addled state, I know that I have to pitch this exactly right. I am clearly dealing with a person who is paid to say 'no' – who possibly even quite enjoys saying 'no' – and I will have to be polite and diplomatic whilst gently ensuring she understands that this is an intolerable situation that requires immediate redress.

'I have bird nok,' I say.

'Excuse me?'

I take a deep breath and try again.

'I'm waiting for a soul,' I say.

She stares at me.

'A bed,' I finally manage. 'I'm waiting for a bed.'

'There aren't any beds,' she says. 'The hospital is full.'

She turns back to her typing.

'But I had one.'

'Had what?'

'A bed.'

'Then you shouldn't have given it up, should you?'

I did not want to have to do this. People with dengue fever certainly require an inpatient bed and close observation, but it could be construed as pulling strings and, anyway, I lost my entitlement to any such privileges when I hung up my stethoscope. Still, my situation is a serious one and I feel I have no choice.

'I'm a doctor and I think this is quite important,' I say. 'I think I'm quite ill.'

There is silence, eventually broken not by a profound apology and a promise that things will swiftly be put right, but by a snigger from somebody in the waiting area. The receptionist turns back to her typing, and I trudge back down the long corridor to my orange plastic chair, where I once again pass out.

The next time I wake, the clock says it is half past two. I wheel my drip stand back up to the receptionist's desk; this time she does not look up from her typing even after I have waited the requisite five minutes. Worse, the people in the waiting room now seem frankly hostile, as if they suspect I am trying to jump to the head of their queue to be told that antibiotics will not be prescribed for viral infections here either. Struck by a feverish brainwave, I walk back down the corridor and knock on the reinforced window in the obser-vation unit door. From inside, I hear an urgent conference of whispered voices, and then the door opens just wide enough for a hand to emerge and pass me two tablets. As soon as I take them, the hand is swiftly withdrawn, and the door hurriedly locked once more.

I swallow the codeine and curl up on my orange plastic chair. At some point, through a nightmare labyrinth of endless corridors filled with armies of toothpick toucans, sour-faced receptionists and white-striped mosquitoes, I hear a gentle voice say my name. It is a sweet and vaguely familiar sound, and I instinctively comprehend that the person speak-ing cares about me and wants only what is best for me; perhaps, I think, this is a lot what dying is like.

'There you are,' I hear the voice say, 'I've been looking all over for you.'

It sounds so reassuring that I decide I must already be dead. Maybe the dengue fever transubstantiated after all, and this is the voice of my angel come to take me to my next paradise. But I am not ready to die yet, and so I vow that I will keep my eyes shut; my long-shot hope is that my angel might think I am merely asleep and leave me alone. I must screw my eyes up too tightly, though, because she notices the movement.

'Oh. Are you awake? Good. I got your blood tests back, and there's some news.'

Reasoning that any genuine angel should have little need of blood tests, I gingerly open my eyes to see the registrar from earlier standing over me.

'You're only bloody neutropenic,' she says.

Neutropenia is the state of having few or no circulating white blood cells. It occurs in cancer patients receiving chemotherapy, patients with immune system disorders, and, occasionally, people with severe viral infections like dengue fever. My normal white cell count on admission had simply been a way station on the decline to neutropenia.

Neutropenia itself is not harmful but it leaves the sufferer at huge risk from secondary infection; devoid of the body's primary means of defence against attack, even a simple winter flu virus can become a life-threatening hazard.

'You've not been exposed to anybody sick in the past few days, have you?' asks the registrar.

'Only them,' I say, and point in the direction of the waiting room full of late November coughs and colds.

The upside of being at high risk of contracting a potentially deadly super-infection means that you must be nursed in isolation. After the bright lights of the observation ward, I relished my side room where I could model my heavy winter coat and elephant-patterned boxer shorts with utter impunity. Here my fever waxed and waned, and my four-hourly codeine accumulated to pleasantly toxic levels. Until somebody rightly took it from me, I passed the time sending occasional messages from my mobile phone that made sense – a warning to my friends in Thailand that I had dengue fever, an enquiry whether anybody else had contracted it – and plenty that did not. I was still missing my soul, but by this point I had come to consider this to be almost a normal state of affairs.

Each day in the hospital followed a predictable routine: at seven o'clock a phlebotomist took a blood sample, at nine my 'get well soon' cards were delivered, and shortly after lunch a young doctor arrived to tell me that I was doing anything but getting well soon.

My blood was being taken each morning to be tested both for the progress of my neutropenia and for any signs of the thinning that would herald the onset of dengue haemorrhagic fever. Mercifully, my International Normalised Ratio – a measure of the thickness of the blood, abbreviated by acronym-obsessed medics to 'INR' – was remaining normal at one, but my white cells had thus far shown no interest in rallying.

Neutropenia is a worrying state to be in, but I had far more pressing matters on my mind. Before the Spanish term 'dengue' came to prominence, the illness was known in some quarters as 'breakbone fever', christened as such by a Benjamin Rush who had ministered to patients in an outbreak in Philadelphia in the eighteenth century; on the fourth day of my illness, I found out precisely why.

Dreaming I had been in a car crash, I woke up wondering if it had been more than a dream, if perhaps during the night they had attempted to move me to another hospital, only for my ambulance to have had an accident on the way. Later, when I looked up dengue in my old medical school text-book, I would find these pains referred to as 'arthralgia' and 'myalgia' – mere 'joint pain' and 'muscle pain' – but Dr Rush's term is far nearer the mark: it felt as if I had broken every single bone in my body.

But fractured bones take weeks to heal, and two days later my pains had started to dissipate. My headache had also begun to improve, the fever seemed finally to be in abate-ment, and my thoughts had naturally begun to turn to when I might be discharged. If only my white cell count could somehow be persuaded to improve, I knew that I stood a good chance of early parole. For days now, the team looking after me had been trying to transfer me to the regional infec-tious diseases unit, and, though it had been made increasingly clear that my side room here was in great demand, I had been stubbornly resisting transfer.

Although the infectious diseases unit was clearly the most appropriate place for me – and might even be staffed with people who would properly appreciate a good case of dengue fever – it was located in the hospital where Dominic had undergone his surgery. It was a building full of fraught memories for all of us, but particularly Mum, and that might have made it difficult for her to bring me my daily sandwiches.

That is something else about dengue fever. The virus also affects the nerves responsible for taste and thereby manages to invest everything with the same monotone metallic flavour. If I had initially imagined that this might be an advantage in a hospital, what I had forgotten to consider was texture: even devoid of any functioning sense of taste, gelatinous mush remains gelatinous mush. Mum was therefore relied upon to bring daily care packages to provide nourishment for the ongoing battle against dengue fever.

On the evening of my sixth day, I am lying in bed plotting my escape when the consultant and his entourage enter in a bustle of white coats and stethoscopes. As the consultant has already conducted a ward round that morning, I am somewhat surprised to see him and idly wonder if he has finally realised he is in the presence of a great and famous illness and returned to show it due deference.

'So your INR today is eight,' he says.

Blood that has an INR of eight might as well be water. The nervous fiddling with tendon hammers and pagers that now breaks out amongst his junior doctors confirms my worst fears, but somehow I feel obliged to ask anyway.

'That's pretty bad, isn't it?'

'We've cross-matched blood for you,' he says, 'and intensive care are keeping a bed on standby.'

Clearly, not nearly enough crossing of fingers has been undertaken on my behalf, for I now have the dreaded dengue haemorrhagic fever. Nor is it just the obvious possibility that terrifies me: if living without a soul seemed bad enough, dying without one is entirely unthinkable. I will become a ghost, possibly even – given the starring role blood looks set to play in my demise – some kind of vampire.

The doctors shuffle out of the room, one or two of the most junior ones smiling apologetically as they go.

As soon as they leave, Barney strides into the room for the start of visiting.

'Evening, mate,' he says. 'How are the old skellybones tonight?'

Poor Barney. He has had to help me through a lot of dark times this past year – and has managed to do so where humanly possible, and joined me in them where not – but the task of cheering me up in the face of an eternity spent wandering with the soulless undead would seem to be beyond even his impressive powers. I tell him what the consultant said and explain what it likely means. Bless him, he is not above having a shot all the same.

'It is probably not as bad as you think,' he says. 'And look, I've brought you a magazine.'

I should call Mum, for I might not get another chance. Any minute now, blood might start pouring forth from my eyeballs and gums. It might start hosing down my nose, or I might even just start vomiting it up. But what could I possibly say to her? Telling her not to worry because I have a reservation in the intensive care unit is unlikely to put her at her ease.

I do not ask to borrow Barney's phone and instead simply warn him about the likely trouble ahead, including the distinct possibility that I will soon begin vomiting bright red blood. Barney is still wearing his good work suit, but he does not flinch.

'Doctors always tell you things are worse than they are,' he says, then leans in closer and whispers. 'That way, when it turns out fine anyway, it looks like they've actually done something.'

We continue in this vein – me on the bed, a cloud of doom hovering above me, Barney in the chair, doing his best to dispel it – for hours. Somewhere outside, the nurse rings a bell for the end of visiting, and yet Barney still sits there, telling me all the good things that he can think of: an old joke, a mutual friend he bumped into on his lunch break, a promising young striker Hearts are rumoured to be buying.

Sometime before midnight, a young doctor enters the room carrying a needle and syringe.

'Your consultant phoned,' she says. 'He wanted me to take the sample again, in case there was some kind of error.'

Barney smiles, stands up and puts on his coat. 'Told you, mate,' he says. 'See you tomorrow.'

Sure enough, an hour later the doctor returns to tell me that the INR on the latest sample has come back as normal. The first result was a sample that did not reach the laboratory quickly enough, a computer malfunction, a typographical error. Despite the evening I have just inflicted on Barney, I was never actually in any danger.

That night, for the first time since leaving Phi Phi ten days before, I sleep soundly. Perhaps I am worn out by the day's excitement, or perhaps it is simply the first night when I have not been jetlagged, when the lights have not been left on, or my bones have not ached as if they were all simultaneously breaking, but I do not think so. Because after the doctor leaves and the nurse puts up the midnight bag of saline, I realise that something has changed inside; it sounds ridiculous but, as I lay my head down on the starchy hospital pillow, the soul that I thought I had permanently lost feels to have been returned to me. And more ridiculous still, that night I am certain that I know what brought it back: it was the short time I spent thinking that I might be about to die of dengue haemorrhagic fever.

Did I genuinely believe that I might die? I think I did, or at least did as much as it is possible for any young and otherwise healthy person to think that they may soon cease to exist. Frankly, it seemed preposterous to me: not just that a random mosquito bite could be my undoing, but the notion that I might die at all. That was why I did not call Mum when I should have: not because I did not wish to distress her, but because the whole thing was so abjectly absurd. And as I fell asleep I could not help but wonder – if there was even any time for him to think or feel anything – if that might not have been what Dominic felt at the end too: not terror, not horror, but a simple disbelief at the absurdity of the situation.

The next morning, the consultant in infectious diseases comes to see me. This, finally, is a man who appreciates a good tropical illness. When, after taking a detailed history, examining me and reviewing my chart, he tells me that I have had a textbook case of dengue fever, I actually blush with pride. I feel as if I have been given an 'A'.

And nor is it merely the pain behind the eyes, the aching bones, the neutropenia. He asks me if I noticed a prodrome, and so it is that I discover the feelings of dissociation I felt for days – feelings that I interpreted as an urge not to leave Phi Phi and the subsequent loss of my soul – can be understood as being a feature of the illness. If I asked him, I am sure he would even tell me that the sudden calm I felt after the INR scare was over was not due to my soul being returned to me, but simply a result of the virus's coincidental defervescence. I do not ask him, though, because I prefer my own explanation of events.

Informing me that my white cells have overnight risen to near-normal levels, he discharges me with a box of painkillers and a warning: I have thus far had a classic case of dengue, and the classic coda to dengue is several days of deep depression.

I am too excited about escaping the hospital to pay this much heed. Half an hour after I call her, Mum arrives with a set of clothes for me. Gathering up my get well soon cards and my elephant-patterned boxer shorts, I put my winter coat on and we head for home.

Two days later, I am floored by the deepest and most profound melancholia I have ever known. It is not just the way the streetlights nightly remind me of boyhood winter evenings, not just the thought of Mum quietly going to work each day with a Dominic-sized hole in her soul, not just the flat Dominic and Eileen bought as their first home which a whole year later remains empty. It is not even just the grave they now share at Colinton that still remains unmarked. It is not just anything. It is everything.

Everything in this world is awful. Dominic is dead, Eileen is dead and so are almost a quarter of a million other people unfortunate enough to have been near the beaches around the Indian Ocean that day. Left behind but blessed with a life of my own, I have done nothing but make a mess of it. At the age of twenty-seven I have had two good careers, and I have already more or less squandered both of them. I have run off to Thailand when I should have been at home to support my family and, to my eternal damnation, I have even gotten cross with Mum when she has brought the wrong kind of sandwiches to me in hospital. I decide that nobody loves me, and, moreover, they are quite right not to. And, absolutely worst of all, it is Christmas time.

More than anything, I cannot stand the fact that it is Christmas. Jesus Christ and his wise men, Santa Claus and his elves, it is as if they are all part of a vast yuletide conspiracy to make me sadder than I have ever been. As a defence, a vaccination against the carollers that seem to line every street, I listen over and over again to a Joni Mitchell song that starts with the melody from 'Jingle Bells' and the killer lyrics:

> It's coming on Christmas
> They're cutting down trees
> They're putting up reindeer
> And singing songs of joy and peace
> Oh I wish I had a river
> I could skate away on

173

My flight back to Bangkok, I decide, will be my river. I will skate away on it.

This is the thought that gets me through these days. This, and a few specific other things besides: Barney's front room, the door to which is never closed, emailed pictures of our burgeoning garden and the thought of my good friends there.

But the first thing that makes me smile again is a crackling phone call from Mon. Despite the fact that nobody else on the island seems to have contracted dengue, he has somehow arranged for the whole of Phi Phi to be sprayed against the white-striped *aedes egyptii*. He proudly tells me it is safe for me to come back, but reminds me again to wear my amulet. I tell him, truthfully, that since the day he gave it to me I have only ever removed it to shower or sleep.

Only as I begin to recover do I recall the warning the infectious diseases specialist gave me. Looking it up in my textbook, I read that there are several reported cases of people suffering from post-dengue depression committing suicide. It takes another full week before I can be in the same room as a Christmas tree without crying, and, as far as I am concerned, the river that will take me back to Bangkok cannot freeze quickly enough.

But before it does there is something else to do. On a chilly morning in December, a coroner's court is convened in London's Earl's Court to review the cases of British people killed in the tsunami. That it is a venue more commonly associated with rock concerts again only underlines the scale of the disaster, and perhaps even hints at the disproportionate number of young people killed. We, their brothers and sisters, ought to be here to watch the rock band of the hour but instead we are dressed again in our black clothes and in the darkened auditorium we sit and listen to a litany of the dead, the names changing but the circumstances – a bungalow, a hotel, a last phone call, a last email – endlessly repeating themselves.

I arrive back on Phi Phi wearing long sleeves and trousers in the noonday sun. Ben wants to know why I am dressed like this, and makes no attempt to conceal the fact that he thinks I look ridiculous. Mon, insistent that since the spraying there is absolutely nothing to worry about, seems mildly offended by my outfit. Toy, who has himself had dengue at least three times, is more philosophical: even if I do get the dreaded dengue haemorrhagic fever, I will simply have to spend a few extra days in the hospital in Phuket. It is, he says, no big deal.

One night at Sunflower Bar, the conversation turns to how strange it is that with so many of us spending all our days and nights together, I should have somehow been the sole person to contract dengue fever. A girl who worked in the garden in early December mentions that she came down with the flu around the time I left, and suggests that this might have endowed her with some kind of immunity against dengue.

Intrigued, I ask her to tell me a little more about her illness.

'It was awful,' she says. 'I had this high fever and a terrible headache.'

'Where was your headache?' I ask.

'Right behind my eyes,' she says. 'And, God, I felt miserable for days after it.'

She does not want to believe me when I tell her that what she had was dengue fever. It cannot possibly have been dengue, she says, because everybody else had it too.

Later that same night, I walk around the bar to look for our bird nok bird, but his cage is empty. Mildly perturbed, I call across to Ben to ask where he is.

'Flew away now,' he shrugs disinterestedly.

175

'Do you think that's safe?' I ask him.

Though it had drifted from the front pages, the papers and the internet had continued to feature daily updates on the progress of the illness that the bird nok bird being locked in his cage was supposed to protect us against.

'Come on, Simon,' Ben sighs. 'The bird nok bird has gone himself. He is not coming back now.'

Sure enough, the door to his cage was hanging open, as if our bird nok bird had somehow found his wings and departed of his own volition.

It is still dark when I awake on the twenty-sixth of December and step out on to the balcony. The stray cats, the whirring mosquitoes, even the last drinkers have all turned in and the town is sleeping silently.

Dinner yesterday was pizzas brought down to the bar, but we had not felt much like eating. That is the kind of Christmas Day it was: there had been no talk of presents, and the sole signs of yuletide were the carols blaring from the speakers outside empty restaurants and a pair of misplaced tourists gambolling through town in red Santa Claus hats. Over at the far end of Loh Dahlum Bay we had worked in the garden, sweeping the paths and raking the leaves in our quiet solidarity. If the Son of Man really had been born on this day two thousand years ago, well, we had our own anniversaries to consider now.

A year. For months we have been anticipating this moment but in the dark before dawn it now seems to me worse even than we could have foreseen. If we had fortified ourselves against today being a day when our sadnesses came into sharp focus, what strikes you most acutely on such a morning is the realisation of what an anniversary actually is: a proof of time passed, a marker of days lost. Tangible evidence that we were now further from our lost ones, that we had not heard their voices, seen their smiles nor held their bodies to ours in four full seasons, in an entire circumnavigation of the sun, in a year.

A year. As dawn slowly broke, the island held its breath and waited for this day to unfold.

Our fellow bereaved would be coming today. Some of them would be returning to the soil that had borne them, others visiting from distant continents and for the first time. They would be coming by longtail, by passenger ferry and by speedboat, some with eyes red even before they stepped on to the pier, others determined to make it through this day with eyes dry in tribute to the unknowable strength of their dead. They would be coming clutching flowers and other offerings; they would be bringing with them their grief, but they would also be bringing with them their love.

A year. I pulled on Dominic's old Bob Marley T-shirt and made my way down to the garden.

Yesterday, in the late afternoon, Carol tied bright yellow ribbons around the shell-shocked coconut trees that still line the torn-up road. Yellow for the King of Thailand and yellow for the missing, their bows now blossom like opening flowers in this rising sun. By the time I reach the garden I am starting to think that I have already seen all the beauty I can cope with, but early on a twenty-sixth of December the memorial garden is inevitably at its most handsome.

You enter by passing underneath an archway that is already overgrown with chrysanthemums. From here, a path of red slate flagstones curves an avenue flanked on one side by a bamboo thicket and on the other by a bed of roses; follow this for ten yards, and you emerge into the garden proper.

The red flagstones continue, summoning you forward across the grass, but your feet have stopped moving. The lawn – flat, green and trimmed as the cricket square in Grandma's English village – would itself have been enough to halt you, but what has really done for you is the luscious flora.

Hedgerows enclose the garden like monastery walls and in every direction you look there are plants both exotic and familiar: roses and hollyhocks, traveller palms and date palms, sweet peas and begonias. Around you are young trees staked to bamboo poles, blossoming bushes fragrant as they are nameless, bright flowerbeds bordered by walls of miniature brick. Dragonflies hover and honey bees buzz, and in the centre of it all there is the pond.

To look on the pond it is difficult to believe it has not been there for generations. Tall and verdant reeds shade its cool waters, flying saucer lilies float languidly across its surface, and a handsome bamboo bridge spans its widest point; step up on to its strong wooden slats and you can see the goldfish swimming beneath and the hand-crafted mosaics that mark the boundaries of their world.

You carry on, over the bridge towards the memorial wall. Constructed of bricks of polished yellow onyx, it is flanked by two ornamental stone elephants, but what you notice first are the names.

Dozens of small rectangular plaques of black marble sit atop the onyx in neatly regimented columns and rows, and inscribed in gold leaf on each of these is a name. Dominic's and Eileen's names are there and so are the names of many others: names you recognise from the newspapers and the coroner's inquest, names you do not. Thai names and Australian names, British names and Scandinavian names, American names and European names; several plaques repeat the same surname and these hint at untellable tragedy. If each plaque here represented one life lost then this wall would be a stark reminder of the scale of what happened here, but in fact only a small fraction of all those who died on Phi Phi are listed, for the custom of the local Muslim people is not to write individual names on graves or memorials. It is thought that a thousand people died on Phi Phi, and there are a little less than two hundred names on the wall.

But even with so partial a roll call of the dead, the names

you read there somehow bring it all a little closer still, remind you anew that what took your loved one was not individual illness nor private tragedy, but a disaster on the scale only nature can create. You stand there early in the morning, and look from the wall to the sea and back again; perhaps a little to the right of the wall you notice where two trees that look a lot like Scots Pines stand, matching yellow ribbons tied around their trunks like the saddest of Christmas decorations.

One year. At ten o'clock a handful of people begin to gather in the garden for a small ceremony of remembrance. Few will be joining us here today, for on this first anniversary an official event has been organised in the shade of the grandfather banyan tree at the far end of the beach. The services there will cater to all faiths with prayers and chants from monks, imams, ministers and rabbis, but our place today is here, amongst these new plants, these chest-high saplings. My family, Carol's, Ben's: at a certain point our journeys were joined and this garden became the place where we and many others belonged together, the place where the living might finally hope to meet with the dead.

Last year the water arrived at half past ten in the morning, and so this is the time our ceremony begins. Twelve months ago there would have been noise, so much terrible noise, and we remember it now with silence, our collective gaze drawn to the names on the wall and the still sea beyond. Our silence lasts only a minute, but carries for an eternity that will echo down through all the quiet moments of a lifetime.

Rat-a-tat-tat rat-a-tat-tat rat-a-tat-tat
In the basement of Uncle John's house in France, Dominic and I once discovered an unopened industrial-sized box of firecrackers. Boy teenagers that we were, we smuggled them

out to the derelict barn, all fifty packets of them, and there set them off in an orgy of destruction, lighting the first couple of fuses and letting the ensuing chain reaction account for the rest. It was a glorious bombardment, their powder sparking bright in the dark, their machine-gun burst the loudest noise we had ever heard. Better still, every fresh report was a confirmation of the ingenuity of our scheme: if the box had been discovered open with two or three missing we would surely have been caught, but nobody could reasonably accuse us of having used up fifty packets of the things.

Rat-a-tat-tat rat-a-tat-tat rat-a-tat-tat
It is the sound of those firecrackers from a decade and a half ago that breaks the silence in the memorial garden. At least, that is what I first think of when I hear the staccato of the firecrackers that Hang has discreetly lit. If I quickly realise that they are not the nostalgic contraband of our youth but rather are of the same brand as the fishermen detonate before they depart the piers at Phuket and Krabi, what they signify comes to the same thing: an offering for those the ocean has taken for its own and a prayer for those who remain in peril from the sea.

Music now comes, drifting over from the bar. Whatever intentions they came with, everybody is crying now: today is a day for weeping, and not only for those who died. We have kept to our part of the bargain, have built this garden and come here clutching our flowers and incense, and yet even now, at this moment on this day, the dead are still only absent. We are here together in our grief, but we are here alone.

Carol takes a pair of roses from the baskets she has had sent over on the morning ferry and lays them at the foot of the wall. The rest of us take turns to follow suit and soon the red flagstones are awash with white roses.

Afterwards, in the bar, there is the sky after the rain and all the relief of a wake. Even if the dead have not yet appeared for us today, we the living have made it through the hardest part of the hardest day of the hardest year. Frankly, we deserve a drink.

Later, we walk west along the beach, the hot sand burning at our toes as we pick our way through the dune line. In the waste ground at Charlie's Resort we find the driftwood shrine that Ben built for us back in October. As we lay our flowers here, Mon appears in the distance, hurrying towards us clutching armfuls of ripe fruit, two cans of Coca-Cola and what will turn out to be a pair of grilled cheese sandwiches. For a moment I wonder if he is proposing a picnic, but he carefully sets his provisions at the shrine, opens the Coca-Cola and reassures us that these offerings will keep Dominic and Eileen sustained in their next paradise.

From Charlie's we cut back up to the main street. The official services have now finished and the road here is thronged with people. The ambience is that of a carnival, the same wake we had taken part in down at the bar apparently now occurring throughout town. Stalls have been brought out to line the road. There are smiles and there is reggae music, but most of all there is food.

Food is how the Thai people tell you that they love you, that you are welcome here, that they will share in everything with you, be it rice or deepest sorrow: just as the dead require sustenance in the next paradise, so too, it is understood, do the living in this one. Every business has set its stall and from all sides people are jostling to offer rice, fish curry, lemonade, beer. The cooks and the dishwashers, the owners and the busboys, they are all facing anniversaries of their own today, and yet they want only for you to feel loved and welcome here in their home with them. We pick up paper plates and eat all that we can.

Afterwards our family group separates. Some of them go down to the beach, some over to the grandfather banyan tree where the monks still sit, some back to their rooms. I return to the garden.

People have been drifting in and out all through the late morning, and each has brought their own tribute. The wall is no longer a mere roll call of the dead but has become another kind of shrine to them. Atop the red flagstones, our white flowers themselves are now blanketed with football shirts and compact discs, handwritten letters and unsmoked cigarettes, laminated photographs and prayers.

One year, and all these offerings, and yet still the dead have not come. I close my eyes. Music goes on for ever, but on this day of days I cannot feel them. I cannot feel them. This was supposed to be the place where the living might meet the dead, but if they have not appeared today then surely they never will. I leave the garden and walk across to the bar to drink a beer with Ben.

One year. My beer with Ben becomes several and in the late afternoon I return to my room to sleep them off. When I awake it is eight o'clock and dark outside, but our anniversary is not yet done.

I hurry back towards the bar, but en route find myself drawn once more into the garden, for a pair of burning torches now flank the entranceway. Inside, candles and paraffin lanterns flicker throughout the darkness. They line paths and perch on the handrails of the bridge, sit on the walls around the flowerbeds and hover in the branches of trees. There are hundreds of them, and they look like the visiting souls of the departed.

At the memorial wall, glimpses of pictures are visible in this candlelight and so are fragments of poems and prayers: '*love*', '*tomorrow*', '*miss you*'. In front of a photograph of Dominic and Eileen two tea lights burn, their glass bodies bearing notes Caroline wrote to each of them and asked us to bring here in the sure knowledge that on a night like tonight and in a place such as this one, the message could not fail to get through.

And if I am alone still, I am not alone, not entirely. At this precise moment, on this precise night, I can feel them here with me. Dominic and Eileen, my big brother and his precious girlfriend. By candlelight in the evening of the first anniversary, our memorial garden has finally become what Hang foretold it would: a place where the living can meet the dead.

One year. As midnight approaches, we carry the *khom fai* down to the beach in front of Sunflower Bar.

Made of tissue paper and bamboo, khom fai are crepe paper and bamboo hot-air balloons, their propane burners flaming blocks of paraffin suspended by the thinnest of wires. If you grew up suburban in the eighties, similarly diaphanous structures hung from the ceilings of your youth, but their wires held only sixty-watt bulbs and they never floated off anywhere.

All around the hard wet sand are paraffin blocks being lit, lanterns held low to the ground by crouching figures, and Thai voices urging, *not yet, not yet*. The crepe paper is highly combustible and many will learn tonight that the trick of a successful launch is to listen to the local people and not let the lantern go until it tells you that it is ready, until you feel the hot air inside tugging at your restraining fingers, tugging for levity, for release. If this is technique, it is the simple technique of all grief: to be patient, to be slow, to wait, and then, when the time comes, to let the velvet cord run through your hands without attempting to hold on.

184

The khom fai work to their own timeline and our lanterns do not leave this earth as one. Instead, they depart individually, as pairs, sometimes in threes and fours. From Loh Dahlum beach they make their way up into the sky and somewhere above the town they join the trail of the others that are tonight being released all over the island: from Tonsai, from Long Beach, from Viewpoint, from all the nameless places around the headland. They rise through the black night sky with a reassuring swiftness; these ancient khom fai know the place to where the bright things that disappear must go, even if we earthbound mortals cannot. Somewhere high in the ether they will join with those from Phuket, from Khao Lak and Karon, with those from Aceh, from Unawatuna, from Galle, and somewhere beyond that they will carry their prayer to the stars and perhaps to our lost loved ones too.

A few days later, Dominic's friends arrive on Phi Phi and we decide that we will go fishing. Not mere shoreline fishing, for this year we have been doing plenty of that back home, but big game fishing: the kind where your quarry weighs as much as you do and is so averse to the notion of becoming your dinner that you must be strapped into your chair whilst you battle him, lest you become his.

That evening we walk down the Front Street comparing the advertising boards in front of the various tourist agencies. The names of the boats vary – *Andaman Adventure, Deep Sea II, Kingfisher* – but each seems to offer more or less the same thing: a full day's package with rods, lunch and cold beer included. Priced at a consistent three thousand baht, it is one of the more expensive ways to pass the day on Phi Phi, but split four ways the charter becomes affordable. Besides, money quickly starts to seem an immaterial currency in light of the day out that the photographs on the boards seem to pledge: the ocean is blue, the boats are universally gleaming white cruisers and the fish suitably monstrous.

As we start to settle on the *Kingfisher* board, a lady from a rival agency hurries over with a proposition for us. Her good friend owns a charter boat, and tomorrow's customers have just cancelled on him. His vessel, she tells us, is fuelled and cleaned, his lines wound taut, his cooler stocked deep with beer; if we would care to go out with him, she says, he will be able to give us a fine discount.

Naturally, we enquire how much of a discount constitutes

a fine one. The price she quotes us is precisely half the going rate and so much of a bargain as to make us mildly suspicious.

'Is it a proper deep-sea boat?' Paul asks.

'Of course it's a proper deep-sea boat!' she says.

'And it is fifteen hundred with beer and lunch?' enquires Graham.

'Of course it's fifteen hundred with beer and lunch!'

'And it's definitely a boat like that?' Neil points at the glistening gin palace depicted on the *Kingfisher* board.

'Yes,' she says, seemingly growing a little irritated, 'it is a boat just like that!'

If we harbour reservations, it is still a deal too good for four thrifty Scotsmen to refuse. We pay half up front and agree to return to the shop at nine the next morning.

Neil, Graham and Paul: Dominic's friends since even before they were teenagers. I would call them his blood brothers, but by the time they met at eleven and twelve they were already all a little too worldly to bother with the Swiss Army knife ritual and their fellowship anyway rapidly ran far thicker than blood. Call them something more, then: call them the brothers of his heart.

Growing up, his room was always full of them, of these three and a handful of other cherished lads besides. From under the door an intoxicating concoction of music and laughter blended with incense and illicit cigarette smoke crept permanently out, and in that furnace of their most formative years, bonds were fused that mere water would never be able to dissolve.

They did everything together, these friends close as siblings. If anybody invited a single one of them to a party, the whole group arrived on the doorstep; when they were old enough to go on unaccompanied holidays, it was as a pack that they boarded the ferry to the Netherlands or the plane to Spain. Finally, when the time came, these remaining three stood strong as they held the ropes that would lower their missing quarter into the ground at Colinton.

Brothers of my brother's heart and now, by inheritance, of mine. Strange that it should work out like that, as if love could be passed on like goods and chattels, but it surely has and since Dominic died, a little of their bond has somehow found its way to me. It is an unsought legacy, and terrible in its cause, but it is yet invested with a magical grace.

Because in the months that followed the tsunami, even as their own grief wreaked its havoc upon them, these brothers of my brother's heart took me under their collective fraternal wing. Traditional Scottish lads who are as taciturn as Dominic was when it came to discussing such things as emotions, they did this in the way they knew best: by simple doing. By shin-bruising games of five-a-side football on a Thursday night. By going out drinking on a Saturday night then sitting in the dark together at the movies on a Sunday afternoon. By yelling for red shorts or blue shorts at a Muay Thai fight. By making plans to get ourselves tattooed. And – perhaps this more than anything – by going fishing.

In this, Neil was the driving force. His were the rods and the permits, his the ability to distinguish a trout from a salmon by the way it rises in a brackened glade; he, more importantly, was the one amongst us who knew how to tie a fly that did not fall off at the first firm cast.

Neil took me fishing a lot that first empty summer, into his fast car and down to the Borders and a particular spot opposite the house where Graham's brother then lived. Here, far enough removed from the road which brings you from the city that you hear only the occasional buzz of a distant motorcycle, the rushing brown Tweed slows to form a small oxbow as it turns southwards to the town of Peebles.

Fishing. You stand in the river, in silence but not solitude, and the water rushes around your waders as you cast your line endlessly back and forth. It is perhaps the ideal way for grown men to grieve together, a special kind of outdoors church where nobody has to speak, but every member of the congregation feels what is passing just beneath the surface. You wait and you wait: for a bite, a sign, an epiphany, religion. It never comes – in all the afternoons we spent there not a single fish was caught – and in a way you are glad, because however much you wish for a message, you wish more deeply for nothing to disturb the stillness, for the river to keep rushing, for this quiet afternoon never to end.

On the appointed morning we turn up in the Front Street at nine, but the lady who took our deposit is nowhere to be seen. The shutters on the shop she seemed to have been working out of are locked and, recalling our transaction conducted entirely in the street, we begin to wonder if she even worked there at all.

After a few minutes, a young girl of seven or eight comes sauntering down the road. Pausing in front of us, she looks us up and down and then makes a one-word announcement.

'Fishing.'

Without waiting for our response, she sets off back the way she came. We shrug at each other and follow her, catching up with her a few hundred yards down the street where she has stopped in front of a small convenience store.

'Buy beer,' she says, sitting down on a nearby empty crate. Her English is rote-learned, and as none of us know the Thai for 'We-sort-of-thought-we'd-agreed-with-your-mum-that-beer-was-included', we cut our small losses and purchase a few packs of Singha. Given that we are getting a deep-sea trip aboard a gleaming white cruiser for a mere fifteen hundred baht, it is still a bargain, even to four thrifty Scotsmen.

The little girl leads us off the Front Street, down a narrow passageway and through the ground floor of one of the houses the local government provides for the island's indigenous Moken population. We pass through a dark living room into a brighter kitchen where an old lady is shelling shrimp and a naked toddler is playing with a kitten; apparently entirely used to tourists tramping through their domain, none of this triumvirate pays us any attention.

The rear porch of the house gives on to a dock on Tonsai Bay, and here a tethered longtail boat bobs ominously in the water. The little girl motions for us to climb aboard, her youth and the fact that none of us knows the Thai for 'But-aren't-we-going-in-a-fancy-white-speedboat?' combining to ensure we do as she bids. By the time we look back, she has disappeared.

I try to reassure the others that our current vessel is merely a launch that will be used to take us to our real boat, but they are sceptical and understandably so: last night the deal seemed too good to be true, and it is hard not to think that we have just discovered why.

Still, it is at least peaceful, sitting there on the shore, the water gently lapping around our longtail. Beyond the shelter of the bay, the sea is cresting with white horses, and Ben has warned me many times that when there are white horses the longtails should not enter the open water. I decide not to mention this to my shipmates, and instead we raise a toast to Dominic and Eileen with the first beers of our fishing trip.

After some time a Thai man emerges from the little house. Wiry, with a weather-ravaged face, he is wearing traditional fisherman's trousers, an oil-stained shirt and an old baseball cap. He too seems entirely disinterested in our presence, boarding the longtail without greeting us and immediately moving astern. There he lights a cigarette and starts to slosh yellow liquid from a plastic bag into the boat's fuel tank. It is a slow and messy process, and a gathering overhang of untapped ash at the end of his cigarette keeps us edging ever closer to the prow.

These preparations complete, our captain then commences to yank the starter cable on the engine. On the third try it spews into life, vomiting soot, water and fumes aft and rear. The painter that joins us to the dock is untethered and slowly, slowly we putt-putt out into the bay and towards the white horses of the Andaman Sea.

As children, somewhere not long after BMX-biking but shortly before skateboarding, Dominic and I went through a fishing phase. Or, a little more truthfully: Dominic went through a fishing phase and I followed him headlong into it, as I always did.

Discovering a cache of old rods in the attic, we spent days at the kitchen table tying weights and floats until our rigs were charm bracelets of fluorescent orange plastic and rough-milled grey steel. We cycled down to the muddy river that ran through the dell beneath Colinton village, cast out our lines and braced ourselves for the onslaught of the perch and bream and monster pike that had spent their entire lives in patient wait for us. When the fish proved reticent, we recalibrated our floats and weights and tried once again. The most that ever happened was that we snagged our lines on the riverbed debris but we kept at it, staying out until evening in a fruitless attempt to achieve some mythical perfect depth. In the months that followed we would fish in the reservoirs of the Pentland hills and the sea off the Isle of Skye, but it all came to the same thing, and that thing was nothing. We kept earnestly waiting for a bite or a splash, some tangible sign to tell us that we were not wasting our time, but it never, ever arrived.

It would be a full year later before we finally caught anything, at a fishery near Grandma's house where the pond was stocked so full that a line could not be dropped without it piercing an unfortunate trout through some random part of his anatomy. Hauled ashore, the wretched things flipped violently in the dust until we had to beg Dad to remove our hooks from their fins and tails and throw them back in so that we would not have to look at them any more. If finally we were receiving our desired sign, it seemed only to tell us that fishing was not the right pastime for us.

It was easy to understand it that way because by then our interest had already waned. With hindsight, I see now that if our experience at the fishery that day was indeed any kind of sign, we interpreted it incorrectly: the lesson was not that we were not cut out for fishing, but rather that by not catching anything we had not actually been missing out on anything. The river in Colinton that contained only supermarket trolleys and imaginary pike was probably the ideal watercourse for us. We were too young to know it, but we did not require a bite to tell us that we were not wasting our time; how could we possibly have been wasting our time when we were two brothers sat on a riverbank together on a summer afternoon?

We'd set our collective hearts on a gleaming white cruiser, but in truth the humble longtail is a vessel possessed of more grace than any tycoon's yacht could ever hope to aspire to. Variations of its design are popular all over Southeast Asia, but those found in the coastal south of Thailand have long since become picture editor shorthand for 'tropical paradise'. In the most iconic image – one that you see on cereal boxes, television gameshows and even occasional London buses – two boats have been pulled up from a turquoise sea on to a beach of pristine white sand. The boats in that picture are longtails and the beach, more often than not, is Loh Dahlum Bay.

Fashioned from planks of coconut wood stretch-dried to a gentle curve, longtails run twenty-five feet long by five feet at their widest midpoint. They have the footprint of an ellipse and their most immediately striking feature is actually an imposing prow, a wooden projection that sweeps up from the hull and from which garlands and flags are hung for blessings and good fortune.

In the stern of the boat, the swivel-mounted engine stands proudly exposed and unashamedly filthy. A short handle protrudes forward to allow the captain to steer, whilst from the rear emerges the eponymous 'longtail', a fifteen-foot-long fixed driveshaft that terminates in an almost comically small propeller at its end. Besides gifting the vessel its unforgettable moniker, this exaggerated length sits the propeller just below the surface of the water and thereby enables the boat to access shallow bays such as Loh Dahlum.

The longtail has always been Phi Phi's beloved workhorse, its motor the engine that drives all commerce on the island. Fully half of the island's fleet was lost in the tsunami, and it is another kind of heartbreak to see these boats in the photographs of the aftermath: upended and split in half, their proud prows snapped and their bows fractured, they litter the beach like so many broken and discarded balsawood toys.

Several organisations comprehended the significance of this loss, and used funds raised in the aftermath to purchase boats to replace some of those lost. Many of the recipients responded in kind, bestowing the high honour of naming the boats upon the people purchasing them. To this day you can travel around Phi Phi and see boats with names that initially seem incongruous – for every *Songkram* or *Pichamon*, you will also pass an *Anna* or a *William* – until you realise that they commemorate somebody lost that day. Due to the generosity of a bereaved father from England who found himself with a small flotilla to name, there is also, somewhere, a *Dominic* and an *Eileen*. By the time of the first anniversary, I had spent months enthusiastically interrogating every longtail captain I encountered but was still yet to see either boat, and had reluctantly resigned myself to the fact that I never would.

Iconic and cherished as they are, nobody would claim that longtails are built for comfort. Those rustic wooden benches may appear inviting on the postcards, but the little propellers give the boats a surprisingly zippy top speed of up to twenty miles an hour, at which velocity their relatively flat hulls do not cut through the water so much as bounce and slap their way across its surface. Factor in a beer-based breakfast and the fumes from an engine still convalescing, and even before we have left the relative shelter of the bay, we four intrepid fishermen are already feeling a little queasy. Our captain seems to sense this, because he now turns to look at us for the first time and, proudly tapping himself on the chest, proclaims what we will later discover are the only two words of English he knows: 'Sea Gypsy.'

The implication is clear: he is a Sea Gypsy, a member of a noble Moken race who, thanks to the salt water running in his veins, is physiologically incapable of feeling unwell aboard a boat; we, by contrast and to our eternal and irredeemable shame, are lily-livered tourists who merely think that we are fishermen.

'Sea Gypsy.'

He repeats it for good measure; then, gunning his engine to its top speed, fixes his gaze on the white-flecked horizon.

Somewhere in the Andaman Sea.

We have been bouncing across foot-high waves and trying not to vomit for over an hour when our captain switches off the engine and drops his anchor. We wait for him to produce the modern graphite rods we will require to land a barracuda or tuna, but instead he rummages deep in his pockets and produces a knotted length of old fishing line. Getting down on his knees in the bottom of the boat, he then scrabbles around amidst the bailing bottles and triumphantly retrieves a single rusty hook. To this he deftly ties his line, and then he removes the lid from a small wooden compartment on the floor to which we had hitherto paid little attention.

The compartment is about the size of a shoe box. Inside it, swimming in eight inches of water, is the most astonishingly handsome fish that any of us four landlubbers have ever seen. An inch long, it is striped brilliant red and pristine white, and has the gas-flame shape of an angelfish. Our captain scoops it out and, grasping it in one gnarled hand, threads his hook through the unfortunate creature's tail. Keeping a firm hold of the other end of the line, he then hurls the fish as far from the boat as he can.

He turns and grins at us and, apparently believing we have fallen silent because we have not understood his intent, performs an exaggerated mime to demonstrate that his purpose is to use the small fish as bait to catch a larger fish. It is the fishery near Grandma's all over again, except Dad is not here to fix it. We opt instead for another round of beer and wait for our captain to receive a bite.

None is forthcoming. After an hour it starts to rain and our captain stands up and moves to the back of the boat. Cold and hungry, we are more than glad to be heading in and quietly smile at each other as we jostle for shelter under the boat's tiny canopy. Our captain hauls his anchor in and starts the engine; the line with the unfortunate fish at its end is left trailing, and slowly the realisation dawns that we are not heading back in, but rather further out to sea.

For twenty or thirty minutes we motor on at top bouncing-across-the-surface speed, a velocity that shifts the rain from vertical to horizontal and renders our canopy useless. Soaked through and now openly shivering, we drop anchor at a place that seems indistinguishable from the last.

This, then, is our big game fishing trip: our captain sits in the stern, smoking and holding in his hand a line that is attached at its far end to an extra from *Finding Nemo*. We sit up on the bow, riding the rough waves and wondering if it is desperately unseamanly to ask if we might now be taken in. Every once in a while we motor to a different patch of choppy grey sea, but they are all equally devoid of fish. There is no lunch, and we quickly run out of beer. At one point our captain stands up to relieve himself off the starboard side and the wind whips his piss back with such force that it actually stings our faces as it hits us. This is the second most exciting thing that happens all day.

Still, though, we wait. We sit in the longtail and we wait for something to happen. This, after all, is what we have really come for, this is the church of fishing. We might have preferred to be aboard a gleaming white cruiser, but it all amounts to the same thing: you sit in a boat in the Andaman Sea, you stand in the River Tweed, or you lie on the riverbank in Colinton Dell and you wait for something to happen. Nothing usually does, but still you go home fulfilled, built up, reborn or baptised. Fishing for pleasure may indeed be nothing more than the art of hopeful anticipation over realistic expectation but all that silent companionship, all that deep, still water; it cannot help but be good for you.

Except on this particular day, just over a year after Dominic died, something does happen. By half past four we are miles out from Phi Phi in the deep backwaters, a place few vessels ever reach. An hour ago we passed some squid boats at anchor, and in the far distance a purse-seiner is setting out its nets for the afternoon's final go-around, but other longtails are as conspicuously absent as the toothy monsters we had expected to spend today reeling in. Whatever the fish's excuse may be, the longtails' absence is easily explained: there is no reason for them to be out this far. Beyond where we are now there is only open sea and then, after untold hours of incredibly rough putt-putting on a day white-crested as this one, there is Phuket.

And yet we now notice a longtail approaching from the open water. From her original bearing she should pass us at a distance of about a kilometre, but something makes her captain shift course and he comes close enough that we can read the name written along her side: *Dominique*.

Finally, finally, here is our sign, our once-in-a-lifetime giant barracuda. It is spelled incorrectly, but this is Thailand and the generous father's boats were donated via a French charity.

It gets away. My camera is stashed in a waterproof bag and our captain is enjoying his day's fishing so much that he pretends not to understand when we implore him − with both words and gestures − to follow that boat. But perhaps it does not matter anyway: this is a fishing story, and the best things always get away in fishing stories.

Or at least you are meant to believe that they get away. More recently I have begun to think that the unexpected

197

appearance of a longtail boat bearing an approximation of Dominic's name might not have been that much of a sign to us after all. I had been searching for this boat for months, so perhaps it was inevitable that I would come across it sooner or later, and its presence that day was mere coincidence. Maybe the captain of the *Dominique* simply had important business in Phuket and veered close on his return because he thought he recognised the colleague piloting our boat.

Once again, though, it comes down to fishing: the point is not what you do or do not catch on any particular day, the point is simply the being there near the water with your companions quiet beside you. And if we ourselves should have ever wished to send Dominic a sign then maybe the four of us sitting there in the rain in the Andaman Sea a few days after Boxing Day would say everything that the missing brother of our hearts would ever need to know.

A few days later I leave Phi Phi, and once again find that I am doing so with a heavy heart. This time around, however, I at least know the reason for my discomfort.

Lean times had followed the tsunami on Phi Phi. The island had remained evacuated for several months and when the ferries eventually did start running again, they mostly did so empty. Businesses did whatever they could to survive, and for the bars this had meant trying to differentiate themselves from every other empty establishment selling generous measures of bootleg Jack Daniels. Reggae Bar did it with its Muay Thai nights, Sunflower did it with its shambolic charm, and the nameless place that inevitably became known as 'Tattoo Bar' did it by setting up a tattoo parlour at the end of the bar.

'Have a drink, have a dance, get a tattoo' read the sign outside, and it was a pitch that packed the customers in every night, the seats along the bar all taken, the erstwhile dentist's chair permanently occupied. Perhaps such success was inevitable, for there was a symbiotic logic to the arrangement and not merely in terms of the predictable relationship between the number of drinks a customer consumed and the likelihood of a souvenir tattoo seeming a good idea. Peak tattooing time on Phi Phi is the hours either side of midnight and many of the tattoo artists will tell you that they do their best work after a shot or two of the local rum. Once you have spent a little time observing them, it is difficult to discount these claims. As an art, tattooing is all about slowness, about a particular – almost lethargic – kind of patience; might it not then be somehow possible that the first numbing and dulling alcohol brings, the first inhibiting of neurotransmitters and depressing of synapses, could actually help them achieve the required state of mindfulness?

Before the tsunami, I would have laughed at the idea that I might ever consider getting a tattoo. Working as a junior hospital doctor, you spend a proportion of each day looking at bare flesh and inevitably begin to take something of a curator's interest in tattoos: the merchant navy anchors, the badges of football teams now relegated from any meaningful league, the names of long-forgotten lovers.

If these designs sound outmoded, it is because they were: hospitals are a province of the old, tattoo parlours belong to the young, and passions tend to decay quicker than ink placed under the skin. Nor was such ephemerality the sole reason a medical background might put a person off: in postgraduate picture tests, tattoos are inevitably examiner shorthand for 'blood-borne virus'.

I had more personal disincentives, too. For all that I can earn my living piercing other people's skin, approach me holding so much as a toothpick and I am liable to pass out. Worse, I am the kind of shopper who will spend an hour deliberating the purchase of a pair of socks, only to end up apologetically returning them a week later anyway. The notion, then, of actually paying somebody to stick needles into me to create a design that I would be obligated to wear every day for the rest of my life was always unlikely to appeal.

Yet on an evening in early January, a week after the ceremonies to mark the first anniversary of the tsunami and my last night before I returned home, I had found myself at Tattoo Bar. I'd had neither a drink nor a dance, but I was now awaiting my turn to get a tattoo.

I was apprehensive, but the tattooist at Tattoo Bar is acknowledged to be the best on the island. He did Carol and Toy's tattoos and, though he utilises the traditional bamboo method, his lines are as straight as those of an architectural draughtsman, his calligraphy precise as any laser-printed font.

More reassuring still was the fact that he is an old friend of Ben's. Earlier in the evening, Ben had introduced the two of us, and this had felt significant as I awaited my turn in the dentist's chair. To ask of somebody that they mark you for life seemed an absurdly intimate request, and I was calmed to know that I had a connection with the person who would do this to me.

But as much as he was the right person to tattoo me, Tattoo Bar was the right place for him to do it. Reclining in the dentist's chair, you can look straight across a hundred yards of dune line to the spot where bungalow A12 stood. For all the times I had previously been to Tattoo Bar, I had somehow failed to appreciate this geography; noticing it properly when I arrived that night, I had taken it as a sign that I was doing the right thing.

But that was all an hour previously and as my turn approached I became acutely aware of all the things that could go wrong. What if it hurt? What if it more than hurt, what if it was agony? What if the tattooist suffered a lapse in concentration and I ended up with a tattoo that said 'Dominique'? What if the authors of my guidebook had not merely been indemnifying themselves when they wrote that nobody should consider getting a tattoo in Thailand? Overwhelmed by these doubts, I had finished my beer and slipped out of the back exit.

This, then, is my regret on the morning ferry: that I am leaving unadorned. The sea is rough, and as we depart the boat hugs close to the prehistoric limestone cliffs and their song of permanence, of how certain right things can last for ever. It is a refrain that only makes me feel worse. We had built our garden, laid our flowers and lit our candles, set the khom fai sailing into the night sky and even witnessed Dominic's longtail boat, but I had singularly failed to do the one thing that would last for the rest of my life.

On a balmy midnight towards the end of a hot summer I am stood on the pavement of an olive-groved street in downtown Athens. I am attempting to send a telepathic communication to Mum, lying deep in coma on the other side of a thick breezeblock wall. A year and a half after we first came to understand what a thing a tsunami could be, my message to her is a simple one: you are not allowed to die too.

The earthquake that occurred that Boxing Day erupted with such violence that it tilted the entire planet on its axis. Perhaps then it should come as no surprise that eighteen months later we are still experiencing the aftershocks. Already now they are felt in our lives mostly as simple tremors – the predictable sadness of birthdays and anniversaries, the occasional days when we must slip home early to look through a shoebox of old photographs – but certain of them yet retain the potency to do further untold harm.

This particular reverberation begins in exactly the same way as its first forebear did: the downstairs telephone in our house in Edinburgh ringing a little too early, a little too insistently. In bed upstairs, half recalling the last time I answered such a call, I sleepily choose to ignore it; if I close my eyes and fall back to sleep, perhaps the harbinger will evaporate like a barely recalled bad dream.

It does not, and when later that morning I switch on my own phone, I have a voicemail message from Rob.

'Si, there's an emergency,' he says. 'Phone John.'

Yesterday I had driven Mum and Rob to the airport to

catch a flight for Greece, where they were to join some old friends on a sailing holiday. Mum has remained fragile since the tsunami, and the summer term that finished a week previously appeared to have left her exhausted. A fortnight of boating, of snorkelling, of drinks on deck whenever the sun got anywhere remotely near a yardarm, had seemed like it might be the tonic that she needed.

Uncle John fills me in: in the small hours of this morning, Mum suffered a subarachnoid haemorrhage, a bleed into her brain. At a local hospital in Corfu a hole was drilled in her skull and a drain inserted to relieve the pressure that the pooling blood had created. Mum has remained unconscious since this procedure was undertaken, and at this moment is aboard a Hercules plane en route to Athens, where an angiogram will be performed in an attempt to pinpoint the source of the bleeding.

Subarachnoid haemorrhage classically presents with a 'thunderclap' headache: the worst headache of the patient's life that comes on so abruptly they can often tell you what they were doing the very second it began. A condition most commonly caused by the bursting of an aneurysm of one of the cerebral arteries, it carries a chilling prognosis. One in ten patients will not live long enough to reach hospital and of the nine that do, a further four will die before the first fortnight is out; of the five that do live, an overwhelming majority will suffer significant long-term disability. Put another way, Mum has a half chance of surviving this, far less than that of surviving intact.

That she even made it to hospital, then, is something to be thankful for. It is further good news that the drain has been inserted, and that this has been done swiftly. (Later, Rob will tell me just how swiftly: when the ambulance arrived at the hospital in Corfu, he was directed to a waiting area; after a few minutes a doctor emerged and began to talk rapidly about the need to insert a drain. Rob had initially assumed this doctor was seeking consent for the procedure but, noticing the blood and bone splinters splattered across the man's scrubs, realised he was being informed of what had already been done.)

But there remains a very long way to go before any of us can think of relaxing. The risk of dying peaks in the first twenty-four hours, usually as a consequence of further bleeding from the original aneurysm. The angiogram Mum is to undergo in Athens involves the injecting of dye into the blood vessels of her brain, followed by the taking of a series of X-ray pictures to look for any such aneurysm. Until this test is performed – and whatever remedial procedures it indicates undertaken – rebleeding will hover a constant spectre at her bedside.

An hour later, I am driving to Edinburgh Airport. It is no exaggeration to say that if I do not manage to get on this plane – the last one on which I can make my connection in London, which in turn is tonight's last flight out to Athens – I might well never see Mum alive again. This time I do not risk the self check-in machines, but go straight to the assistance desk.

On a Friday afternoon at the beginning of July my flight from London to Athens is chaos, the plane crammed full of children fighting over portable DVD players and spilling fizzy drinks over one another. Across the aisle from me, two young brothers are sat between their parents, quietly swapping their comic books back and forth according to the rigid barter system known only to boy siblings. We spent a summer holiday in Greece when we were growing up, and it occurs to me that twenty years ago we were the family beside me. I put my headphones in and select an album that Mum likes.

Somewhere over Italy I find myself thinking of Uncle Bob's desperate journey to Thailand eighteen months earlier. Athens is east of London, Bangkok is east of Athens, and it follows that Bob must have passed this way. Even in the midst of today's tumult, the intimate connection between our two journeys looms large in my thoughts. A pathologist might seek to explain Mum's current condition by saying that a period of hypertension caused a congenitally weak artery to burst, but that would be no more truthful than claiming that the swollen abdomen of pregnancy is caused by the baby growing inside. The root cause of Mum's current predicament is the earthquake that occurred off the coast of Indonesia eighteen months ago; if the tectonic plates had not slipped on the morning that they did, Mum's life would not now be in jeopardy. I listen to the album that she likes again and again; Greece, it turns out, is a faraway place.

Later, I attempt to distract myself with the airline's in-flight magazine. Amongst adverts for calling cards and local taxi cabs, it reminds me that Athens is named for Athena, the ancient Greek goddess of war. According to legend, she quarrelled with Poseidon for this honour until a contest was agreed: they would each give the city a gift, with the deity whose present most pleased the citizenry granted eponymous naming rights. Poseidon, King of the Sea but apparently as hopeless at picking out gifts as his more mortal male brethren, gave the city its salt water – and hence its poor soil – whilst Athena gave it the olive trees that line its streets to this day.

By the time we come in to land, the two brothers across the aisle are fast asleep. Their heads rest one atop the other in the same way ours used to in the back seat of Mum's car, and their treasured comic books lie temporarily forgotten on the floor.

Out at the kerbside, the night is hot and chaotic and the taxi driver cannot discern the name of the hospital I am asking him to take me to. I try everything – speaking loudly to him as if he is deaf, speaking slowly to him as if he is an idiot, speaking loudly and slowly to him as if he is both deaf and an idiot – but none of it works, and a hopelessly optimistic attempt to reverse-translate the hospital's English name back into the ancient Greek letters I barely remember from high school falls predictably flat. Eventually one of his colleagues takes pity and comes across to reveal that whilst I have been pronouncing the name of the hospital with a soft 'g' sound, it is actually properly pronounced with a hard 'g'; everything in Athens, I will quickly discover, is going to be harder than I had hoped.

In the small hours of a Friday night, the hospital's emergency corridor is overflowing. It takes a long time to even push my way close enough to a member of staff that I can explain my purpose here: my mother, very sick, bleeding in her brain, aeroplane from Corfu.

At the intensive care unit, a weary registrar buzzes me through the door and ushers me into a small office. Rob must have told him that I am a doctor, because he simply snaps Mum's CT scan up on the light box and stands back.

'You see where they inserted the drain,' he shrugs.

It is clear that he intends the pictures to speak for themselves. I cannot see where they inserted the drain, though, because I cannot get past the very first image.

CT scans arrive on the wards printed like photographers' contact sheets, twenty-four small black and white squares to an A2 page. The latter twenty-three of the squares are cross-sections of the brain, but the first shows a frontal view of the skull that demonstrates the places from where these horizontal slices have been taken.

In this plain X-ray view, ordinary teeth show up with the same ghostly translucency as bone. Like many a sweet-toothed child of the 1950s, however, Mum has gold fillings in her rear molars, and here their precious metal is rendered a bright and brilliant white. In daily life these teeth remain hidden unless you really make her laugh, but when we were young she used to show us them and tell us that she was the daughter of a pirate. By their teeth and their fingerprints, by their tattoos and their DNA; this is how we will know our sick and our dead.

'Bed three,' the registrar says, flicking the switch to turn the light box off.

I look at him, expecting more, but he only shrugs at me.

'We wait and see,' he says.

We wait and see. He is right. When a loved one is very unwell we want to be told immediately and categorically that they are only going to get better, but no good doctor can tell such a lie. The only guarantee that ever comes with being very sick is the one which says that if recovery does eventually occur, it will happen neither as quickly nor as straightforwardly as you would like.

I approach the patient in bed three tentatively, for she does not seem to be my mum. Mum is the smiling woman I waved off at the airport in Edinburgh a day and a half ago. She is a mother, an aunt, a sister and a wife; she is the head teacher of a primary school full of happy children, and she is a survivor of unimaginable grief; she likes old songs and young children, Paul McCartney, red wine on winter nights and family lunches that go on all afternoon. This pale, eyes-shut woman, by contrast, is simply one of six bodies laid out in a foreign intensive care unit: a name misspelled on a whiteboard at three o'clock in the morning, a list of deranged electrolyte measurements, a somewhat less than half chance of survival.

This woman in front of me is breathing spontaneously, but the rest of the living dead paraphernalia is firmly in place: the suckering electrodes, the dripping bags of saline, the stigmata where any number of needles have already pierced her skin. A bandage is wrapped around her head, and from somewhere deep inside a thin tube emerges to terminate in a milk-bottle-sized drain that lies on her pillow.

I stand and stare at her, instinctively counting her breaths and tracing the tangle of wires back to the readings on their respective monitors. As I am doing this, Mum opens her eyes and smiles at me.

'Hi, Simon,' she says, as nonchalantly as if I have just walked into her Edinburgh kitchen.

'Hi,' I say, trying not to betray my surprise. 'How are you?'

Mum has to consider her answer, and this makes her frown.

'I don't know,' she whispers. 'But I'm in hospital,' she continues, quietly conspiratorial, 'I think I had food poisoning.'

Later, I will learn that this is what the very first doctor who examined her suspected she was suffering from, and therefore was the only diagnosis she heard before losing consciousness. Something else now occurs to her, and she frowns again.

'But aren't we in Greece?' she asks.

I nod and take her hand.

'So have you come all the way from London?'

I nod again.

'Good God,' she says. 'Then it must have been serious food poisoning.'

Mum squeezes my hand and we laugh together. If it is not the greatest joke either of us has ever made, it is still not bad going for somebody who eighteen hours ago was actively bleeding into her brain.

But there is something else troubling Mum. She is struggling to locate the right words – a common symptom of subarachnoid haemorrhage is a word-finding difficulty that will hopefully prove transient – but eventually she manages to get her meaning out.

'Where is my other Simon?' she asks.

The question hangs between us for a moment. I know exactly what she is asking me, but it seems too cruel to answer her honestly.

'I'm Simon,' I smile.

'No,' she says, more determined this time, 'I know you are here. But my other Simon. Where is he?'

I can only shrug. 'He's not here just now.'

Mum is puzzled and visibly disappointed, but exhaustion and confusion win the moment; she closes her eyes and drifts back to sleep.

Athena was a daughter of Zeus, a great-great-granddaughter of Chaos himself.

Warned by a prophecy he would one day be usurped by his own offspring, Zeus lived in such fear of his progeny that he turned Athena's pregnant mother into a bee and gulped her down whole. Months later, he suddenly found himself suffering from the worst headache of his life, a prostrating pain that left him screaming for mercy.

To relieve the pressure building inside her brain, Mum was rushed to hospital in Corfu and had a drain inserted. Ancient medicine preferring a more direct approach, Zeus ordered Hephaestus, god of blacksmithing, to cleave his head open with his axe. Hephaestus obliged and out sprung the goddess Athena, armour-clad and prepared for battle.

The morning after I arrive in Athena's city, Rob and I meet with the neurosurgeon overseeing Mum's care. Somewhere in his forties, he is straight of back and steady of hand, old enough to have amassed experience, young enough it has not yet wearied him. In an ideal world nobody would need to cut open your mother's skull; in this imperfect one, where somebody needs to, you pray for a man like this one.

Our Hephaestus, however, has come bearing the unexpectedly good news that Mum's angiogram showed no aneurysm. This, he says, suggests the blood in Mum's brain likely came from the rupture of a minor vein small enough to have already sealed itself off; in turn, this places Mum in the rare diagnostic category of non-aneurysmal subarachnoid haemorrhage.

This is better news than we had dared hope for: with no aneurysm, the chances of a rebleed are minimal. Better yet, as there is nothing to operate on, the neurosurgeon will be able to leave his axe in the fire. What Mum requires now is simply a period of observation and recuperation.

Aunt Catriona and Uncle Bob have been travelling in Thailand and outside I raise them on the phone. I start to break the news of all that has happened as quickly and gently as I can, but it transpires Catriona already suspected something was amiss. This does not come as any major surprise: on Boxing Day she had woken at home in Glasgow as the tsunami would have been making landfall in Thailand, sat up in bed and told Uncle Bob that something terrible had happened. Likewise, yesterday whilst I was dozing through Rob's fraught early morning phone call, she was struggling through the worst headache of her own life. Catriona and Bob want to come to Greece straight away, but we agree that they will hold off on making the arrangements; if Mum now recovers as swiftly as her doctors seem to be anticipating, we could already be safely home in Edinburgh by the time they arrive.

The next few days pass in a strange kind of bliss. Outside it is summer, the olives are ripening on the trees and in the late afternoon the long hospital corridors are dappled in sunlight. On the second day Mum's drain is removed and she is stepped down from the intensive care unit to a six-bedded bay in the main ward. Here, if you look out of the windows by the nurses' station, you can see all the way to the Acropolis and, atop it, the Parthenon of Athena. If Mum is not able to come and take in this view for herself, she is at least interested to hear of it, and her language difficulties seem to be evaporating with each day that passes. She still seems to think she might yet get back on the boat with her friends this summer, but whether this is residual confusion or simply her usual indubitable optimism, I cannot tell. If she has not yet mentioned Dominic or the tsunami, there has been no further mention of any other Simon either. Rob and I have agreed that we will tread carefully here: if she asks us anything we will not lie to her, but neither will we bring up the subject until we have found the right way and the right moment to do so.

On the third day Mum asks me to bring in her radio and late in the afternoon she even manages to talk on the telephone to Aunt Catriona. Tentative arrangements are made for everybody to be reunited in Edinburgh in a week, and the unspoken belief is that we have finally had a little of the luck that the gods must surely owe to us. And then, on the fourth day, everything goes to shit.

I had been up early to visit the British Embassy in order to renew the passport that had expired the day after I arrived in

Greece. The security guard had required me to turn in my phone and my bag, and all I'd had to keep me entertained in the waiting room was my old passport. For all the hours it had lately spent in economy airline seat pockets in front of me, for all the cartoon purple stamps from the entering and the leaving of Thailand, somehow I had never appreciated that the shield on the front was held aloft by a lion and a unicorn.

We had a history with the lion and the unicorn, and I made a mental note to remind Mum of it later. It would be an indirect way of talking about Dominic and, as we would soon be going home, the time to broach the subject had arrived.

Our nursery school was a high-ceilinged Victorian building in Colinton village. At the end of my first year there I am almost four and Dominic, destined for school proper after the long holidays, is already five. As the proud mothers gather in the doorway, our teacher announces a farewell talent show to be performed by the leavers. Dominic is first up on the small stage and recites, word perfectly to the back of the room, a nursery rhyme that Mum has taught him, 'The Lion and the Unicorn'.

The rest of Dominic's class now take turns: tell knock-knock jokes, sing songs, make animal noises. Perhaps the children are just anxious to be released into the summer holidays, but nobody comes close to being as well received as Dominic. For my own part, I can feel rising in me a sensation that I will later come to know as envy. When the teacher asks if everybody has had their turn, it overwhelms me. Sensing my one and only chance at greatness for ever slipping by me, I climb up on the stage.

From my new vantage point I can see that some of the

parents are frowning, but I remain undaunted. The teacher tentatively asks what I intend to do for my turn, and I proudly announce that I am going to recite a nursery rhyme of my acquaint, a little piece I call 'The Lion and the Unicorn'. As I say this, I notice Mum take a step towards the back of the group of parents and there sort of conceal herself amidst the cloakroom coats.

She is right to hide. I do not know the words to 'The Lion and the Unicorn'. For weeks I have been dimly aware of Mum and Dominic practising it, but Dominic's recital fifteen minutes previously is the first time I have sat and listened to the whole thing.

I certainly manage to mention a lion and a unicorn, but that is as far as it goes before I descend into a word salad of the names of any classmates who happen to be in my sightline mixed in with my ambitions for the summer holidays and a bold claim about having once seen a real unicorn at Edinburgh Zoo.

In the embassy a buzzer sounds and I collect my passport. Downstairs my belongings are returned to me and I find that Rob has left several messages on my phone asking me to come back to the hospital, for Mum does not seem right to him. Rob is an engineer by trade, but it was he who called the first doctor back and insisted that whatever Mum was suffering from must be more than food poisoning. Where Mum's health is concerned, Rob has something as useful as any medical training: he is married to the woman, and knows her as well as anybody.

From the point when I left the embassy, my recollections of that day become fractured and slow-motion, as if it were a car crash in which I had been a front-seat passenger. In a way, that is exactly what it was.

Mum complaining of a headache worse than the one she had been admitted with. Mum making mistakes in conversation that she would not have made yesterday. The resident responsible for her care refusing to come and review her, though he is stood in the corridor outside. The chief resident refusing to come and review her, though he is stood in the corridor talking to the other resident. Mum becoming increasingly confused. Searching the hospital for Mum's consultant, not knowing that he worked that day at a different hospital in another part of the city. Mum declining as fast as I have ever seen anybody go. Still nobody coming to see her. Standing in a corridor in the country of Hippocrates and Apollo the Physician, begging passing doctors and nurses to come, to come, to please do something. Nobody coming. A passing doctor taking an interest, noting that Mum could barely now open her eyes, and ascribing it to the normal fluctuation of recovery. A nurse growing nervous and slipping me the consultant's private mobile phone number. The thought that we are saved. A message in Greek that seems to mean that the phone you have called is switched off, please try again later. Nobody coming. Rob struggling to keep Mum's oxygen mask in place, for oxygen was all that we had to give her. Nobody coming. Telling Mum that we love her, though I know that she cannot now hear anything. The stressed nurse shouting at me that she has other patients to think of besides my mother; shouting back, asking how many of the others are dying in front of her. Nobody coming. Feeling Mum's pulse grow thready and irregular. Watching her blood pressure on the monitor begin its final dive. Nobody coming. The resident nonchalantly arriving back on to the ward; screaming at him that she is dying, my precious mother is fucking dying, how can he possibly not see that she is dying? Physically grabbing his hand and placing it on her grave-cold arm. Begging him to take bloods, perform tests and immediately infuse industrial-strength antibiotics. And all the time Mum drifting away. Nobody coming. Mum no longer even fighting the oxygen mask. Nobody coming. At last reaching the horrified consultant on the telephone, but the relief tempered with the knowledge it is likely now all far, far too late. A twenty-gauge needle stuck into Mum's spine that should flow with crystalline fluid but instead draws a viscous stream of frank pus. Mum's pretty face swelling, her beautiful sun-freckled arms ballooning white. The look on the face of the anaesthetist who comes to fetch her back to the intensive care unit. Outside the unit the resident proudly telling us that this was a difficult case and he was pleased to have performed the test which sealed the diagnosis. Managing to restrain ourselves from attacking him, but only just.

Mum now has meningitis, an infection of the membrane that surrounds the brain and spinal cord. In health, the skin and skull together constitute a physical barrier impregnable to invading microbes, but the drain that needed to be inserted in Corfu created the breach the bacteria required.

All through this day the bacteria have been multiplying, feasting on the rich cerebrospinal fluid that is supposed to keep the brain nourished with glucose and oxygen. If antibiotics had been started earlier things could have perhaps been controlled, but worse even than the infection itself, Mum's body has now started to react to the presence of the bacteria. Of all things, this is the catastrophic part.

Blood poisoning. Sepsis. Septic shock. The systemic inflammatory response syndrome. There are any number of names for the process now taking place inside Mum's body, but none of them adequately conveys the awfulness of it. On meeting certain invading pathogens, the reaction of the white cells charged with orchestrating our immune response – the same cells that hide when faced with the dengue virus – is to panic and to scream as loudly as they possibly can. If it seems surprising that white cells should scream, they surely do, and do so by releasing vast quantities of chemicals called cytokines. These shrieking prophecies of doom echo around the body and their effects are quickly disastrous. They cause veins to massively dilate, dropping the blood pressure to levels incompatible with life; they shift fluid out over capillary walls and congest the tissues, swelling arms, legs and pretty faces; most wickedly of all, they actively encourage the circulating red blood cells to form clots in the very lumens that they are supposed to travel through: just stop here, they say, sit down, give up, there is nothing ahead for you, no point carrying on.

The inciting infection is treated with antibiotics, but the only treatments for the systemic inflammatory response syndrome itself are supportive: fluids to replace those that have been persuaded into the tissues, mechanical ventilation to take over the work of breathing, inotropic drugs that keep the blood pressure up by constricting veins at the cost of occasionally causing fingers or toes to drop off. Even if these basic measures can buy enough time to bring the infection under control, however, there is no guarantee that any of the havoc so wreaked will be reversible; more commonly, the patient's organ systems will sequentially begin to fail. And when that happens, Mum will die.

Outside in the evening we make the necessary phone calls. As always, Aunt Catriona barely requires one; by the time the infection started to take its firmest grip on Mum, it was night in Bangkok and Catriona felt too feverish to sleep. She went through the hopeful motions of sending Uncle Bob out for paracetamol, but she already suspected that her discomfort had no local cause.

Mum survives her first night back in the intensive care unit. In the morning, the intensive care doctor tells us what we already know: that we are, in the very best scenario, in for a long haul. People in Mum's condition spend days, sometimes weeks, ventilated in intensive care; sometimes they survive, but mostly they do not. As it was a few days and a lifetime ago, we wait and see.

For all her armour-clad springing from the skull of Zeus, Athena was not merely the goddess of war but was also the deity of wisdom and of crafts. This did not mean she was in any way peaceable; Ovid wrote that she had a 'vengeful mind' and it is hard to disagree when you consider what she did to poor silly Arachne.

Arachne was a mortal girl whom Athena had schooled in the art of weaving. Young and naïve, Arachne grew boastful, and started to brag that she could produce tapestries more beautiful than those spun even by her divine tutor. Word of this impudence reached Athena, who disguised herself as an old woman and called upon her former pupil to enquire if the things she had heard could really be true. Delighted that her fame seemed to be spreading, Arachne proudly repeated her bold claim; when Athena revealed her true identity, Arachne only compounded her sin by agreeing to a weaving contest that would be judged by Athena's sister goddess, Envy.

In her tapestry, Athena piously wove the scene of her triumph over Poseidon: the saltwater spring, the olive tree and the gods sitting in their glory on Mount Olympus. Ominously for Arachne, she filled the corners with images of mortals who had previously offended the gods: Haemus and Rhodope, turned to mountains in Thrace; Antigone, rendered a stork; the daughters of Cinyras, reduced to prostitutes by Aphrodite.

Seemingly undaunted, Arachne effectively doubled down, portraying the senior gods at the wicked indulgence of their basest desires. She wove Athena's own father Zeus as a bull, a satyr, a swan and a snake – some of the various disguises he had taken on to father his assorted children. Poseidon was a horse, a bird and a dolphin; Apollo, esteemed god of medicine, was reduced to a humble shepherd.

Despite its inflammatory subject matter, Arachne's tapestry was technically flawless. Even Envy, duty bound to side with her divine sister, could find no fault in the work and adjudged the contest a draw. This sent Athena into a rage: smashing Arachne's loom to pieces, she used its shuttle to thrash her former protégée. Defenceless, humiliated and now abruptly aware of her own terrible impudence, Arachne attempted to hang herself with the very yarn from which she had woven her tapestry. Taking a peculiarly ancient kind of pity on her erstwhile pupil, Athena turned the yarn to web and Arachne to a spider, thereby condemning her to pass out the rest of eternity weaving tapestries that would forever be torn down by the wind and rain.

We rent an apartment near to the hospital, and the days pass in a languid haze of anguish. We fill our time by doing the things that Mum would do if she were awake: Rob befriends the neighbourhood stray cats and starts to feed them; I find myself drawn to the Sudoku puzzles Mum enjoys and I have until now never seen the point in. The focal point of each day, though, is our afternoon visit to the intensive care unit.

Shortly after two o'clock the nervous relatives begin to assemble in the hospital hallway. Half-smiles are occasionally exchanged, and a father whose son has been injured in a motorbike accident sometimes talks to me about football, for his AEK Athens have been drawn to play my Hearts in a

Champions League qualifier. For the most part, though, we are all too caught up in our own worries to much notice one another.

At half past a security guard arrives and unlocks the door to the intensive care corridor before taking up position at the entrance to the unit itself. We wait here again until a doctor emerges – usually the same registrar from the night Mum was admitted, sometimes a consultant, sometimes a petrified junior – and one by one each set of relatives is taken into a small side room to be updated on the changes over the last twenty-four hours. Occasional families emerge with tear-stained eyes, but for the most part they come out as they entered: staring slightly downwards, not cheered but not yet entirely broken either. Things happen slowly in the intensive care unit.

At a certain point, Mum's name is called – *Stefanson*, they pronounce it here, *Mrs Stefanson*, the way they say it in Thailand too, as if we are a family of holidaying Swedes – and we go into the small room to make our daily communion with her temperature and white cell count. Up is bad and down is good, but there is rarely a discernible trend. The doctors begin to fear that the infection has spread to the deeper, fluid-filled spaces of Mum's brain; now another hole is drilled in her skull and a tube re-inserted in order to deliver antibiotics directly to these areas. This reduces Mum's white cell count and temperature, but not by enough; it is decided that she must have a second focus of infection that the antibiotics are still not reaching, and a further tube is now inserted into her lower spine.

We are reconciled to the fact that we are in this for the long haul, but I am equally aware that as the days add up Mum's chances of survival are falling. Doctors are fond of declaring that hospital is a dangerous place to be if you are sick, and nowhere is more dangerous than the intensive care unit. Besides the ever present dangers of blood clots in the legs and lungs, for every day Mum spends on a ventilator the likelihood of her developing a life-threatening pneumonia increases exponentially. The only saving grace is that Mum's kidneys appear to be holding up so far. In the systemic inflammatory response syndrome, organ systems tend to fail in a predictable order and Mum's kidneys – parched by her low blood pressure and poisoned thrice daily by bleach-strong antibiotics – are likely to be the tipping point. Each afternoon I am grateful anew for their surprising resilience.

In the evening, there are phone calls to be made. Each night I spend hours going through each aspect of Mum's care with friends who work in relevant medical specialties, discussing every little decision that has been made or might need to be made in the coming days. Mum's consultants are excellent, but after the day we watched her get so sick, it is hard to let go.

Afterwards, when the phone calls are done, I go down and stand in the street outside the hospital. Her window is too high for me to see in, but I know that she is there, and it somehow calms me to be able to stand close to her. Sometimes I worry that she will not make it, but mostly I just miss her. And to begin with, this is what I tell her when I go and stand outside the intensive care unit, this is what I say to her: I miss you.

I miss you. Already I miss you in the same way that I miss Dominic. At some point during these weeks, I turn twenty-eight and it occurs to me that I should not be going through this alone; only I don't mean alone, because Rob is here and we face each day together: I mean without Dominic. Neither of us should be going through this without Dominic; eighteen months ago we were four going on six and now we are three going on two.

And this thought inevitably leads on to another: that perhaps Mum herself does not wish to wake up. Perhaps from wherever you go to stand on the precipice of death you can glimpse Mon's next paradise, whatever that may or may not be. Perhaps halfway dead Mum feels closer to her lost sons. You could not blame her if she did, could not blame her if she wanted to simply slip away and be with them. But my mum is too precious to this world to leave on such a note; I need her and Rob needs her and her school full of children needs her. I alter the message I am sending: you are not allowed to die too.

Subarachnoid haemorrhage.

'Arachne' became the Greek word for 'spider', and so it is that the tale of the weaver girl also lies at the root of the name for the condition that has brought us to her tormentor's city. 'Sub-' means 'beneath', and '-oides' means 'like'; a subarachnoid haemorrhage, then, is *a bleed beneath the spider-like thing*, the spider-like thing being one of the membranes that surrounds the brain, its tiny veins and arteries giving it a characteristic cobweb appearance.

Mum has never boasted about anything in her life, but she did once take an evening class in weaving at a local college. Walking at midnight through the streets that surround the hospital, lighting candles in the Orthodox church at six o'clock in the morning, sleeping on plastic chairs in a hospital corridor, it is hard not to wonder if we have somehow offended the gods. Certainly all our webs, all our tapestries, seem to be being torn down with alarming alacrity.

Now the family arrive in Greece, Mum's siblings and two of her nieces.

On her first day, my cousin Kathleen – Aunt Catriona's daughter and sixteen years old that summer – does not come to our standing appointment at the intensive care unit. She has travelled for over twenty-four hours to get here, and it is agreed that the sight of her sick aunt might be a little too overwhelming at the end of such a long journey.

Kathleen stays in the apartment, falling asleep on a soft couch in a dark room to dream that she is asleep in a hard bed beneath a high window. Somewhere in the distance a radio is playing foreign pop music and, amidst a chatter of whistles and beeps, Catriona is whispering to her, stroking her hand, reassuring her that everything is going to be all right. Kathleen has an overwhelming feeling that she wants to wake up, to open her eyes and tell Catriona that of course everything is going to be all right, she just needs to sleep a little longer, but somehow she cannot.

When we return to the apartment, Catriona confirms that this is indeed how things were when she took her turn at Mum's bedside in the intensive care unit. If this necessarily means that Kathleen is a white witch like her mother and her aunt before her, it is nevertheless also the first hint of good news that we have had in weeks.

July turns to August and Mum does not get better, but neither does she get worse, remaining instead in a netherworld somewhere between the city of Athena and the next paradise, the forces of living and dying stalemated over her soul. The relatives who congregate in the corridor at two o'clock all now have different faces from those we came to know when we started here, and it has gradually become clear that we have once again travelled beyond the normal boundaries of human experience. Other family members tentatively begin to ask me how long Mum's body can possibly sustain itself in this way and I tell them the grim truth: the longer this continues, the less likely a happy outcome is.

Kathleen's dream notwithstanding, we have no real reason to hope or expect that Mum will ever be well enough to be evacuated home, but if such a time does ever arrive, we want her to be ready to travel the moment that it does. Everything here in Greece is too foreign, too unintelligible, too hard; if Mum is to recover, it seems intuitive that she will best do so in familiar surroundings.

Mum would need to have woken up before she is moved, but we also require to be certain that there is no risk of rebleeding. In the past weeks, the relief provided by her initial angiogram has imperceptibly turned to nagging doubt. Angiograms will miss about one percent of aneurysms, and it seems inevitable that Mum would be that one. Moreover, several doctors have noted that the fact that she even required a drain in the first place implies the presence of the larger volumes of blood usually associated with an aneurysm.

So it is that at midday on what will transpire to be the hottest day of this heatwave summer, I am attempting to cross downtown Athens's busiest road whilst clutching an A2 envelope that is as heavy as it is unwieldy. Red lights and green men seem to count for nothing as the motorbikes and taxis race past so close to the kerb that they repeatedly make a sail of the precious envelope, pulling it from my hands with their slipstreams.

The envelope that I keep dropping is precious because it contains the original of every scan Mum has had since she first arrived at the hospital in Corfu. My destination is a specialist copy shop on the other side of the road, for a British expert on subarachnoid haemorrhage has agreed to provide a second opinion. A visiting cousin is flying back home tonight, and if I can only make these copies, she will have them in his eminent hands within forty-eight hours. Unfortunately, I am almost certain that the copy shop does not exist; there seems to be a rapid turnover of businesses in Athens, and none of the other five I found on the internet and have spent this morning searching for were still in operation.

There are six lanes of traffic, each of them moving at motorway speed. There is a pedestrian crossing, but each time the green man comes on I step out and am immediately met with a wall of blaring horns and on-rushing metal that forces me back to the kerb. Nobody else seems remotely interested in crossing this road, and, indeed, why would they need to when the copy shop on the other side is surely another hoax?

This, then, is my breaking point. For days now I have been wondering when it would come, and I now have my answer. For the past eighteen months I have held it together as best I knew how through all the unfolding chaos. I have waited and endured. I have begged and I have prayed to gods I have not believed in since I was eight years old. I have told news to people who should never have to hear it. I have written my twenty-seven-year-old brother's eulogy. I have visited the places he and his beloved last stood on this earth. I have laboured in the tropical heat. I have writhed in hospital with fever. I have discussed my mum's chances of survival as dispassionately as if she were nothing more to me than a name on a whiteboard at three o'clock in the morning.

I have managed it all, but now this road has me beaten. I cannot cross it and, more than that, there is no point in crossing it for a shop that does not exist and a mother who will clearly never make it home anyway. Another passing bus plucks the envelope from my hand and when it falls to the gutter, spilling images of Mum's brain and pirate teeth here and there, I do not bother to pick it up but simply sit down on the kerb, broken, alone and feeling so very far from home.

It is then that my phone starts to ring, an international call that is no doubt Mum's insurance company seeking their daily update on the nothing that has happened since I spoke to them yesterday. More accustomed to dealing with the broken legs of skiers and the occasional cruise ship heart attack, I have lately started to suspect that the main purpose of their calls is to see if Mum has yet passed away so that they can call time on the account.

But the voice on the other end is Carol, and then it is Toy, and then it is Ben. They are calling from the bar beside the garden at the end of the beach, where tonight the sun has already started to go down and even right now the reggae music is drifting out across the water. They talk to me about all the happiest nothings we know: old jokes and stories retold, bird nok birds and toothpick toucans, Ben's latest building project. Carol tells me that yesterday they all sat silent in the memorial garden and sent some luck our way; she says that she does not know how long the karmic post between Thailand and Greece takes, but thinks it ought to be reaching us soon. We speak for an hour and as we do, a curious thing happens: the buzzing motorbikes become longtail boats, the downtown tall buildings limestone karsts, the scorching black pavement the cool shaded square of grass at the far end of Loh Dahlum Bay.

When I hang up the phone I am restored. With the help of these friends I have made it through impossible things in the past, and I will do so again today. I retrieve the envelope, gather up the scattered sheets, and at the next green man I walk out into the traffic which parts for me like a biblical sea. The shop is precisely where the internet said it would be, can make my copies whilst I wait, and I am back at the hospital in time for our afternoon appointment.

But in the intensive care corridor, things quickly take

another turn for the worse. The resident is seeing the relatives today, and the security guard instructs us to return in an hour because she has asked to see us last. From experience, we know that this means only bad news: a rise in Mum's white cell count, a spike in her temperature or perhaps now – given how long this has all been going on for – something much worse.

Sure enough, when we eventually enter the stuffy little room, her face is lined with worry. Mum's white cell count and temperature have remained relatively settled, but as of this morning she has started to pass litres of water. The resident admits that this is a little outside her own clinical experience but tells us that she is gravely concerned. For weeks they have been warning us daily that if a problem develops with Mum's kidneys, the prognosis will become exponentially grimmer; this, she says, would seem to be exactly that problem.

I have to restrain myself from hugging her. A long-term intensive care patient suddenly passing a great deal of water is a sign almost as reliable as any in clinical medicine, and it does not mean that there is any problem with Mum's kidneys. On the contrary, it means that Mum is about to get better. In the systemic inflammatory response syndrome vast amounts of the fluid that ought to be in our veins spills into our tissues; doctors desperately run in more fluids to replace this in an attempt to keep the blood pressure up, but this is akin to trying to fix a breach in a levee not by repairing it but by pouring more water into the sea. A body getting rid of this excess fluid is a sign that a decision has been made to live, that the cytokines have ceased their screaming, that a human being is ready to re-engage with the world on their own terms. It means thank you for all your efforts, your toxic antibiotics and your uncomfortable breathing machine, but I am going to be taking things from here. This is the moment when I know that Mum is going to make it.

After this, things start to happen quickly. Mum's white cell count and temperature rapidly drop to normal and remain there. The doctors turn off her sedation and she begins, slowly, to wake up. One fine morning she opens her eyes independently and is stepped down to the high dependency unit, a halfway house on the road to full parole. Our expert in Britain confirms that the scans show a non-aneurysmal bleed, and a day later two men in flight suits arrive on the ward wheeling the most expensive-looking stretcher I have ever seen.

Now it is our turn not to stop for red lights as a wailing ambulance carries us through the streets of Athens. At the airport, a polished silver jet that looks a lot like the one Professor Xavier flies in the X-Men films awaits us; inside, it is better equipped than many hospitals. Our journey lasts three and a half hours and I sleep for every single minute of it.

In Edinburgh it is already autumn and the cool breeze on the runway feels as welcome as a turned-over pillow on a hot night. Hearts are this evening hosting AEK Athens and in the day room of Mum's new ward I glimpse moments of the match in which our best player gets sent off and we concede an injury-time winner. For tonight, the result barely registers and I only find myself hoping that my friend and his son who was hurt in a motorcycle accident have also made it home and are watching this match too.

As the second anniversary of the tsunami approaches, I make plans to return to Thailand. Friends and colleagues who hear that I am going back take me aside and tell me that it must be difficult, that I am brave, that they will be thinking of me. Quickly I learn that if I tell them the truth – that I can barely wait to get back to the place that feels so curiously like home – they will simply not believe me.

Mum is recovering rapidly but not yet up to the trip, and this winter I have a new travelling companion. Caroline was Dominic's university flatmate and perennially close confidante; it was Caroline who phoned us on that first Boxing Day morning, who gave the first reading at Dominic's funeral, who inscribed candles for Mum to light in Thailand on the first anniversary. For some time now we have been aware of an increasing chemistry between the two of us, but our shared instinct has been to avoid it, to deny it, even occasionally to run from it. Caroline and Dominic's relationship had always been entirely platonic, but we have both felt that it ought to be left undisturbed; dead people do not have the chance to make new friendships, and we would seem to have the whole wide world in which to find romance.

That, anyway, had been our unspoken understanding. This autumn, however, our own feelings have become impossible to ignore and so it is that we now travel to Thailand not just as two people who loved Dominic, but as a couple ourselves. Their friends tell us that they are happy for us, and that they think Dominic would be too.

On Phi Phi we tend the garden, lay our flowers and launch our khom fai, and then on our way home we stop off in Bangkok. There, we walk through the crowded Khao San Road to the New Siam guesthouse, the last standing building where Dominic and Eileen rested their precious heads.

It is another station of the cross, another bungalow A12, but it is also a workaday hostel: clean rooms with fan, shared bathroom, weekly rates available. A radio plays in the bar downstairs and with the bottles of beer lined up in the glass fridge and the people greeting each other as they come and go, it seems like it would have been an easy place to pass a day or two. Still, if it is pleasing to imagine Dominic and Eileen here, it is not the reason I had wanted us to visit Bangkok. Jim Thompson, an American expatriate who disappeared almost forty years ago, is the reason I had wanted us to visit Bangkok.

Inevitably, it had been Uncle Bob who had first told me about Jim Thompson: Uncle Bob, who himself had been a traveller and an expatriate, who had sat in the backstreet bars, smoking his roll-up cigarettes whilst listening to and telling the tales that keep the guesthouses full; Uncle Bob, who had a desk drawer full of old passports, the pages bursting forth with colourful stamps, a corner of the front cover snipped from each of them.

And Southeast Asia was not the only place Uncle Bob had heard the story. There is a Jim Thompson in Kinshasa, in Guatemala City, in Vanuatu: a man in a white linen suit who one day vanishes and is never heard from again. The name and the place may change, but certain plot points remain inviolable: the silver cigarette case left on a chair, the cup of tea forever steaming on a table. Such a story is an explorer's inheritance, passed down not merely on the tongue, but also in the blood. It is both a threat and an incitement to the adventurers of this world, a warning and a promise that it could happen to any one of them, and at any time.

In his Bangkok heyday, the soirées that Jim Thompson held at his celebrated canal-side home were considered the highlight of any trip to Thailand. If you had been short-sighted enough to arrive in the city without a letter of introduction then either you went to the Jim Thompson Silk Company shop on Soi Surawong and bought scarves and dropped hints until you hopefully no longer needed one, or you perhaps had a second name – Beaton, Capote, Merman – that was itself an invitation.

These days Jim Thompson's house is a popular tourist attraction and significantly easier for the unconnected to enter. Caroline and I gain access to his famous home simply by purchasing a pair of one hundred baht tickets, taking off our shoes and waiting for one of the hourly tours to begin.

But did Dominic ever visit? Certainly he too would have heard of Jim Thompson from Uncle Bob, and no doubt the story would have intrigued him. Had he needed any further reason to take a tuk-tuk across the city, he surely would have had a professional interest in seeing a house universally acclaimed to be a masterpiece of traditional Thai architecture.

Yet I cannot remember Dominic ever talking about it, and for that reason alone I can be certain that he did not go. If Dominic ever glimpsed so much as a doorway he liked, he would be sure to describe it to you in intricate detail; if he saw a noteworthy building, well, you knew you were going to be on the telephone for a while. No, my brother spent at most a handful of days in that eastern city of angels, and on each of those he would have been either recovering from a long flight or preparing to undertake another one. Perhaps, then, like so many other jetlagged or sun-kissed travellers, he did not get much further than his pleasant guesthouse court-yard.

But that makes me a little sad, for Dominic would have been fascinated by Jim Thompson's house and, more self-ishly, I would have liked to hear what he had to say about it. Certainly he would have appreciated the fact that it is not really a house at all but rather an amalgam of six houses, each antique component handpicked in the distant countryside and here fused together to make a dwelling somehow more resplendent than the sum of these already precious constitu-ent parts. And no doubt my superstitious brother would have comprehended, too, the prophecy seemingly implicit in its setting: built on a particularly verdant piece of land, the house's red-stained teak stands out against the surrounding foliage bright as blood freshly spilled in the jungle.

When it came his turn to disappear, Dominic left a home behind too: the one-bedroom flat in Edinburgh that he and Eileen had bought a month before the tsunami. On the late November weekend that they took possession, they had excitedly shown us around before we went for dinner at the restaurant on St Mary's Street.

It was a wreck. The flat's last occupant, an elderly lady, had moved to a nursing home a year previously and the property had lain dormant since then. Junk mail clogged the letterbox, patterned carpets swirled over sagging floorboards, and the grease-splattered kitchen was a graveyard of condemned appliances.

When Dominic and Eileen looked at it, they did not see these things. They saw opportunity and the chance to put Dominic's years of training into practice. They saw white walls and pure lines, clean sanded floors and restored period features. Their enthusiasm for this next stage of their life was visceral and infectious, and somehow after fifteen minutes of being there with them, we started to see these same things too.

Jim Thompson was also an architect. He did not complete his postgraduate studies, but he was a Princeton alumnus with a patent talent and a contacts book to match. During the 1930s he practised up and down the eastern seaboard of the United States, designing summer houses for the society families amongst whom he had been raised.

It was a pleasant and productive decade, but in 1941 Jim Thompson felt the call to service and enlisted in the army. When he first arrived in Thailand then, a few weeks after V-J Day, he did so as a soldier in a war that was already over. He was forty-one years old, spoke no word of the language, and had a young bride waiting for him back in America; Bangkok itself remained full of disgruntled Japanese troops, and yet it did not take him long to fall in love with the place. After only nine months in the country, Jim Thompson went back to the United States to receive his military discharge and ask his wife to move to Bangkok with him. She declined, and they divorced.

Returning to Thailand alone, Jim Thompson moved into Bangkok's Oriental Hotel and joined a consortium seeking to restore the establishment to its previous state of grandeur. For preceding decades, Bangkok had been the crossroads at the centre of the world and the hotel, which had been desecrated by the billeted occupying army, had once been as opulent and celebrated as any on the planet.

A quarrel with one of his partners meant that Jim Thompson's involvement in the scheme ultimately proved short-lived, but this does not seem to have been much of a setback for anybody. The Oriental quickly flourished and today it is a grande dame again, with a rate card to match; Jim Thompson continued to reside at the hotel and now discovered the vocation that could truly serve as a counterpart for his love of the country. Learning that the traditional Thai craft of hand-spinning silk had all but died out, the task he set himself was the resurrection of this once proud industry.

Using his connections in the United States, he first lined up buyers in the worlds of American interior design and fashion and then he went out and raised an army of weavers in the backstreets of Bangkok and the silken heartlands of north-east Thailand. Most of his craftspeople had long since abandoned the only trade they had ever known, but Jim Thompson supplied his employees with the materials and dyes that they required to start practising their timeless skills anew.

If this sounds a singularly ambitious undertaking, the project swiftly met with the kind of success that would ultimately make the Jim Thompson Silk Company as much of a Bangkok institution as the Oriental itself. As the orders arrived from hoteliers, film producers and even royalty, Jim Thompson further established himself in Thailand by building his Bangkok house; here he hosted his nightly parties and between his business and social lives he rapidly became known as the most famous *farang* in Southeast Asia. 'Farang' is a Thai word that approximates to 'foreigner', but Jim Thompson's celebrity was nevertheless closely intertwined with the country that he had adopted: when *Time* magazine profiled him in 1958, they did so under the headline 'The Silk King of Thailand'.

What is this thing that calls us to Thailand, that calls us there and then makes us fall so irrevocably in love with her?

It is unique for each of us, of course – it is a sunset, or the sewer-stink of a rainy afternoon, or the sight of a sea eagle circling a limestone cliff – and yet in another way it is all exactly the same thing; it must be the same thing, because it happens to every one of us. It happened to Jim Thompson, and it happened to Uncle Bob; it happened to Dominic and, despite the grief that first took me there, it happened to me too.

What I think now, more or less, is this: nobody goes to Thailand without falling a little in love. You hear it in the sighs of the departing travellers in the airport lounges; you sense it when you sit down beside them on the overnight coaches, where they lay their heads against the windows but do not sleep; perhaps most of all, you see it in the glaze that gets in their eyes in the bars under the stars when evening segues into night and candlelight starts to flicker on bamboo.

For some visitors, it quickly runs deeper still. Even after his first nine months in Thailand, Jim Thompson could not have gone home to live in America. How could he, when he already was home? That vast, free land across all those oceans was by now no more than a country he had once known, a place where the summers were hot and the winters were cold and at five o'clock architects left their offices to catch the railroad out to the suburbs.

Home now was here. It was the light on the klongs at dusk, the dogs in the marketplace, the reek of durians in November. The bond Jim Thompson shared with the place he knew as Siam had already gone beyond mere love or infatuation – whatever the thing it had been was, whatever abstract noun you wish to name it with – and had become the most pro-found thing a person can hope to feel: a sense of belonging.

It creeps up on us, the feeling that we should be there, that the people we see in our European supermarkets, in our

North American malls, are not the ones that we are most like, not the ones we want to be most like. We want to talk in the singsong, move with the gentle grace, and know instinctively how to balance three young children in front of us on a moped. Only duty or industry has dragged us away from this place we now live in our hearts, and we yearn for it daily: we pin unwritten postcards to the walls of our workday cubicles, dine in inauthentic restaurants just to hear the waiters' unintelligible melodies, and count the days until a parade of planes will return us to the place where we feel that we ought to be.

Back in Thailand, once we have spent more than a little time there – long enough that friends and acquaintances greet us in the street, that we now know the words for 'food' and 'room', for 'shower' and 'milk' – we even begin to let ourselves think that we have finally started to achieve it, that we are now somehow less alien than those unfortunate enough to still be wielding rucksacks and communicating entirely in English.

I have felt as Jim Thompson did. Pushing my cart back through town from the pier with Mon, calling out our greetings to the people we pass. Eating monk's rice in the morning or drinking coffee at dawn with Ben and the men who are all his cousins. Repeating my dozen words of Thai over and over again, as if they would, if I only say them often enough, coalesce into an entire language, as if they would somehow carry me straight to the innermost sanctum of the impossible temple that is Siam.

As they found it, Dominic and Eileen's new flat in Edinburgh had a kitchen in the back, a bedroom in the front and a pair of storage cupboards between the two: adequate accommodation for a single old lady living alone, but hardly ideal for a young couple who liked to have their friends over as often as possible.

With Eileen visiting her grandmother in Hong Kong, Dominic had worked on his drawings late each night through the first weeks of December. His earliest private commissions had all been similar conversions for the starter properties of his friends, and by now he was something of a master at maximising the potential of the humble Edinburgh tenement. His design for their own home seemed simple but effective: the bedroom would be moved to the back, the brighter room at the front would become the living room, and the large cupboards between them would be knocked together to form an internal kitchen that a fenestrated wall would simultaneously render part of – and yet distinct from – the living space. Finishing the plans the night before he left for Thailand, he printed and packed a copy to show Eileen.

A plethora of Buddha and Bodhisattva images. Screens silk-painted with feudal scenes. An ancient Chinese mouse house. A family of North American diplomats who insist on pointing out the similarities between each object and one they saw in Vientiane or the Chicago Institute of Art. Mostly, though, what Caroline and I see inside Jim Thompson's house – rather, what we feel – are ghosts. A chair that Somerset Maugham once sat in. An empty wicker bird cage wherein Thompson's pet cockatoo lived. The spirit house where untold generations of stray cats have eaten the offerings. And, above all and transcending everything, the shape and feel of a man who disappeared almost forty years ago.

Were he still alive, Jim Thompson would be a hundred now, bent double with arthritis from his wartime exertions, spluttering with emphysema from his unfiltered cigarettes, and yet his house still patently expects him to walk through the door at any moment. 'Home is so sad,' as Grandma's Larkin has it, 'It stays as it was left,/Shaped to the comfort of the last to go.' We pause in Jim Thompson's bedroom, let the tour drift ahead of us. We feel like intruders and perhaps that is exactly what we are.

At the end of the tour we wait our turn then collect our shoes, lace them up as quietly and slowly as we can, but still find that we do not know what to do with ourselves. Feeling as misplaced as the noisy diplomats seemed in the silently heartbroken house, we run our hands through the smooth silks in the Jim Thompson Gift and Souvenir Shop and pick at plates of too-perfect pad thai in the Jim Thompson Restaurant. We sit in the courtyard, disconsolate amongst its plants and ponds, and watch a puppet show written and performed to mark the anniversary of Jim Thompson's birth, a hundred years ago in a faraway country.

After they had died, we did not know what to do with Dominic and Eileen's new home. We walked around its dank and empty rooms, remembering the trouble they'd had finding it and the dreams they'd had for the house and the lives that they would live there. We recalled the plans Dominic had drawn up and Eileen's ideas on how they would decorate it. We agreed that the only practical thing was to sell it, but when the moment came we could not bring ourselves to do so. It was the last design that Dominic had worked on, his most personal, and it needed to be completed. I still had a little television money left for a deposit; we had it surveyed again, and I bought it from their estates.

A friend who had known Dominic carried out the building work for me. Back living in London by that time, I did not see the flat again until it was all but completed and walked in from the station one bright spring morning to find the home we had previously seen only through their eyes rendered perfectly solid: spotless walls, smooth floors, a period fireplace.

What neither the plans nor even their enthusiasm had been able to convey was how well the space would work. In practice, Dominic's design had made the flat feel double the size it was previously and his masterstroke – the fenestrated wall in the kitchen – provided precisely the right balance of light and concealment. If Dominic had not been blessed with Jim Thompson's address book, it was another reminder that he'd had no shortage of talent.

But there was something even more striking about the place, and that was that it missed them. They had never lived there, had likely not spent more than an hour in total there, and yet somehow its emptiness cried out for them: for their pots and pans in the kitchen, for their belongings in the cupboards, their coats and shoes in the hallway. Here, too, were ghosts.

Just as Dominic would later do, Jim Thompson boarded his last short flight at the old Don Muang Airport and vanished whilst he was supposed to be on a well-earned holiday.

He had travelled with friends to a cottage in the Cameron Highlands of Malaysia. The others in his party went for an afternoon nap, and when they woke up he was gone. They assumed that he had taken a walk and would return by suppertime, but he did not appear, and when his host drove down to the golf club at the end of the road there was no sign of him there either. They were sure he could not have gone far, however, because he had left a cup of tea on the table and the silver cigarette case in which he kept the medicine for his stomach ailment on his chair. Only when he had not returned by nightfall did they contact the police.

The search for Jim Thompson continued for days, and then months, and then years. Everybody lent whatever expertise they had – policemen with dogs, the local witch doctors, survey teams from the British Army – but nobody found anything. The Jim Thompson Silk Company offered an increasingly large reward, but this only caused more problems: the case had already been heavily publicised around the world and it now rapidly became the province of charlatans. One of these, an obese Dutch psychic called Hurkos, was even hired by the desperate Thompson family themselves. Emerging from a trance in which he seemed to speak in tongues, Hurkos claimed that Jim Thompson had been kidnapped and taken to Cambodia. Still nobody found anything.

Nobody found anything, but it is not entirely impossible that there was nothing to find. In its profile, *Time* magazine had asked Jim Thompson about his motivation for becoming involved with the silk trade. His response had been as simple as it was devastating. 'It disturbed me,' he had said, 'that production of this wonderful material had stopped.'

It is as noble a reason as one can imagine – what greater gift could a man give the country he loved than the preservation of its disappearing heritage? – but some commentators have raised the possibility that there might have been a little more to it than that.

Jim Thompson had indeed first arrived in Bangkok a soldier, but not a soldier in the conventional sense. He was OSS, the Office of Strategic Services, the organisation that would later grow up to be the CIA. In those early years it was a rather Baden-Powell affair, but the fact remains that Jim Thompson was a trained spy. He had operated behind enemy lines in France, and when word crackled through the radio of the Japanese surrender he was preparing to parachute into Thailand where he had been tasked with leading the liberation.

The Japanese surrender rendered that liberation unnecessary, but for the months between the end of the war and his discharge, Jim Thompson served as OSS station chief in Bangkok. It was a time of great intrigue, the first beginnings of the dark paranoia that two decades later would wreak such devastation across Southeast Asia. In the course of his duties, Jim Thompson necessarily cultivated many friends and contacts in the north-east of Thailand – particularly amongst the Vietnamese and the Laos – and more than one writer has suggested that his fledgling silk business might initially have simply been a convenient way to travel frequently to the region without arousing suspicion.

Everybody who has ever repeated the story of Jim Thompson has wanted to disappear, and I am no exception. In the darkest moments of my grief I have wanted to vanish, to walk into a jungle and never come back, to walk away from loss, from funerals and responsibility. Perhaps this much is understandable, but if I am entirely honest, I have known the feeling at other times too, and I had known it before I ever knew what a thing a tsunami could be.

In the months before that December, a friend and I collaborated on a screenplay based around the idea of disappearing. A man emerges unscathed from a rail disaster, hesitates for a brief moment, then tosses his wallet back into the burning carriage and walks past the onrushing sirens into a world in which he can be whoever he wishes. Initially we motivated our character to go missing by endowing him with a heavy burden of financial debt, but we quickly came to understand that such a plot device was not necessary.

We came to understand it was not necessary because we enjoyed writing the piece as much as anything either of us had ever done. Shorn of all duty and responsibility, our character could do anything that he liked: he could travel anywhere, talk to anyone, and take any job that he chose. He could, in short, reinvent himself in his own image, and we felt the thrill of absolute escape vicariously through him. When he stood at a crossroads and knew he could go left or right, a significant part of us wished that it was ourselves standing there; when other characters speculated about what had happened to him – what important thing had called him away – we imagined our own colleagues talking wistfully about us in such terms.

Only after the tsunami did I learn what a terrible thing it must actually be to disappear. To leave the words unspoken, the letters unposted, the shirts in the wardrobe and the books by the bed, pressed open at the place where you last put them down; it is not a form of heaven at all, but hell itself. The good thing is not to go missing, but to be found safe and well; the good thing is not to be able to disappear for ever, it is simply to be able to come home after work each day.

'Today almost every ship or plane that leaves Thailand carries Thai silk to some seventeen countries.' So wrote *Time* magazine in 1958, and it is the same on this today, except that the ships and planes now carry Jim Thompson's silk to far more than a mere seventeen countries.

Awaiting a flight home from Bangkok's gleaming international airport, the Jim Thompson Silk Company concession store is as unavoidable as the five hundred baht departure tax that Thailand levies upon all her guests. It sells a seemingly endless ribbon of silk – scarves and shawls, ties and cummerbunds – as if Thailand were a thing that could be bought, wrapped up in fine crepe paper and carried home, as if the greens and blues of her seas, the flickering lamps of her night markets, the cool of her afternoon rain, could be distilled into a duty-free package you purchase with a credit card.

Caroline and I do not buy anything, but sit silent in the departure lounge. Leaving Thailand always feels awful, and I know by now that there is nothing you can do to make it any better.

Back in London a few weeks later, I go to have lunch with Grandma and her friend Ishbel, who have come up to town for the day to visit the galleries.

I think that I am entertaining them with exotic tales of our trip to Thailand, when Ishbel lets it slip that she lived in Bangkok in the years after the Second World War and was an acquaintance of Jim Thompson.

I ask her what she believes happened to him, and she sighs gently. It is clearly a question that she has been asked many times before, and one that for her relates not to a tourist attraction or an airport gift shop but to a sad story involving a very real man.

'James,' she says, 'always had such a fondness for the ladies. A lot of us wondered if a woman – or perhaps her husband – wasn't somehow involved.'

It was not an answer I had expected. Exquisite taste, a wonderful host, a flair for entertaining, an eye for architecture, for fashion, for design, and a short-lived marriage; I had lazily half-assumed, as many had done before me, that Jim Thompson had been gay. The truth that he was not the character I had sketched in my head reminded me anew that this was not an apocryphal traveller's tale, but some family's real and private tragedy.

Yet over and again I have found myself telling people

243

about Jim Thompson. Sometimes I have found myself telling the same people twice, and sometimes they have asked why I am so interested in him.

'Because it's such a mystery,' is the answer I usually give, and one that seems to satisfy people.

'Because he was a talented architect who went to Thailand, fell in love with it and disappeared,' might be a more honest one. And yet 'Because he went to Thailand and never had to come home again' might be the most truthful one that I can give.

In 1987 a writer named Shannon Gilligan published a children's book inspired by Jim Thompson's disappearance called *The Case of the Silk King*. Part of the 'Choose Your Own Adventure' series that Dominic and I had loved when we were growing up, each chapter ends with a predicament, and you plot your own journey through the story by choosing one of several courses of action for your character to follow.

Perhaps it is a valid approach to an unsolvable mystery. If you like realism you choose to believe Jim Thompson was sixty-one years old, in declining health, and had an accident in harsh terrain; if you like anthropology, you choose to believe that he took up with one of the indigenous tribes that haunt the jungles of the Cameron highlands; if you like spies, you choose to believe he was lured back for one last mission that somehow went terribly wrong. Somewhere within it all you remember that there once lived a man called Jim Thompson, and maybe that is more than most of us can – or perhaps even should – hope for after we leave this world.

What I would like to believe – and what some nights still seems to make the most sense – is that he simply chose to walk away. That he did not want to be a farang any more, let alone the most famous farang in Southeast Asia. He wanted to belong entirely to his Siam, and so he walked off into the jungle on a northwestern bearing and challenged the country he so loved to take him as he was, and to do so for ever.

What would be Dominic's thirtieth birthday comes two years and three months after he died and falls on a day that is unequivocally the first one of spring. We have chosen to mark the occasion in a tattoo parlour in Edinburgh's old town; if from its couch you cannot see the spot where bungalow A12 stood, the establishment is only a short walk up St Mary's Street from the room where I sat with Dominic's coffin when it first came home.

Our tattooist is from Eastern Europe, his weapon of choice an oscillating gun rather than a splinter of bamboo, but the stencils he will use today have been posted over from Tattoo Bar. As in Thailand, music plays in the background and eager apprentices hover nearby. Our tattooist does not seem to have been drinking, but at two o'clock on a midweek afternoon this seems only a good thing.

Graham is first on the couch. A red-tagged Muay Thai fighter who gives himself daily injections for his diabetes, he is stranger to neither pain nor needles, and yet visibly suffers exquisite agony as he is tattooed. Neil goes next and, stoically grimacing at me from the chair, confirms that the procedure is indeed little short of torture.

But I am not scared now. Even all these years later Neil and Graham remain my big brother's pals, and in such company I am incapable of feeling apprehension, far less of showing it. When my turn comes I do not hesitate to take my place in the chair; as the tattoo artist fires up his gun I close my eyes and bite my bottom lip in anticipation of the impending hurt.

What I feel is a soft vibration that no more than tickles. Neil and Graham, who have been carefully winding me up all afternoon, fall about laughing. 'Should have seen your face!' they say. 'You closed your eyes and everything!'

When my tattoo is finished we hold out our arms to compare them. All three are the same word written in the letters of the Thai alphabet. Graham's tattoo is on his left arm, the one that he leads with in Muay Thai; Neil's is on his dominant right arm; mine is on my left bicep, as close to my heart as I could get it. Our tattooist advises us to smother them in emollient cream and keep them wrapped in clingfilm for the next twenty-four hours; if it sounds like first aid for a burn, that is exactly how the thing now feels.

And perhaps that is also what it is: a burn, a brand seared into the flesh. It is black ink placed beneath the skin, which turns blue down through the years but never disappears. It is a grown-up version of the pretend silver dog-tags we wore whilst playing soldiers when we were young, lest disaster does ever come calling again. It is all these things and it is something more besides. It is a pledge, a covenant made with ourselves and each other that says whoever we shall be tomorrow, wherever we shall go, and whoever shall be there beside us, we will always carry this today and yesterday with us. It is a promise made on the flesh of a person's body. Writ in the Thai alphabet on the occasion of his thirtieth birthday, ours say 'Dominic'.

People hearing my story for the first time often want to know if Dominic's body was ever recovered. A simple affirmative reply sometimes satisfies them, but more usually emboldens them to now ask the question that they would really like answered: do I know what physically happened to him, the actual mechanics of his demise?

'No,' I tell them. 'Not really.'

This is true enough now, but it has not always been; at least, I have not always accepted that I did not know. In those first years after the tsunami, I was adamant that I knew exactly how Dominic and Eileen's last moments had been: they had gone to bed, happy and a little tipsy on cocktails, and they had woken in the next paradise, the first wave having brought their bungalow down on top of them whilst they slept oblivious. They had never felt a thing, perhaps had even remained dry until afterwards when the water seeped through.

It had seemed to me as plausible an explanation as any, and that as much as anybody could reasonably hope for. In December in Phi Phi the temperature breaches thirty degrees before ten o'clock in the morning and there was simply no time for cataloguing, for noting where a body was found, what lay atop or nearby it. At most, bodies were numbered, swaddled in a sheet, and carried to the pier. Unless you were with your loved one when the water arrived, unless you were there to bear witness and somehow possessed the strength to dig their body out from beneath the debris with your own hands, you faced an inevitable dearth of information about their last moments on this earth.

No matter how much you try to resist it, the unavoidable human response is to turn detective. Late at night you study the internet forums where the survivors recount their experiences, peruse maps and photographs and gather from these whatever clues you think that you can. Lying awake in the small hours you formulate hypotheses and test them out against the known and the half-known facts until you reach an account of events that seems the most likely.

The case I assembled in my head went something like this: the numbers Dominic and Eileen's bodies were assigned were close and this meant that they had been found in proximity to one another; on the telephone they had told us that they were planning only a single nightcap, but it was Christmas and they were both sociable people; at home in Edinburgh they were late sleepers, and under normal circumstances at half past ten on Boxing Day morning it was entirely possible that they would still have been in bed. It followed, then, that the head injury with which Dominic was found must have occurred when their bungalow collapsed in on top of them whilst they slept contentedly late.

Except that it did not follow. There was a flaw in the evidence that broke my entire case wide open: Dominic was found with his wallet in his pocket.

Uncle Bob had smuggled this Exhibit A back from Thailand in early January. A simple fabric design, it had lain with Dominic's body in the heat and the damp until it too had now started to decompose. Even through all the layers of plastic Bob had wrapped around it we had still been able to smell the salt stench of rot; when the time came to open it, we had taken it outside to the workshop.

It had been the first tangible proof we'd had that Dominic was dead, the first piece of evidence that could not be discounted as circumstantial. Here, spilled out across Rob's sawdust-covered bench, were the fossils of the life that Dominic daily carried with him: some intimate, some random, all of them utterly my brother.

A single passport-sized photograph of Eileen. The card of a man who styles himself as Scotland's premier mind-reader. Two Bank of Scotland cards, one that bore his full name, another with the initials he liked to make use of wherever possible: DJ Stephenson. A flyer for a resort on Ko Samet that Graham had visited. A lucky dollar saved from a holiday Mum took us on four years previously. A telephone calling card, unused, to the value of five pounds sterling. A handwritten letter from Eileen, carefully folded into sixteenth-parts. One of Dad's business cards from his new venture in France. A single green Scottish pound note of a kind no longer in circulation.

So much to think about, to forever return to in the years to come, and yet the amateur sleuth in me that night had immediately focused on the fact that this wallet was fairly slim. I took this as further confirmation of what I so desperately wanted to believe: that it would have been possible for Dominic to fall asleep with this wallet in his pocket. Maybe they had been excited at being somewhere so special for Christmas, and maybe he had indeed had more than one or two Mai Tais; whatever the reason, when he came home he had fallen asleep with his wallet in his pocket, and there it had remained until he arrived in the next paradise. It would never stand up in front of a jury of our peers, but then it did not have to. It only had to stand up in front of a jury of me.

But not only would I not consider any other possibility, nor would I allow anybody else to. Mum said that sane people do not generally sleep the night with their wallets in their pocket, and quietly maintained that Dominic therefore had been at least up and dressed when the water arrived. I could not agree with her: if Dominic was up and dressed, he was awake. And if he was awake, he would have survived. He was, after all, young and fit and a strong swimmer.

Young and fit and a strong swimmer. Such were the things we had clung to in those first hours in the living room in Edinburgh as we waited for news. Dominic was young and fit and a strong swimmer. If there was a danger from water, and he was awake to meet it, he would have surely got both himself and Eileen out of trouble.

Except there would come a time when we would learn that being awake or being a strong swimmer did not really come into it. All it was about, ultimately, was luck: you chose one breakfast place that did good eggs and you survived, or you went to another famed for its banana pancakes and you did not.

Even as late as a year after the tsunami, though, I had remained certain of how things had been. At the inquest in Earl's Court I had sat and listened to the eyewitness accounts of other people's losses – the chaos, the confusion, the terror – and counted myself lucky to know that it had not been that way for Dominic and Eileen, that their passing had been so mercifully quick.

At which point, then, did I stop insisting to myself and others that people commonly sleep with their wallets in their pockets, or that Dominic might have drunk enough not to know the difference? Sometime after the first year, certainly, but it is hard to say with any greater precision, for there was no Columbo moment where it all clicked into place.

Considered logically, the wallet in his pocket means simply that Dominic was probably not asleep when the water

251

arrived. The two of them could still have been in the bunga-low, perhaps preparing to go out, or they may even have just returned from an early breakfast. It remains entirely possible, then, that they knew very little about the tsunami.

But there are other possibilities too, and as time has passed I have come to understand that I need to acknowledge them. Ten thirty in the morning is late in Thailand: the streets get noisy and the rooms get hot; however many drinks you drank and however high you crank up the air conditioner, it is difficult to sleep much past nine. It is more than possible, then, that Dominic and Eileen had already left their bunga-low by the time the water came. Dominic could have sustained his head injury in a multitude of ways, and the close numbers assigned to their bodies might be mere coincidence, or might simply suggest that the water carried them some-where together.

Why, then, did I persist for so long in insisting that they were asleep? Perhaps, as with my earlier misplaced faith in the casualty numbers, I was in the psychologists' cherished state of denial. Or, a little less simplistically, maybe we believe the things that we need to for the time that we need to, because sometimes it takes as long as it takes to come to terms with our most difficult truths. And yet the truth does always find us out in the end, builds a momentum until – like a wrongful conviction overturned decades later – we can simply deny it no longer. I can write these words now, but it has taken me a long time to accept them: I will never know what hap-pened at the end, but it is unlikely that Dominic's passing was as simple or as peaceful as I would like to believe.

It remains hard, though, this not knowing, this wondering. I show photographs of Dominic and Eileen to everybody I encounter who was there that day, but nobody ever recalls having seen them that morning. Whenever a new video clip of the tsunami surfaces on the internet, I look not at the on-rushing water but instead scan the fleeing crowds, pausing and rewinding, pausing and rewinding, in the forlorn hope of catching a glimpse of them. I never do.

Maybe I do not need to, because in my heart I already know enough about how it was. I know now that it likely would have been hard and that they likely would have been frightened, but equally I know that they would have been brave and strong, for that is the way they were. Perhaps more than anything else, I know that if there had been any way to survive, any way whatsoever, then they would have found it.

Towards the end of *The Big Sleep*, the greatest of all detective stories by the greatest of all detective writers, Raymond Chandler writes this of the departed:

> 'You were dead, you were sleeping the big sleep, you were not bothered by things like that. Oil and water were the same as wind and air to you. You just slept the big sleep, not caring about the nastiness of how you died or where you fell.'

I hope that he is right, that the dead do not know or care how they died, and I believe that he must be. But I know something else, too: that I do care, and that I must care. I owe it to them to bear witness and to sometimes think of them even in their final moments, to acknowledge that it would likely not have been easy or quiet, and that they would have been as scared as anybody would be in the same situation. Dominic's body was recovered from the sand and the water, the debris and the sun. Now when people ask me if I know what happened to him, I tell them no, not really.

Seven o'clock on an evening in early summer, and we are driving through Oregon's Willamette Valley. Today has been thirty degrees and glorious; as the sun slips down over the cornfields that stretch out west of us towards the Pacific Ocean, the whole world seems to be turning golden. Every mile takes us further from our already distant beds in the city of Portland, but we keep driving. We are making tonight for the town of Brownsville, a dot on the map in my guidebook where our long day's quest will at last be fulfilled.

Ostensibly, I have come to Oregon on holiday, to visit my old friends Paul and James. Really, though, this trip is more than just a vacation: it is another step in the resumption of a life, the first time since that December two and a half years ago that I have packed a suitcase for anywhere other than Thailand. As we continue south into the evening and the conversation turns to familiar and beloved insults about expanding waistlines and receding hairlines, I find that I am happier than I have been in a long time.

We had not planned to visit Brownsville and initially journeyed so far south only because James omitted to write down the location of a swimming hole he'd read about on the internet. Still, he had remembered its name – Three Pools – and had seemed to think that, if only we drove far and fast enough, it would somehow appear at the side of the freeway.

It had not appeared, but an hour south of Portland we had stumbled across a tourist information centre. The shelves inside were lined with leaflets advertising a multitude of nearby attractions, none of which were the Three Pools. Undeterred, James had asked the beehive-haired lady behind the counter for directions.

'I've been working here twenty years,' she had replied, visibly affronted, 'and I've never heard of any Three Pools.'

A man browsing nearby had heard a rumour of it, though, and thought it lay to the east, along the winding course of the Santiam River. Meantime, flicking through the leaflets, I had come across a sentence that stopped me cold and fixed our compass for the evening ahead.

'The town of Brownsville,' it said, 'is where much of the movie *Stand By Me* was filmed.'

A warning: the rest of this chapter will necessarily contain spoilers about *Stand By Me*, a film about a group of twelve- and thirteen-year-old boys who undertake a quest, first seen at a time when Dominic and I were twelve and thirteen and embarking on a quest of our own.

Still, I am not going to tell you half as much about the film as Dominic would have if it came up in conversation and you admitted to him that you had not seen it. Just as he could not let an interesting building pass unmentioned, if there was a film he loved, my brother would want to recount every detail that made it imperative you see it. Sometimes by the time he had finished telling you about it, you would feel as if you already had seen it.

It is a great movie, though. It is lovingly directed by Rob Reiner and its talented screenwriters won the Academy Award for their troubles, but the heart and soul of the thing are transplanted from 'The Body', the Stephen King short story from which it is closely adapted.

The four boys at the centre of the film – Gordie Lachance, Chris Chambers, Teddy Duchamp and Vern Tessio – are nominally on a mission to discover the body of a local teenager, Ray Brower, who has disappeared whilst picking blackberries. Really, though, the boys are out to find out about life: about family, friendship, love, the whole package; back in the Edinburgh suburbs, this was our quest too, only we lacked the body of Ray Brower to bring it into ninety-minute soft focus.

When we were twelve and thirteen, Dominic and I had an entirely algebraic relationship with the movies. Films came only from Hollywood, and were judged on nothing as unreliable as cast or director, but on one factor, and one factor alone: the minimum viewing age certificate they had been issued by the British Board of Film Classification.

Films rated '18' were the undisputed masterpieces of the oeuvre, cinematic triumphs to be savoured and, wherever possible, viewed repeatedly; the little red circles on the posters signified not a danger of moral corruption but inarguable awesomeness. Conversely, if a film lacked that talisman, it was very unlikely to be worth bothering with. Films rated '12', 'Parental Guidance', or – most heinous of all – 'Universal', were beneath even our contempt. If other people mentioned them in our company, we simply pretended not to know what they were talking about.

We were by no means alone in doing so. All over the city, boys our age were in similar thrall to that little red circle. Whenever we encountered one another, our mutual first question was inevitably the same: 'So how many eighteens have you seen then?'

Our problem was that we had barely seen any. With their gratuitous violence, their guns and their colourful language,

18-certificate films were anathema to Mum and therefore utter contraband to us.

Inevitably, this only made us covet them more. At Dominic's new school, a boy with a pair of video recorders and inattentive parents was making himself a small fortune dealing pirate cassettes, and in this way had we recently obtained the canonical treasures *The Punisher* and *The King of the Kickboxers*. When our parents went out we watched them until the tapes wore thin, knowing even as we did so that we would never be able to satisfy our cravings: after even those first two meagre hits, we were utterly addicted.

Like all addicts, we spent most of our time thinking up new and more ridiculous ways to obtain our drug of choice. We set the timer on the video to record the television premiere of the horror film *Omen* and prayed that our parents would not notice when it clunked into action during the ten o'clock news. We arranged complex swap deals with other, equally addled neighbourhood boys, suspiciously leasing out our already almost unwatchable copy of *The King of the Kickboxers* in exchange for a version of *Nightmare on Elm Street* that had clearly been taped from the back row of a cinema. We tried everything we could think of but, after a while, we knew that we could not continue to ignore the video shop in Colinton village.

If we were addicts, it was a pharmacy. A bright, shining pharmacy, with a window filled with shimmering bottles of the morphine we craved. All those precious little red circles, right there in the heart of our suburb. They felt like our birthright.

Although the story proper takes place in the late fifties, a framing device means that *Stand By Me* opens and closes in the present day of the time in which the film was made: 1986.

257

In the opening scene, a forty-something man sits in a Land Rover, writing in a notebook as he looks out over an autumnal Oregon field.

'I was twelve going on thirteen,' his voiceover intones, 'the first time I saw a dead human being.'

Later, we will realise that this man is a grown-up version of Gordie Lachance, first among equals of our four main characters. Grown-up Gordie's voiceover drops in and out throughout the movie, and thus it is through the prism of his bittersweet nostalgia that we view the seminal events of young Gordie's life.

Young Gordie is a writer; rather, he is a twelve-year-old boy with a head full of stories who dreams of growing up to be a writer. For now, life in the small town of Castle Rock is excruciatingly hard for Gordie: his adored older brother Denny has recently been killed in a car crash, and the loss has turned the family home into something close to a mausoleum. If that sounds a touch movie-maudlin, Gordie's situation is worse still: Denny was the only one who ever showed any belief in his writing – and ergo him – and Gordie suspects that his parents believe that the wrong son died.

As we meet the rest of Gordie's gang, we quickly learn that each has his own sorrow to contend with, each is his own Tin Man or Scarecrow: Chris Chambers hails from a rotten family, Teddy's father is a shell-shocked veteran who once held Teddy's ear to the stove, and Vern is overweight and bungling.

The four boys come to know where the body of Ray Brower lies when Vern overhears his older brother Billy talking to his friend Charlie about having seen it whilst they were out joyriding. The alleged resting place is over twenty miles away, a journey that will take our young heroes two days to walk and guarantee at least Chris Chambers physical punishment, but they cannot resist the adventure. What ensues is a paean to male friendship, a hymn to the joys of boys insulting each other, a Y-chromosome symphony set to the storybook background of rural Oregon.

On leaving the freeway the road had narrowed and the country turned to the familiar landscape that the *Stand By Me* boys do so much of their hiking through: the same tall pines, the same sun-dappled glades. As we kept our lookout for the Santiam River, I half expected 'Lollipop', a 1950s doo-wop song that plays in the film, to crackle through on our radio.

After a dozen miles, James stopped the car and triumphantly announced that we had arrived at the Three Pools. None of us had managed to spot the river, but a nearby parking lot overflowed with cars and even from up on the road we could hear splashing. Gathering our towels, we hurried down the path to the water.

Geographically it was indeed a good location: clear, slow and deep, with a sudden drop off that meant you could completely submerge yourself without first having to walk a long and chilling way out. At least, you would have been able to do so were it actually possible to get anywhere near the water. The swimming hole was already full of people and dozens more lined the riverbank in an impatient queue. Worse, we were visibly short of two pools. This was not the place we had been looking for.

The letter was Neil's idea, and his plan was as simple as it was audacious.

Telling his mum that the officious staff at the video shop had started denying him even the 12-rated films that were by then his legal entitlement, Neil had asked her to write them a note giving them permission to rent him such movies.

259

Twenty years later, I can still see her letter clearly: the blue ink on thick cream paper, the inarguably maternal signature at the bottom of the page, and the singularly perfect stroke of penmanship with which Neil had gently corrected her 12 to an 18.

It was an ingenious idea and it ought to have been our passport to a land of endless violence. When it rained, however, as it did torrentially throughout that summer we were twelve and thirteen, the border remained firmly closed. The video shop was too crowded with neighbours to risk using our priceless letter, and, anyway, the endless downpour left holidaying teachers like Mum every bit as housebound as we were; even if we could have discreetly obtained a film about a soldier of fortune now fighting the private army of a South American drug lord, we would have had no safe house in which to watch it. No, when it rained, there was really nothing we could do except stare out of the window and lament the parade of destruction we could right then have been watching had the Scottish summer not so cruelly conspired against us.

'Have gun, will travel' reads the card of a man
A knight without armour in a savage land
As they walk, the four boys sing the theme tune to 'Have Gun – Will Travel', a television series about a gentleman cowboy trying to make an honest way in a dishonest world. It is an apt choice, for our young heroes' journey is fraught with danger: there are trains to dodge, monstrous dogs to outrun and leech-filled swamps to wade through. Worst of all, there is Ace Merrill and his band of hoodlums.

As played by Kiefer Sutherland, Ace Merrill is a bleach-haired switchblade-wielding pool hall villain of the first order. We first encounter him early in the film, when he steals a cap that Denny gave Gordie. Chris responds by calling Ace an asshole and finds himself immediately wrestled to the pavement; when Chris refuses to retract the slur, Ace comes perilously close to extinguishing a cigarette in his eye.

As our young heroes undertake their journey, the action frequently cuts back to Ace and his gang. Each time we encounter them they are undertaking an exploit more wicked than the last: they tattoo each other, they play mailbox baseball, and, in a horrifying game of chicken, they even run a logging truck off the highway. As the tension builds – and Ace's cronies Billy and Charlie glance at each other every time the news bulletins on the radio in his Cadillac mention the missing Ray Brower – we are left in no doubt that Ace's gang will eventually catch up with our young protagonists, and that there will be trouble when they do.

Back in our own car, we continue along the road that winds above the Santiam. It is now approaching late afternoon, four or five o'clock, and under the thick forest canopy the heat of the day already feels to be dissipating. The clock on the paradise promised by the Three Pools is ticking down.

As we drive, we catch glimpses of the silvery river below, but nothing that resembles another swimming hole, let alone three of them. At one point we pass a pair of mailboxes so beautifully weathered we have to reverse back to them. Ace Merrill's gang would have smashed them with a baseball bat, but we merely photograph them with our digital cameras then compete to see who has taken the best shot.

A few miles further up the road we start to notice cars parked in the ditches, one or two at first, but soon they are nose-to-tail. Decades old and fifteenth-hand, they sport bumper stickers that proclaim the names of rock bands and minor league baseball teams. These, we decide, are surely the cars of Three Pools folks, people who will travel the extra mile to find the sweetest spot. The fact that there is no obvious access point must simply be a deliberate strategy to help preserve the Three Pools' mystique.

Hopping over a fence, we clamber and slide down a muddy embankment that brings us out at a shallow and deserted stretch of the river. Paul and I look to James, our thoughts idly drifting to all the abuse we must now give him for messing today up so spectacularly, but he is already wading downstream. We do not have to follow him far before we too hear the sounds that are drawing him on: laughter, and the torrent of waterfalls.

We see the young people as we come around the corner. There must be a hundred of them, an entire high school graduating class drinking beer in the late afternoon and throwing themselves off the twenty-five-foot rocks into a deep pool below. Part of us wants to rush over and beg them not to, to warn them that alcohol, high rocks and deep water are a deadly combination, but we do not say a word: they think they are young and invincible and, for today anyway, such belief will provide all the protection they need.

We maintain a respectful distance and nod a courteous hello, and yet they still regard us strangely. Suddenly it hits us: all three of us turning twenty-nine within the next month, our skin pale from strip-lights and flabby from eating out whenever we like, we look ancient to them; we think they are our peers, our younger brothers and sisters, and they think we are their grandparents.

So it goes, of course, so it goes: yesterday we were Gordie Lachance and Chris Chambers, and last night we were drinking beer and throwing ourselves into deep pools and tomorrow we will all be thirty and some of us will be gone for ever.

Besides, they are right: we should not be here. It looks a private party and, more than that, here again there is only a single pool. This, too, is not the place we have been searching for.

On the way back to the car, walking up the wide path we had somehow failed to spot on the way in, James claims that he overheard some of the high school kids discussing the mystical Three Pools. We tell him that he was hallucinating, that all the sun and the driving have gone to his head, but he is adamant that he can now find it from the things he heard them say.

If Gordie Lachance is *Stand By Me*'s Luke Skywalker – an earnest, centre-frame truth-seeker – his best friend Chris Chambers is its Han Solo, a broodingly handsome hero with a past. Chris is played by the late River Phoenix, acting with an intensity and passion that at moments make you wonder if he is even acting at all.

If Chris's troubles seem to have commenced with the simple fact of his low birth, his personal stock has been further diminished by an episode at school which the town appears to have taken as proof of the genetic character flaw of which they were all anyway already certain.

'He stole the milk money,' Gordie's dad tells him, 'and that makes him a thief in my book.'

Gordie protests his beloved friend's innocence – male friendships may be built on mutual denigration, but woe betide anybody outside the circle who chances their hand at it – but we later learn that the truth is a little more complex than Gordie would have liked to believe. Admitting the theft over a campfire as the movie approaches its climax, Chris reveals a surprising postscript to the incident.

'Maybe I took it to Old Lady Simons and told her,' he says,

'And the money was all there. But I still got a three-day vacation because it never showed up. And maybe the next week Old Lady Simons had that brand new skirt on when she came to school.'

The proof of Chris's tale lies not in Gordie's recollection of their teacher's new skirt but in the fury manifest in Chris's eyes as he recounts the injustice. It is a devastating moment, the last glass cola bottle of youthful optimism shattering in celluloid slow motion against the hard brick wall of adult cynicism. You want to somehow reach into the screen, to hug young Chris Chambers and tell him it will be alright, life will get better, but you can't and, anyway, you know that it won't.

And now the puzzling part: as played by River Phoenix, Chris Chambers could have been Dominic's twin when he was twelve going on thirteen.

To be clear: I am not claiming that my brother looked a whole lot like the movie star River Phoenix. Whilst there were certain physical similarities between the two – both were boys of robust physique and of no more than average height, both had the same short fuzz of dirty-blond hair and both bronzed to the same late summer tone – it was not posters of Dominic that would soon wallpaper the bedrooms of every girl we knew. No, what I am saying is that in the film *Stand By Me*, the character of Chris Chambers – a twelve-year-old boy rendered flesh and blood by a prodigiously talented young actor – is uncannily like my brother Dominic was when he was twelve.

How to account for this? If in terms of simple physical appearance the most you could truthfully say is that they were not dissimilar, how can it be that I still get goosebumps every time I watch that film? How can it be that sometimes, lost in the film, or even just thinking about it, I find that I cannot honestly say where one boy finishes and the other begins?

Maybe a more concrete example will help. There is a photograph of Dominic at twelve years old, taken on the patio at the back of our house in Colinton. Crouched on the ground, he is painstakingly restoring a dilapidated racing bicycle that he has retrieved from a neighbourhood skip to replace one of his that has been stolen. The frame is already almost too small for his fast-growing body and whatever Dominic now does to it, however many more hours he spends stripping and painting and tightening and oiling, it will never last him more than a few months. If he only waited until Christmas – as I no doubt would have cynically done – our parents would have happily bought him a new bike, but even at that age, Dominic preferred to earn things rather than be given them. In that photograph, just as in the movie, he looks exactly like Chris Chambers.

But why should they be so similar? Dominic may not have been born with the troubles of Chris Chambers, but he did sometimes seem to have been born into bad luck. The stork might have dropped Chris Chambers on the wrong side of the tracks, but he dropped Dominic six weeks too soon; though easily survivable today, in the medical dark ages of 1977, six weeks represented an eternity of touch-and-go.

Dominic made it through, but perhaps his card was marked thereafter. He simply was not a lucky person. An obvious example is that by the age of twelve he'd had more bicycles stolen than the rest of the children in our neighbourhood put together. There are dozens more like that, and that is before you get anywhere near his Crohn's disease or the chances of being on Phi Phi on the day the tsunami arrived.

Yet what really united the two boys in this regard was not

so much the various misfortunes that befell them, but rather their reactions to them. Chris responds to the milk money incident by studying harder to prove the town wrong about him; when the surgeons had to remove a section of Dominic's bowel, he threw himself into Muay Thai and six months after being wheeled out of the operating theatre was fitter than he had ever been.

This precocious sense of character manifested itself in other shared ways too, and both boys would have sooner suffered a beating than cower to a bully. I have already written about Chris's early confrontation with Ace; for his own part Dominic received at least one broken arm wrestling older and bigger boys over matters of principle. Allied to this, they each had a healthy ambivalence for authority and a profound sympathy for the underdog: Dominic would never in a million years have stolen any milk money, but if he had known who did, he would not necessarily have turned them in.

A connection that always hits me hard, however, relates to writing. From the earliest days, Dominic took more pride in my fledgling writing career than even I could, celebrating my minor triumphs and soothing my innumerable failures. In *Stand By Me*, Chris takes up this mantle after Denny dies. 'You're gonna be a great writer someday, Gordie,' he tells him, 'You might even write about us guys if you ever get hard up for material.'

I did not grow up to be as great a writer as Gordie – nobody did, for Gordie grew up to be Stephen King – but I think Dominic would be proud that I am writing about him, just as he was rightly proud of that old racing bicycle when he finally got through with it. He painted it up yellow and purple and fitted it with an old-fashioned horn you could hear three streets away; for the short time it lasted him, it was the greatest bicycle any boy in our neighbourhood ever saw.

It was a day too wet even to cycle. We were fraught with boredom and the impending doom of a return to school in a week's time and Mum insisted on driving us to the video shop in Colinton village to rent a movie. We could not tell her why we did not want to go, and so tumbled into her car, consoling ourselves that she was a good sport and would at least vouch for us for a 15-certificate comedy that might have some good swearing in it.

Inside the shop, the rain beating our retreat on the window, we forlornly fingered the boxes of the red-circled movies we really wanted to rent. Over the years I have occasionally wondered which of us first held up the box with the photograph of the four boys on the front, but in Oregon I realised that it could only have been Mum. Dominic and I had both furtively checked it out several times in the preceding months, but neither of us could ever have actually suggested it.

It ought to have been an easy one. The boys in the film were ages with us, the blurb on the back promised a dead body, Corey Feldman – who plays the character of Teddy – had been our favourite in *The Goonies*, and we already knew Kiefer Sutherland from *The Lost Boys*, one of the few worthwhile fifteen certificates we had seen. It ought to have been an easy one, but *Stand By Me* was rated PG for Parental Guidance.

I am surprised we took it to the counter. I am surprised we let Mum pay them actual money to rent it, and I am most surprised of all that we took the cassette home and placed it in the machine. But we did all of that then sat, utterly engrossed, as the story worked its rites-of-passage magic upon us.

By now, the directions James thought that he had overheard were distant memories, and he was driving on instinct alone. He was certain Three Pools was around here somewhere, and we were going to find it if it took all night.

Turning off the blacktop, he started us up a track with a gradient steep enough to confuse even our hired car, the automatic transmission flicking restlessly between gears as if there were any ratio to suit an incline harsh as this one. As we carried on, up into the moonshine country, Paul quietly pointed out that every signpost we passed had been peppered with shotgun pellets.

When the boys do eventually find the body of Ray Brower, it initially seems an anticlimax: we do not see a corpse, but only a pair of white trainers protruding from under a bush. Even on that first rainy afternoon, however, this seemingly broken promise did not matter to us. We now had a new favourite film, and, perhaps emboldened by one of the movie's take-home messages – to never be afraid to be yourself – we did not care if every other boy in Edinburgh knew that our favourite film was rated Parental Guidance.

But can I claim it changed our sensibility? That we stopped choosing films on the basis of that little red circle, and instead began selecting arthouse classics from the foreign language section? Of course not. We lost Neil's letter around this time – confiscated by a sceptical clerk, or dropped from a bicycle on a windy day – but our appetite was not sated. And whilst you would have to find a clever psychologist to engineer a reliable test, I suspect that if today I was given the choice of seeing the same movie with a 15 or an 18 certificate, I would still pick the 18 every time.

Stand By Me did not need to show Ray Brower's body, because the real drama lies in the discovery's aftermath.

Almost as soon as the boys have located the body, Ace and his gang show up to usurp the glory that will come with finding it. Our young heroes boldly resist and here the film reaches its dramatic zenith: Ace pulls his switchblade, and yet Chris Chambers – more courageous than is good for him – still refuses to back down. The stand-off is resolved by Gordie but, in case you have not seen the film, I am not going to give away exactly how he does it.

Suddenly, as if it was the most natural thing in the world, as if we could not have missed it today if we had tried, we found ourselves at the Three Pools.

There was a sign to confirm we had arrived, but we did not need it, for the colour of the water visible through the trees had already informed us that we had reached our destination. This high in the forest it was green: a green of sunlight filtered through emeralds, a green of the deep jungle, a green of pastures beside still waters.

We lay down on the bank for a while, staring at the open, sunny sky and listening to the sound of the water. Then, recalling the high school kids, we took our own turn to leap from high rocks, felt the water burst through our nostrils, up through our sinuses, and perhaps into our memories and there our souls themselves. We were finally in the right place, and there were actually more than three pools: there were dozens of them, stretching up the mountainside as if, if you wanted to, you could swim all the way to heaven.

It felt like the promised land, but even as we were falling through the air to the cool green water, even as we were acknowledging James as the undisputed king of navigation, even as I was thinking how far I had travelled from a phone ringing on Boxing Day morning, we all three knew that we were not yet at our journey's end. Just as the quest of the boys in *Stand By Me* does not finish with the discovery of Ray Brower's body, nor would ours finish with the cool waters of Three Pools.

It takes the boys a solid night of hiking to make it back to Castle Rock, their fictionalised version of Brownsville, and they arrive just after dawn. It takes us two hours in the hire car, and we arrive just as the sun is finally starting to set.

Like all good movies, like all good art, *Stand By Me* resonates. It resonated with our lives as they were at twelve going on thirteen and, if anything, it resonated even more as I approached thirty; driving into Brownsville on a Saturday night, it felt closer than it ever had. Looking out the window, I kept expecting to see Vern lollygagging along the sidewalk or Old Lady Simons in her new polka dot skirt.

Because it is all there, just like in the movie. Here is the alleyway where Gordie and Chris test fire the pistol I was trying not to mention, here is the General Store and, though the sign we will take our photographs beside reads 'Brownsville Saloon', over there is the Castle Rock Pool Hall where Ace's gang waste their days.

Mostly though, here is the bridge at the end of the movie that marks the true and final end of the boys' quest. It is at this bridge – a handsomely practical affair in green-painted steel – that the boys bid their farewells. As they do so, grown-up Gordie narrates an epilogue that reveals his young friends' fates. Much of what has happened is satisfyingly predictable – Vern works for his parents, Teddy has spent a little time in prison and now does odd jobs – but the fate of Chris Chambers is as unexpected as it is true.

Chris Chambers, we learn, stuck with Gordie through school, made it to college and eventually graduated as a lawyer. A week before the time of narration, he intervened in an altercation in a fast food restaurant and was fatally stabbed.

As grown-up Gordie is telling us this, Chris Chambers, walking away over the bridge, is imperceptibly faded out; before you properly realise what is happening, he is gone. Even if you do not think of River Phoenix, who himself died devastatingly young, even if you do not sometimes mix up Chris Chambers with your own late brother, even if I have somehow now inherited an inability to simply say it is a great film about four boys who go on an adventure in the woods and you really should see it for yourself, it might still be the most heartbreaking thing you ever see in a movie.

The third anniversary of the tsunami comes and goes, and we see in 2008 in Phuket Town's Metropole Hotel.

The Metropole is a curious establishment: a twelve-storey superhotel in a grimy port town that attracts at best a handful of overnight tourists. At night she falls asleep to dream of slipping her breezeblock moorings and sailing on down the coast to join the Hiltons and Sheratons in Patong and Karon, but somehow it never happens.

In the dimly lit Lobby Lounge Bar, where impossibly tall Thai ladies swish gracefully past balancing trayfuls of cocktails on the elegant fingers of one hand, New Year's Eve is kara-oke night. On a dais only partially obscured by a Christmas tree fashioned of silver tinsel, a teenage Scandinavian tourist is performing 'My Heart Will Go On', the Celine Dion anthem from the film *Titanic*. She is accompanied in this endeavour by the resident house band which on this auspi-cious evening consists of a keyboard player in dark glasses and a tambourine-shaking ladyboy.

'My Heart Will Go On' is, if nothing else, a technically challenging song, and the impromptu trio engineer a fitting aural extravaganza. The young chanteuse hits enough of the right notes that each wrong one retains its punch, the lady-boy shakes her tambourine too close to the microphone, and the keyboard player enthusiastically punctuates the song with the splintering iceberg and mast-snapping sounds he has earlier programmed into his effects board.

At our table we huddle in a little closer and talk about

moving on somewhere, but the truth is that in Phuket Town there is nowhere much else to go and the drinks here are cheap and good as any that the swells are drinking down the coast. We order another round and toast the band.

My very first night in Thailand was spent in a Phuket Town guesthouse just down the street from the Metropole. Arriving in Bangkok in the late afternoon, Neil and I had immediately taken an evening flight south. Thailand was by far the most exotic place either of us had ever visited, and we were both more than a little green.

Even on the plane itself we had kept our traveller's cheques tucked inside our money-belts, checking them every few minutes lest a particularly foresighted and dextrous pickpocket had booked the seat behind us. On the drive in from the airport, our taxi driver stopped over a dozen times to introduce us to people he said were members of his immediate family; though they all had hotel accommodation, ferry tickets or elephant trekking tours to sell us, we had taken each of their photographs and earnestly told the driver what an honour it was to be meeting so many of his close relations.

When that night we went out to eat, the prices on the menu were so far removed from what we were accustomed to paying at home that we concluded we must be in a tapas situation and ordered half a dozen dinners each. Afterwards, as we attempted to walk off the kilos of squid and shrimp we had inadvertently consumed, a man approached us and asked if we wanted to buy some marijuana; instead of politely declining, we hurried back to the hotel, locked the door of our room behind us, and did not emerge until the next morning. I almost fell out of the tuk-tuk that took us to the docks, and then paid three times the going rate for the privilege. Greenest of all, I actually drank the ten-baht coffee on the ferry, and my heart palpitated all the way to the island.

The ferry docks and the airport: these are really the only reasons a traveller has to visit Phuket Town. On this final day of 2007, this is indeed why we are there, because Mum is to commence her journey home the next morning. Even with the boat ride from Phi Phi out of the way, it is a long way back to Edinburgh and by the time the teenage Swede delivers the last of her encores, Mum is already in bed.

Outside, through the Lobby Lounge's smoked-glass windows, I can see the clock tower which serves as Phuket Town's focal point. Around it, a crowd is beginning to assemble: teenage Thai boys and girls, dressed in freshly pressed jeans and T-shirts, in hair gel and jewellery; they smoke cigarettes, climb on and off each other's scooters, and wait for midnight.

Inside the Lobby Lounge, the keyboard player and the ladyboy welcome a new singer up from the audience, a Thai man who looks to be in his sixties but has quite possibly simply had a harder than average life. On New Year's Eve he is here alone, drinking neat whisky and chain-smoking cigarettes, and the lines on his brow seem a depth chart of troubles. He must have a degree of wealth in order to afford the Johnnie Walker the Metropole sells, but he is dressed simply: his shoes and trousers are in the country style, and his collared yellow T-shirt pays homage to the revered King.

Seemingly without need of instruction, the keyboard player starts an effect that sounds like falling rain, the ladyboy gently shakes her tambourine, and then this ordinary-looking man – with his glass of whisky in one hand, and the microphone paired with a cigarette in the other – opens his mouth and starts to sing. The musical scale used in Thailand has seven notes, but this singer uses only two of the most closely placed ones to hint at a melody, and requires no more than that. His song is the saddest and most profound sound that any of us in the Lobby Lounge have ever heard.

The lyrics are entirely in Thai, but whatever he may be singing of, it is pure and unadulterated heartbreak of a kind too acute to provide the soundtrack to any Hollywood movie. There are a dozen verses and the singer does not raise his head once, lest we see the tears we have all long since realised that he is crying. Halfway through, the keyboard player silences the falling rain effect and the ladyboy gently lays down her tambourine, but the man keeps singing.

Perhaps more really do die of heartbreak.

Earlier that day, on the short taxi ride from the docks to the hotel, I had picked up an English-language magazine from the seatback pocket. It was a publication aimed at visitors to Thailand, particularly those considering extending their stay. The cover promised *Entertainment, Lifestyle* and *Property* and bore a picture of a sunlounger on an invitingly empty beach. Inside, the adverts were predictable enough: language courses, beachside condominiums, and lawyers who specialised in circumnavigating Thailand's complex visa and property ownership rules. One particular advertisement, though, stood out.

At the top of the page, across a background of autumnal sunlight filtering through a glade of magnolia trees, the words 'For when life is unpredictable' were scrolled in the gentlest of fonts. Beneath a small sepia headshot of an avuncular-looking Australian, a series of bullet points pledged such benefits as 'Detailed knowledge of individual nations' requirements' and 'Qualified foreign embalmers with disaster experience'. The advertisement was for a firm of inter-national undertakers who specialise in the repatriation from Thailand of the tourists who die during their stay.

At the end of a year, on a bright sunny day of hotel drinks and promises for the future, it was a stark reminder: Thailand may be a magic kingdom, but it is not Disneyland. Even with the stillest of seas, the simple truth is that not everybody who steps off a plane in Suvarnabhumi Airport will get back on to one, at least not by walking down the jetway.

People arrive in Thailand from far away and they have a drink and they sit in the sun and they somehow come to believe that because they are so happy, because they are having so much fun, nothing too bad can happen to them here. They climb aboard overloaded boats, they rent scooters and drive them fast without wearing helmets, and they find themselves having public arguments with people to whom loss of face is a mortal insult. They take strange and potent drugs and they go scuba diving then board planes without having allowed themselves adequate time to decompress. They pay to have their picture taken petting a tiger and tell themselves that if it was not safe then they surely would not be allowed to do it. Sometimes they simply sleep in on a morning in late December, and sometimes that is all that it takes.

All of our distant Hogmanays at home.

The street party in the centre of Edinburgh, a million rev-ellers pressed into a few square miles. The afternoon phone calls trying to locate enough wristbands for your friends and visitors. An evening house party somebody knows about, and then that long, freezing walk into town over the Meadows. The spraying lager and sparkling wine, the kisses at the bells, the fireworks. The brief, primal fear as the crowd surged and you felt yourself momentarily flattened up against a crush barrier. Me out with my friends, and Dominic with his, but always then the coming home, the reuniting at two or three or four o'clock in the morning. The gleeful scavenging of the leftovers of Mum's annual party, and then a last beer, a last whisky. And always, always, some peaked-too-soon Graham or Paul or Neil asleep in my bed; roll him out, if you can, otherwise shove him over and climb in beside him. It is at least warm.

And when we were younger still, staying up with all the children we knew like cousins. Upstairs, in their smoky living room, the adults drink their drinks and tell their noisy stories, but in the little dormitory downstairs we have our own party. On the black and white television with the dial you turn to change channels and a coat-hanger in the back for an aerial, Rikki Fulton is pretending to be a minister. We understand no more than half of the jokes but he is still the most hilarious thing that any of us have ever seen. Tonight, we are staying up till midnight.

In the Lobby Lounge, the man with the yellow shirt and the insoluble pain in his heart appears an impossible act to follow, but two game Thai ladies are willing to give it a try. Perhaps as an insurance policy, they pick the one song near-guaranteed to win them adulation in this part of the world: 'Take Me Home, Country Roads'.

What is it about Thailand and John Denver's 1971 hit? You hear it everywhere: not just in the bars, but in the taxi cabs, the supermarkets, the dentists' waiting rooms. When Hang lifts up a guitar, it is the song his fingers instinctively first chord out, and if you search on the internet, you can even find a clip of a group of long-necked Karan hill tribe women practising a choral version of the song for a talent competition.

Almost heaven, West Virginia
Blue Ridge Mountains, Shenandoah River

Perhaps it is the ears that hear it as much as it is the song. For all the buzz of its neon and the secrets of its back streets, Thailand remains a rural nation, a kingdom of country dwellers where most every citizen yet carries some village in their heart. The sprawling megalopolis of Bangkok is a place you go to – for work, for love or to study – rather than one that you come from. At the city's Chatuchak Market urban Thai cowboys pass the weekend wearing western shirts with boot-lace neckties, picking banjos and singing lonesome of dogies and prairies, of homesteads left behind.

And yet all those singing Karan women – many of whom will never have been further than twenty miles from home – cannot really be missing the countryside, can they? Maybe, then, it is not the evocation of arcadia that draws people to the John Denver song at all, but rather the notion that a person might belong somewhere and at a certain point be returned there; perhaps the key phrase in the first line of the chorus is not 'country roads', but the universal plea to 'take me home'. Noteworthy, then, that John Denver and his co-writers indeed inverted this phrasing in the song's title: though the first line of the chorus runs 'Country roads, take me home', the actual title of the song is 'Take Me Home, Country Roads'.

We all want to be taken home. We want to travel to exciting places and there have our adventures, but we also want to belong somewhere. And if the worst must happen to us, we certainly do not want some corner of a foreign field to be for ever England; we want to know that we will be taken home, that an expert qualified in the field of international repatriation will be able to make the necessary arrangements for us.

In the Lobby Lounge, the song has the desired effect. Around the room feet are tapped, notes are hummed, and when the two Thai ladies reach their first chorus, the entire bar joins in joyful as a gospel choir:

> Country roads, take me home
> To the place I belong
> West Virginia, mountain momma
> Take me home, country roads

The old churchyard at Colinton, where Dominic is buried amidst influenza victims and fallen First World War infantrymen, is a pretty spot, a quiet garden in a wooded dell with a river running nearby. Its mossed stones are misted with morning light and gentle rain and local history all, but that is not what matters. Nor, even, is it the fact that three years after we buried him we found a local artist who had himself known loss, understood instinctively what we needed and carved a stone memorial that is a thing of quiet and gentle beauty.

What matters is that it is a place saturated with our own personal history, that together we once knew it so well. That when we were very young, Mum formed a playgroup in the church hall and named it after a yew tree that still stands nearby. That when we fidgeted and dozed through all our endless Easter and Harvest services, we did so on the wooden benches of this church. That just beyond those tall trees is the video shop from where we tried to rent our beloved 18-certificate movies, the barber's shop where we received our identical haircuts, the doctor's surgery we visited when we were sick. That Mum's cars spent half their lives in the garage up the street, that Dominic used to have a friend who lived atop the steep hill over there. That if you walk along-side this river we used to never catch any fish in, that if you pass the weir that each winter threatens to break, that if you then climb the steep and muddy wooden stairs you come back out at the old railway line whose dark, empty tunnel haunted our childhood dreams. That if you are brave enough to walk through it alone then beyond it you will come to the wide park where we ran our races on long sunny afternoons in June.

By country roads or aeroplane, it counts for something to be taken home, of course it does. As far as such things go, the only thing that matters more is that his precious Eileen lies there beside him.

At ten minutes to midnight in the Lobby Lounge, the key-boardist removes his sunglasses, the ladyboy steps down from the stage, and the pair of them usher everybody outside.

In front of the Metropole, a fair that had looked tentative when we entered a few hours previously is now in full swing. The emphasis is on aqueous fun: darts accurately thrown at water balloons win you a stuffed toy, target-shooting with water pistols draws lengthy queues, and there is even a stall where you can throw a ball at a coconut and, if your aim is true, an unfortunate bellboy will be plunged into a human-being-sized barrel of water.

As midnight approaches, the hotel staff abandon their stalls and join us on the Metropole's steps. Here and there a few bottles of sparkling wine are brandished, ready to pop at the stroke of midnight, but most of our fellow revellers are clutching what seem to be candy canes, foot-long miniature walking sticks wrapped in festive red and blue paper. As the countdown begins, cigarette lighters are produced and the ends of these apparent confections hurriedly lit.

The countdown itself, initiated by the ladyboy but quickly taken up by the assembled crowd, is made in a mongrel mix of Thai and English – *ten, kao, paet, seven, six, ha* – and the fuses fizzle as it proceeds. The first fireworks launch on the stroke of midnight, a volley of them streaking away from us towards a point only slightly above the heads of the teenagers assembled around the clock tower. Simultaneously corks burst forth, toasts are raised, and handshakes and kisses exchanged.

And then the next volley of fireworks hisses into the air, and a moment after that the next, and the next again: the candy canes are not merely individual rockets, but are sort of handheld Roman candle repeater guns. At some point, one over-enthusiastic reveller moves too high on the steps; instead of sailing across the road to explode above the heads of the teenagers, his missiles now ricochet off the Metropole's entrance canopy and back down into the crowd stood immediately in front of him. Nobody seems to mind very much: it is New Year in Thailand, and, blinded by smoke and soaked in wine and the promise of another year, we are happy.

I wake on New Year's Day, groggy from a last drink and coughing from the air conditioner we forgot to turn off, and switch on the hotel room television. The default station is an international news channel and it is now New York City's turn to enter 2008.

I sit up in bed and watch as the immaculately coiffured correspondent works the barrier, meeting and greeting the revellers. All ages and races, they have travelled from far and wide to be in Times Square at this moment. They are visibly as happy and excited as human beings can be, and in their collective fifteen seconds of fame the single thing on their minds is to wish the whole world a wonderful New Year;

more than that, they seem in no doubt that everybody is going to get it.

Perhaps this is the truly great thing about being human: Celine Dion, whose heart will merely go on, is a minority of one. The rest of us expect more. Against overwhelming evidence, we all believe that this year will somehow be greater than every other we have known. This year nobody will fall ill, and nobody will get divorced. Nobody will be knocked down, and nobody will be sent to prison. Next New Year's Eve, not one single man on our entire planet will find himself singing to a hotel bar full of strangers, crying as he does so. This year we will drink all the drinks we desire and not suffer so much as a hint of a hangover. Perhaps more than anything, this year nobody's body will be required to be repatriated from a faraway land.

In the evening rush hour I am driving south out of Seattle in the company of Dr Brian Atwater, a writer and United States government geologist. Lashed to the roof of Dr Atwater's truck – itself a weathered green pick-up driven straight off the pages of a John Steinbeck novel – is an ancient and battered aluminium canoe; we are making tonight for the Cascadia coast, there to search for evidence of a three hundred year-old tsunami.

Et in arcadia ego: even in the midst of life, I am surrounded by death. A year earlier, Paul, James and I had seen the signposts as we drove home from Brownsville along the Oregon coast a few hundred miles south of here: TSUNAMI HAZARD ZONE, EVACUATION ROUTE THIS WAY, IN CASE OF EARTHQUAKE GO IMMEDIATELY TO HIGH GROUND. Browsing in a Portland bookshop a few days later, I had picked up the journal of the local historical society to find a version of an Indian folktale that the translator believed concerned a tsunami that had affected nearby Coos Bay in 1700. Back in London, I had found that I had carried fragments of the lines I had read that afternoon – that 'when the flood tide came there was no ebb tide', that 'wherever the top of a fir tree was sticking out, there they fastened their canoes', that 'some people were without braided ropes', that 'some people drifted far away' – home with me.

I had carried them home because I had been stunned to encounter such resonating history when the Indian Ocean tsunami had always seemed entirely without precedent.

When we had first heard the newsreaders start to speak the word aloud, it had taken collective and concerted effort to cast our minds back to a footnote in school geography lessons about natural disasters, more still to properly process the notion that this phonetic curiosity might infer such grave consequences. Even the people who were stood on Loh Dahlum beach on Boxing Day morning struggled to comprehend what was happening as the waters rushed towards them; the Indian Ocean tsunami occurred two years after the Bali bombing, and most survivors say that their first thought was that they were experiencing an act of terrorism.

Two and a half years had passed between that December morning and my trip to Oregon, but despite all that I had come to learn in the interim, the Indian Ocean tsunami had somehow remained in mind a catastrophe set for ever apart from those that had come before it. In the British Library I had read of the tsunamis in Chile and Alaska in the 1960s, but had always done so in the distancing language of science: in Richter scales and moment magnitude, in casualty numbers logarithmically lower than those around the Indian Ocean. Perhaps it mattered, too, that I had seen no emotive home video from Alaska or Chile, no shaking camcorder footage of onrushing tides, of people running and screaming; the primary visual records I had found of those events were the sober black and white photographs taken by insurance company loss adjusters long after the flood tides had finally ebbed away.

This, then, is why I have returned to this Pacific Northwest only a year after I was last here: because I want to understand more about this tsunami that seems somehow to be the event most intimately connected to the one that affected Phi Phi on Boxing Day. I want to bear witness to the water that ravaged this place and to the lives it inevitably took. And, more than anything, three centuries after the flood tides came with no ebb tides, I want to feel the firm ground beneath my feet and know that all things in heaven and on earth will surely pass.

We stop for dinner on the outskirts of Olympia.

Dr Atwater, who throughout our trip will valiantly battle a cold, is in need of a dose of chilli, and a friend has recommended a Thai restaurant. It takes us the best part of an hour to find it, for the address we have seems to correspond only to a sprawling suburban shopping mall; between us, we should deduce that the restaurant is actually located inside the mall far quicker than we actually do. Flanked by a shop selling cut-price perfumes and a miniature golf concession, it is a location so absurdly incongruous for a well-considered restaurant that the only other place I can imagine such an establishment existing is in Thailand itself.

But if from the outside this could be the MBK mall at Siam Square, inside the room the accoutrements of higher-end Thai restaurants the western world over are all in their tick-box place: the waft of incense, the stone Buddhas, the water features that trickle into pools where white orchids float. It is a version of the country as manufactured as any airport souvenir, but it is one for which I have come to feel a deep affinity: in Europe, too, such places are often the nearest you can get to Thailand without boarding an aeroplane. Nevertheless, if at home I have visited such restaurants solely for the ambience and often received no more than that, here the tom yam's arrival is heralded by an aroma of fresh lemongrass and Dr Atwater's massaman curry contains all the fresh red chilli a suffering man could wish for. Closing my eyes and travelling by taste alone, I could be at Papaya Restaurant on Phi Phi, where the proprietor cooks manna at a hotplate by

the entrance and his cat makes her home on the cool bottom
shelf of the drinks refrigerator.

I had come across Dr Atwater back in April. Searching the
internet for information about the Coos Bay tsunami, I had
stumbled upon the programme for a tsunami-preparedness
conference at the University of Washington at which he was
speaking. A footnote mentioned that Dr Atwater would be
taking a group of delegates out to the Cascadia coast to inspect
the geological evidence of that 1700 tsunami; that trip was two
days hence and impossible for me to join, but I had emailed
him and he had generously extended an open invitation.

In the intervening weeks that it had taken to organise my
travel, I had found myself reading and re-reading a book that
Dr Atwater and an international team of colleagues had
together produced about a geological detective story in
which they had been involved.

The tale began with a mysterious tsunami that made landfall on Japan's eastern coast in 1700. Japan had always known
itself to be at risk of tsunamis – the word 'tsunami' itself comes
from the Japanese, in which language it translates literally as
'harbour wave' – but no preceding earthquake had been felt
locally and for subsequent centuries this event was therefore
considered an 'orphan', a tsunami of unknown provenance.

In the 1980s, geologists working on the opposite side of
the Pacific started to accumulate evidence that the northwest coast of America had also once been affected by
earthquakes and tsunamis. A significant proportion of this
evidence – found at sites from California to Oregon –
carbon-dated to a window centred around the end of the
seventeenth century and this posed an immediately pressing
question: did these findings represent multiple small events,
or a single and much larger one?

A group of Japanese researchers were able to suggest an answer. By careful study of the historical evidence, the Japanese researchers concluded that the orphan tsunami had arrived in the small hours of the 28th of January 1700, and could only have been triggered by a massive earthquake involving almost the entire Cascadian Subduction Zone, the fault line that runs alongside coastal Oregon, Washington and British Columbia. Back in America, by further interrogation of the geological record, Dr Atwater and his colleagues had subsequently been able to confirm that a huge earthquake and tsunami had indeed occurred in Cascadia between the growing seasons of 1699 and 1700.

This was big news not merely for geologists, but for residents of the entire Pacific Northwest and indeed coast dwellers everywhere. The received wisdom had always been that the Pacific Northwest was at low risk of suffering a major tsunami, for the Cascadia Subduction Zone was thought unlikely to be capable of generating the necessary moment magnitude. The investigative work undertaken by the Japanese and American researchers, then, was the reason we had seen so many warning signs as we drove home from Brownsville last year.

Yet for all the contemporary implications of their discovery, what kept drawing me back to their book had been the sources from which they had discerned these things. On the Copalis River on the Washington coast, Dr Atwater and his colleagues had located what would come to be known as a 'ghost forest', a grove of dead red cedar trees that still stood three hundred years after they had drowned in salt water. In Japan, weathered books of mulberry-bark paper had been unearthed in municipal attics and family chests: diaries and official documents that spoke of panicked villagers, of houses swept away, of a desperate need for supplies with which to build temporary shelters. Like the folktales of the Coos Bay Indians with their canoes and their braided ropes, this primary evidence sang of people as real as our own lost ones, people lifelike in a way that dates and figures or the black and white photographs of loss adjusters could never be.

We stay the night at the Olympic Inn in Aberdeen, Washington, hometown of the late Kurt Cobain, my early teenage idol.

When I was growing up and bought it religiously every Thursday, the *New Musical Express* invariably described Aberdeen as a 'depressed logging town'. Fifteen years on, the term just about still fits: though the logging has now all but gone, the economic downturn remains.

It was Dominic who broke the news to me that Kurt Cobain had died, outside our house on a grey day not long before Easter when it seemed to my teenage mind that if on the third day he did not rise again, such unspeakable tragedy must surely cause the world to end; Dominic, who himself would later also die at twenty-seven and teach me what it really meant to feel that the world was ending. That teenage April I had worn my Nirvana T-shirt for weeks, just as I would later do with Dominic's Bob Marley T-shirt. The Nirvana T-shirt is long since lost, but I have learned my lesson and take better care of the Bob Marley one, keeping it back for special occasions, for anniversaries and the days when I require the extra support it invariably provides. Abruptly jetlagged and emotionally overwhelmed, I could do with it tonight but instead fall asleep in the Aberdeen motel to dream of a time when all the dead twenty-seven-year-old brothers and rock stars are alive again.

Last year's trip to see Paul and James had not been my first visit to the Pacific Northwest.

At twenty I had spent a month in Vancouver assisting on a medical research project at the University of British Columbia. If I cannot claim the study ignited in me a passion for the daily rigours of laboratory research, I had nevertheless come home with a new interest: the folk mythology of the first peoples of the Pacific Northwest. The university had a museum of anthropology on campus, and I had lost myself there almost every afternoon.

Haida. Chinook. Coast Salish. Tlingit. Tillamook. Years later the names of the tribal bands and their geographical boundaries begin to merge, but what indelibly remains is the communal mythology with which they attempted to make sense of the lethal beauty that surrounded them.

Raven was the trickster, a shapeshifter who stole the sun and moon and threw them high in the sky. Bear was a spirit who disappeared each winter by turning back to his ghost form. Salmon was the holiest fish, his complex life cycle a measure of his unique importance. Earthquake was a giant sasquatch who lived high in the Olympic mountains and shook the world when men came too close. Killer Whale first lived in the rivers, but ate all the salmon and brought the people close to starvation; Thunderbird plucked him up in his claws and carried him out to the deepest ocean. Thunderbird himself created the wind with the beating of his wings and had lightning flashing in his eyes; he was powerful above all creatures, and only the most revered chiefs were permitted to display his likeness on their totems.

On a downtown street packed with souvenir shops, it had taken me the best part of a day to find the perfect Thunderbird for Dominic. Most of those on offer I could not afford, and

289

those that I could did scant justice to the regal creature that they were intended to depict.

Dominic had not asked me to bring him anything home – let alone anything perfect – but I had been determined to fetch him a gift that would somehow carry with it a message. Whilst I had been exploring Vancouver he had been ill with his Crohn's disease, battling the pain and the ever-looming scalpel with his usual quiet stoicism. The Thunderbird that I eventually found for him was a carved icon, framed in wood and painted in the bold black, red and white of the Haida. At only a few inches square, it was far smaller than any of the others I had seen, but it had obviously been made with respect and love.

I had hoped that Dominic might appreciate it, but it turned out that he did far more than that. After the tsunami, when I walked around the empty rooms of his flat, fingered the clothes still hanging in wardrobes and read the notes he and Eileen had left for one another on the bedroom mirror, I noticed the Thunderbird that I had long since forgotten, hanging proudly on their wall.

At the Olympic Inn we are awake early, for by noon the rising tides will have obscured the things Dr Atwater has to show me. From Aberdeen it is a half-hour drive to our putting-in point in the Copalis River, and a little before seven o'clock in the morning we are already on the road. At this early hour the journey ought to be restful but, fuelled by reverse jetlag and an overdose of motel coffee, I am wide awake and full of questions for Dr Atwater.

Dr Atwater has lately been working in Indonesia, and when I ask him about this he tells me that his brand of geological detective work has proven particularly challenging in the countries around the Indian Ocean: between the heat, the unshifting mangroves and the constant to-and-fro of the fiddler crabs, it can be a challenge to infer much about what happened in such places a decade ago, let alone several hundred years ago.

I have another question too, one that I have previously always stopped short of asking anybody who might know the answer, lest the enquiry sound like an accusation. Perhaps it is the fact that Dr Atwater is giving up his weekend to take a stranger into the wilderness, but I feel able to ask him.

'Couldn't the Indian Ocean tsunami have been predicted?'

In truth, it is a question to which I think I already know the answer. The location of the fault line was known, as was the fact that it had not ruptured in a long time; at the very least, the benefit of hindsight must surely have had the experts lamenting a collective failure of imagination.

Dr Atwater, however, only shrugs and shakes his head. 'No,' he says, 'I don't think it was really on anybody's radar.'

Dr Atwater goes on to explain that the reason for this was not inattentiveness or indeed any failure of imagination, but comes back to simple science. Minor earthquakes involving small sections of the fault line were known to occur around the region relatively frequently, and it was believed that this regular release of energy likely provided a safety valve against massive accumulation. At that time there was no evidence to suggest a twelve hundred mile rupture was even possible, let alone impending, and if anybody had stood up to propose such an event as a likely occurrence, the scientific community would probably have given them short shrift.

What he tells me dovetails with something else that I had lately discovered. I had long suspected that the lack of an effective tsunami warning system in the Indian Ocean was a reminder of everything that was wrong with our world: the Pacific Ocean, bordered by rich countries, had a warning system it had no apparent need for; the Indian Ocean, bordered by poorer countries, had clearly needed one that it did not have.

As I researched the 1700 tsunami, I had come to understand that it had not been a question of poverty but rather one of history. There is a reason why geologists speak of a Pacific Ring of Fire, and, equally, there is a reason why until now the Indian Ocean has had no corresponding moniker. The Pacific warning system was created as a direct response to the Alaskan tsunami of 1964, at a time when the Indian Ocean had suffered no similar event for centuries. If there was no tsunami warning system in the Indian Ocean, it was because nobody knew that there was a need for one.

We turn off from the highway, bounce down a dusty slip road and pull up overlooking the Pacific Ocean, grey and violently at odds with its name in the early morning light. Somewhere two miles in front of us, the Juan de Fuca Plate is right now grinding its way beneath the North American Plate, storing up the energy that will one day again be released as house-shaking tremors or an almighty lifting of the seabed. Dr Atwater tells me that he harbours grave concerns about what will happen if and when the latter occurs: for all the signposts on the highway, for all the Japanese scrolls unearthed from dark attics, there still remains a sense in the local community that such a thing could not possibly happen here.

When the logging money left Aberdeen, it left its nearby coast too. The short journey from the ocean back to the Copalis River takes us past closed-down general stores and petrol stations, patched-up homesteads and wrecked cars. A few hardy enterprises still offer oceanfront accommodations and these places are strangely reminiscent of the family-run enterprises that lead from the highway down to the beach on

Ko Lanta, Phi Phi's poorer neighbour: the paired rows of bungalows, the hand-painted signs promising free cable television, the silver pickup trucks the owners use to run their errands. At the height of what ought to be high season, however – and at a time when Lanta can barely provide the peace and quiet its visitors seek – most of them seem entirely empty.

At our putting-in point it rapidly becomes apparent that the woollen hat I bought in an army surplus shop in Seattle yesterday is going to provide little protection against the elements. Too late, I realise that whilst I have been cheerfully referring to this journey as a 'boat trip', the phrase Dr Atwater used in his emails was 'canoe expedition'. Mercifully, Dr Atwater has come prepared and the back of his truck is a veritable outfitter's shop, albeit one specialising in lovingly muddied equipment. Dressed in fisherman's waders, a road-mender's overcoat, and a pair of thick gloves, I follow him down to the water, pick up a paddle and climb into his aluminium canoe.

Canoes and kayaks are memory boats. Dr Atwater and I are on the Copalis, a tidal river that winds its way through Washington State estuary land. Sometimes as we paddle I am barely there at all, and each stroke pushes me back into the streams of my mind.

I am ten years old and Dominic is twelve. It is Easter time, and we are having a week of lessons on the duckweed-filled pond at Craiglockhart, learning how to paddle, to capsize safely, to put the oar in on the side we wish to turn to, to put it in and hold in there. Partly we are here because Dominic is now an accomplished skier and I have no need for any more Grade Five certificates, but mostly we are here because we have recently obtained our own kayak, a hulking neon orange wreck that Uncle John built when he was a boy and now hangs suspended from the roof of our suburban garage like the strangest of UFOs. When summer arrives, Dad will strap it to the top of his car, and drive us down to the Union Canal. There, we will take turns to proudly show him all our new skills except safe capsizing: boys at Dominic's new school have warned us that, due to unspeakable acts the bankside rats perform, the canal water is deadly if you swallow so much as a single drop.

On the Copalis River we are turning, heading in to one of the muddy banks. I put in my oar and hold it there as we learned to do so many years ago.

Dr Atwater climbs out of the boat. He is carrying an old army entrenching tool, its handle painted in ten-centimetre stripes in order that it might demonstrate scale in the photographs of the treasures he inevitably finds; at low tide the bank of the Copalis River tells a story to those who speak its language.

Using the entrenching tool, Dr Atwater gently scrapes at the riverbank to reveal a cross section of three distinct layers. Moving downwards from ground level, the first two feet is composed of brown mud, deposited here by three hundred years of coming and going tides. The bottom foot, almost coal-black, is formed of petrified roots that are the remnants of the trees that stood here before the tectonic plates shifted; the viscous black sludge that binds them together was once the rich soil of a forest floor.

A centimetre-wide line of white-yellow sand, clear to the eye as cream in a chocolate sponge cake, separates the upper brown mud from the lower black sludge. This line of sand, Dr Atwater tells me, was carried here by the tsunami of 1700. Out in the Pacific, the North American Plate slipped over the Juan de Fuca Plate, simultaneously raising the seabed and causing the land behind it to fall; when the tsunami waters reached this estuary they found the forest already part submerged and were able to travel miles inland.

We push off and start to paddle again. Dominic and I are in France, visiting Dad the summer before the tsunami. With Laurie and Samantha we hire kayaks and paddle around a muddy estuary beside the beach. We race and splash each other, and later I capsize Dominic, and he capsizes me. It is a good day, with hindsight an unforgettable one, the last time we are all together.

Left and left and left and left. I am on the left side of the boat, Dr Atwater on the right. We keep paddling, following the curves of the Copalis River and passing under the decaying bridge of an abandoned logging railway. That day in France we did not reminisce about our lessons on Craiglockhart pond, our alien kayak suspended from the garage roof, for we assumed there would be time for that in all the years to come. Now I paddle beneath broken bridges and wish I had somebody to remember these things with.

Dr Atwater steers us up a tributary, angles us into the bank and takes out his entrenching tool once more. My eye properly in now, I can make out the line of tsunami sand even as Dr Atwater digs. This time, though, he has something more to show me: running his fingers through the dark black sludge, he picks something up and, polishing the dirt from it, holds it out to me.

It is a piece of broken pebble, and it looks as unremarkable as it sounds. I turn it over in my hand, puzzled as to why he has given it to me, and then Dr Atwater reveals its significance. The breaking of stone requires tremendous heat, and this pebble was fired in the hearth of a native fishing camp that once stood on this spot. 'The people drifted far and wide,' ran the folktale from Coos Bay, 'the water carried them far away.'

We paddle on. Left then right, left then right. Now it is a week after the first anniversary of the tsunami and, feeling restless, a few of us have hired two-man canoes. Toy is paired with Neil, Graham and Paul are together and Mon – yet to realise quite how short a straw he has drawn – is with me. We came out from Loh Dahlum Bay and paddled to Monkey Beach. It was a distance not far enough to cure our wander-lust, and anyway the monkeys had long since retired to the jungle's shade. Somebody suggested we continue on, around the side of the island and back in to Tonsai Bay. Left then right, left then right.

Two hours' solid paddling later, the sea is growing rough and our sole landmark remains the steep limestone cliff we do not want to hug too closely lest we should be wrecked against it. The sea eagles that hover above us have taken on the vague appearance of vultures, and when now we shout at passing longtails for help, we are no longer entirely joking. Mon and I form the rear of our flotilla, just close enough that the other boats in our fleet can still hear his increasingly fre-quent suggestion that we all change canoe partners 'for fun'. The circuit we are attempting is in fact the shorter half of the island – the head of Ben's alien rather than its body – but by the time we turn the final corner into Tonsai, we look like castaways from a distant shipwreck.

Our canoe crunches aground in the mud. We clamber out, scramble up on the bank.

The ghost forest stands on an island in an oxbow in the Copalis River, a few miles inland from the ocean. There remain now perhaps a hundred of the trees; shorn of almost all their limbs, bleached white by three centuries of sun and rain, they yet stand as proudly defiant as the wounded soldiers of an unvanquished army. In life these were red cedars, the trees from which the Haida carved their famously unsinkable battle canoes; in death they are a last testament to the world that disappeared here.

Dr Atwater finds some business on the beach and I walk on alone, into the ghost forest. Three hundred years after this land was submerged, the ground on which it now stands is a marshland meadow. I make my way to the middle of the ghost forest, through reeds and rushes, over fox holes and streams, and there sit down on the trunk of a fallen tree. Excepting the faraway rumble of the breakers in the Pacific and the whisper of the wind blowing through the meadow grass, the world is abruptly quiet.

There is an aura here, mystery and history combined, and it occurs to me now what a ghost forest is and, perhaps, the real reason I have made this long journey over again: it is a place where the living can meet the dead. It is another place where the living can meet with the dead, and it is something else besides: it is a warning from nature, a testimony that terrible things happened here and, if we are not vigilant, will surely do so again. It happened here, just as it would three hundred years later in a different kingdom on the other side of the world: 'the people fastened their canoes to the tops of fir trees', but 'some people were without braided ropes and drifted far away'.

A few yards from where I am sitting I notice a lone faded flip-flop, perhaps carried from one of the bungalow resorts and beached here during last winter's flooding. In the first years after the tsunami I searched for signs from Dominic everywhere: in cathedrals, on beaches, in the memorial garden and in the names of passing longtail boats. Now I no longer look for them, have learned that my brother travels with me and in me, and yet somehow they come more abundantly than ever.

We climb back into the canoe. I have a paddle in my hand

and I am an Indian, a Tillamook paddling into the future on unsinkable red cedar. I am a bear that changes back to spirit form in winter. I am a Thunderbird that looks down from the wall in a tenement hallway.

Left and right, left and right, left and right. Now it is the fourth anniversary of the tsunami, and at close to midnight we are paddling out into the dark waters of Loh Dahlum, four of us in two canoes. Khom fai have this year been deemed a fire hazard and banned from the beach, so our idea is to launch one from the safety of the middle of the bay. We paddle hard but the night is dark, the current strong and the sea choppy. For three-quarters of an hour we try to light the thing but are constantly washed back to shore until our lantern becomes so torn and waterlogged that we have to give up. Tomorrow I leave on the early ferry and for the first time since the tsunami we shall release no khom fai on the twenty-sixth of December.

But Ben has witnessed all this and later calls me up on to the roof of his landlocked boat where together we light a lantern he has kept back for the occasion. It lifts a little then sails perfectly horizontally, as if indeed intent on setting the town aflame. We hold our breath, but as it passes over the memorial garden, it pauses and then, as if caught by a prayer, carries itself straight to the stars.

Left and left then right and right. It is early evening by the time Dr Atwater and I paddle back down the tributaries, under the broken bridge and down the Copalis to where his green truck awaits. It is a long drive back to Seattle, and yet the important part of this journey is already done.

The world changes when you lose somebody you love. Whether or not your loss begins with an earthquake, the planet tilts on its axis and remains there. At first this is dizzying: life is suddenly so strange that all you can do is desperately cling to the earth's spinning surface and hope not to fall off yourself. Over the months and years, you can learn to live in this unfamiliar orbit, to walk upright again, to carry your grief as a tattoo on your arm or an amulet around your neck. In this way time passes.

Sometimes it even seems to pass too quickly. I find my way back to the medical work I had always missed and one winter morning I finish another hospital nightshift to discover that it is now December and it has been almost five years since the tsunami. Five years to accept that it all really did happen, and yet still I wake sometimes in the small hours and cannot quite believe that they are gone.

A few weeks later I arrive in Thailand perplexed and apprehensive. Perplexed that so much time has passed, apprehensive that a fifth anniversary seems like a particularly significant occasion and I have not been able to think of any meaningful way to mark it. Typically, Carol already has an answer for the latter, and tells me her idea as soon as I arrive at her house in Krabi: this year, we will light a candle for everybody that died on Phi Phi that day.

'But that would be hundreds of candles,' I say.

'I know,' she says. 'I've got them in the garage.'

'But how will we manage it?' I ask. 'What about the wind?'

'We'll work it out,' she says. 'Like we always do.'

She is right, of course: we will work it out, like we always do.

Over the next few days at their house, I am gently reminded that neither is the passage of time necessarily anything to be perplexed about. Their son, a toddler and our shy mascot when we were making the garden, is now a talkative schoolboy of six, and this year there is somebody else very special to get to know too. After years of waiting and praying, Carol and Toy have been able to adopt a beautiful girl who has the most infectious laugh of anybody I have ever met. Carol believes that fate has brought them together, says that their bond is all the stronger for the troubles they have each known; when you see them gently sleeping next to one another on the Phi Phi ferry, it is impossible to disagree with this sentiment.

On Christmas Eve, the waitresses at Reggae Bar spend the afternoon tying balloons around the ground-floor railings. Passing by, I imagine that they must be Christmas decorations, but later that day I see Mr John hurrying through the town, and I know then – because Mr John is not a man who hurries anywhere – that something must be up.

At Sunflower that night, I find out what was afoot at Reggae Bar: an evening of no-holds-barred Muay Thai, organised to raise money to replace the island's police box which had burned down a year previously.

At ten o'clock, Caroline and I walk up to town. The balloons – craftily placed to stop people viewing the fights from the street – have done their job, but when we get inside the view is scarcely better; with an entrance fee of five hundred baht, this is no exhibition match and Reggae Bar is packed to its literal rafters. We can hear the pi chawa, the

300

thundering impacts and the raucous cheers, but can see nothing of the action. It seems like wasted money but, more than that, I have the feeling that I have somehow let Dominic down. Tonight I'd had a chance to watch some proper Muay Thai, but have squandered it by arriving so late.

But through the crowd comes Mon's voice, calling out my name. He is sitting in the second from front row, the place I used to sit when I first arrived in Phi Phi and would come to Reggae Bar to watch the exhibition bouts and feel close to Dominic. Pulling us in through the crowd, Mon chides and hustles his friends along to make a space for us.

And what a night it is. Fuelled by a partisan and capacity crowd, the fighting is simultaneously more graceful and more spectacularly violent than anything I have previously seen. The fighters twist and turn, dance the dances of ritual and combat; again and again the bell rings, and again and again Mr John raises a victor's triumphant hand. There are knockouts, flying elbows, and a legendary but seldom-seen roundhouse kick. The beer flows like water and we make ridiculous bets with Mon and Chai and their friends, picking red trunks – *denang* – or blue trunks – *namode* – on a whim, and scream maniacally for our man in the ensuing bout.

And, of course, I think of Dominic. Five years on I think of how much he would have liked it, to sit there with Caroline and me and Mon and Chai and shout for denang or namode, old and new friends united in appreciation and enjoyment of his beloved Muay Thai.

In truth this remains one of the hardest things to live with, not whatever I or even their parents lost that day, but what Dominic and Eileen themselves lost: the dreams and plans that will now for ever remain no more than that. The buildings he would have designed, the places they would have visited, the birthdays, the anniversaries, the thousand nights out. That they had such a short time on this planet still seems nothing short of outrageous.

In the email that he sent me from Phi Phi on Christmas Day, Dominic had spoken of his plans for Boxing Day:

> Tomorrow I may go to a yoga class on the beach, windsurf or get a boat to a bay. Or maybe just lie on the beach and drink Bahama Mamas all day, I can't seem to decide.
>
> Anyway man, take it easy and get enough rest over the festive season.
>
> Peace and season's greetings,
>
> Your man in the field

Sometimes that is how I choose to think of him now: my man in the field, sitting with Eileen on the garlanded prow of a longtail boat as it moves across a turquoise bay towards a white sandy beach on the brightest of days in the high season. After all these years, I do not think I believe in any afterlife other than the one of memory, but who is to tell me that is less valid than anybody else's interpretation of heaven?

On the morning of the twenty-sixth of December we gather in the memorial garden as we have done for the last half decade. At ten thirty we fall silent and a minute later Hang lights the firecrackers. We cry our tears, lay our flowers, and then repair to the bar to together remember our loved ones and our shared loss. Later, we go our separate ways to think our own thoughts and make our private communions.

As evening starts to fall, we congregate down on the beach. Longtail drivers are laying their boats at anchor, oblivious tourist couples are strolling arm in arm, and children are playing down by the tideline. Carol's children are amongst them, and so is Ben's young daughter, for a few years ago he met and fell in love with a woman wise enough not to ask a buffalo how it is feeling but strong enough to reach one all the same.

Slowly, purposefully we begin to mark out an area of sand in the shape of a heart. Toy erects a windbreak of yellow fabric around its perimeter, calling for more bamboo stakes as he does so. Soon Carol's boxes of candles are fetched from the bar too, and now a dozen people climb into the heart to set these out, kneeling as they twist them down into the sand to ensure that each remains upright.

Carol walks across and stands beside me.

'Do you think it's going to work?' I ask her.

'No idea,' she says.

Once the sun sets the light quickly fades; as the squid boats line themselves along the bay and illuminate their lamps, the children are called in. Nearby a match is struck, and then another and another. One candle is alight, now three, now fifteen. A breeze blows along the beach. Carol and I hold our breath but, though they flicker, the candles remain aflame. We exhale. Thirty candles. Fifty. A hundred and fifty.

An enthusiastic ten-year-old tries to join in the lighting and Hang has to move quickly to lift him out before he catches fire. Two hundred. Three hundred. Five hundred. Seven hundred. A thousand.

We sit down to look at them. Rather, they make us sit down: they mesmerise us. I am dimly aware of the faces that flicker through them and around me. We are brothers and sisters. Parents and children. Husbands and wives. Friends and strangers. We are a family brought together by a common tragedy and five years on we remain united by our determination to remember our departed not with mere sorrow but with the love and joy they each brought to our lives. We sit there in silence until at some point Ben declares that everybody must half-close their eyes. We do as he bids and see what he has seen: that once you do this, all our individual candles combine to look like a single giant burning heart.

Above us, illicit khom fai drift through the night sky to the stars, and we sit by our flaming heart in the sand until late in the night, listening to the reggae music that comes drifting across the bay. I will miss my brother for ever.

Afterword

The United Nations now estimates that 230,000 people died in the earthquake and tsunami that occurred on the 26th of December 2004, a figure that equates to more than two people for every single word in this book. Each of those lives was every bit as important as the ones I have written about here and if in these pages I have told only our story, I have done so in the certain knowledge that endless variations of this tale are daily carried in hearts around the Indian Ocean and the wider world.

I think of our fellow bereaved and their lost loved ones often, but I have heard the story of the buffalo and the two birds too many times by now to ever claim to speak for anybody else's loss. Besides, just as Richter scale seismometers are incapable of measuring earthquakes above a certain strength, perhaps the only way to write of a catastrophe on the scale of the tsunami is to do so similarly empirically, to examine the tiniest fraction of the whole and then acknowledge it to be no more than that. Here I make that acknowledgement.

We do not forget them. Not Dominic, and not Eileen, and not any of the other precious souls who were lost that day. They are always with us, and we with them.

Notes

My thanks to all the writers, publishers and estates who allowed their works to be quoted. Amongst the many other publications consulted, the following were particularly helpful:

Jim Thompson: The Unsolved Mystery by William Warren (Editions Didier Millet, 1998) is both the definitive work on Jim Thompson and a poignant portrait of life in post-war Bangkok.

The Orphan Tsunami of 1700: Japanese Clues to a Parent Earthquake in North America by Brian Atwater, Satako Musumi-Rokkaku, Kenji Satake, Yoshinobu Tsuji, Kazue Ueda and David Yamaguchi (United States Geological Survey and University of Washington Press, 2005) is Dr Atwater's team's fascinating − and beautifully rendered − account of their investigations into the orphan tsunami.

The Coos Bay folktale was published in the *Oregon Historical Quarterly*. Recorded by the linguist Leo Frachtenberg in 1909, the version I quote was researched and lovingly re-translated from the Hanis language by Patricia Whereat Phillips.

On a personal note, to list here all the people I have reason to be grateful both to and for would be impossible. Perhaps, then, they will all indulge me once more if I simply say to all those friends, family and colleagues who shared in these things, who picked up shovels, who lit candles, who stayed up late, who taught and inspired, who allowed me to write these stories without condition, who read and re-read and offered opinions, who took such care of this book and me, who understood: *khob khun maak khrap*.